Pleasure, Reward, Preference

Main speakers at the symposium on "PLEASURE, REWARD, PREFERENCE," Korsør, Denmark, 1972.

From left to right: K. B. Madsen, J. Nuttin, H. Helson, H. J. Eysenck, J. Olds, E. L. Walker, D. E. Berlyne, H. Heckhausen.

PLEASURE, REWARD, PREFERENCE

THEIR NATURE, DETERMINANTS, AND ROLE IN BEHAVIOR

Edited by

D. E. BERLYNE

Department of Psychology
University of Toronto
Toronto, Ontario, Canada

K. B. MADSEN

Royal Danish School of Educational Studies
Copenhagen, Denmark

ACADEMIC PRESS   New York and London   1973
A Subsidiary of Harcourt Brace Jovanovich, Publishers

ACADEMIC PRESS, INC.
111 Fifth Avenue, New York, New York 10003

United Kingdom Edition published by
ACADEMIC PRESS, INC. (LONDON) LTD.
24/28 Oval Road, London NW1

Library of Congress Cataloging in Publication Data
Main entry under title:

Pleasure, reward, preference: their nature,
        determinants, and role in behavior.

        "Derives from a symposium . . . held at the
Klarskovgaard Training Institute, near Korsør,
Denmark, on June 5-9, 1972. The symposium was
organized under the auspices of the Advisory Group
on Human Factors of the Scientific Affairs Division
of the North Atlantic Treaty Organization."
        Includes bibliographies.
        1. Pleasure—Congresses. 2. Reward (Psychology)
—Congresses. I. Berlyne, D. E., ed. II. Madsen,
K. B., ed. III. North Atlantic Treaty Organization.
Advisory Group on Human Factors. [DNLM: 1. Pleasure-
pain principle—Congresses. BF515 S9891 1972]
BF515.P46   152.4'4   72-13607
ISBN 0−12−092550−8

Contents

CONTENTS

List of Contributors

Numbers in parentheses indicate the pages on which the authors' contributions begin.

D. E. BERLYNE, Department of Psychology, University of Toronto, Toronto, Ontario, Canada (1)

*SUITBERT ERTEL, Institute of Psychology, University of Goettingen, Göttingen, West Germany (115)

H. J. EYSENCK, Department of Psychology, Institute of Psychiatry, Denmark Hill, London, England (133)

HEINZ HECKHAUSEN, Ruhr University, Bochum, Germany (217)

HARRY HELSON, El Cerrito, California (167)

*E. LEEUWENBERG, Department of Psychology, University of Nijmegen, The Netherlands (99)

K. B. MADSEN, Royal Danish School of Educational Studies, Copenhagen, Denmark (275)

JOSEPH R. NUTTIN, Department of Psychology, University of Leuven, Leuven/Louvain, Belgium (243)

JAMES OLDS, Division of Biology, California Institute of Technology, Pasadena, California (35)

*ALBERT SILVERSTEIN, Department of Psychology, University of Rhode Island, Kingston, Rhode Island (189)

EDWARD LEWIS WALKER, Department of Psychology, University of Michigan, Ann Arbor, Michigan (65)

* These authors did not deliver their papers at the symposium.

Preface

This book is derived from a symposium on "pleasure, reward, preference: their nature, determinants, and role in behavior" which was held at the Klarskovgaard Training Institute, near Korsør, Denmark, on 5–9 June 1972. The Symposium was organized under the auspices of the Advisory Group on Human Factors of the Scientific Affairs Division of the North Atlantic Treaty Organization. The book contains revised versions of the papers delivered by the eight main speakers, together with three shorter papers by other participants who had done recent, and as yet unpublished, research close to the theme of the Symposium.

The objectives of the Symposium were set out in the following brief statement, which was sent to all participants:

> The crucial role of pleasure in behavior was stressed by the long hedonistic tradition that can be traced back to Plato and Aristotle. The early introspective experimental psychologists paid a great deal of attention to "pleasantness" and "unpleasantness" as aspects of "feeling tone." The last comprehensive book on this topic seems to have been J. G. Beebe-Center's *The Psychology of Pleasantness and Unpleasantness* (1932), although a book entitled *The Role of Pleasure in Behavior,* consisting mainly of physiological contributions, was published under the editorship of R. G. Heath in 1964. Some of the most important currents in 20th-century behavior theory have, like earlier hedonism, maintained that the probability of a particular kind of behavior depends primarily on its consequences. Their central concepts have been *reward value* or *reinforcement value,* shown by the capacity of an event to promote learning. Various ways of measuring *preference* have been devised by specialists in social psychology, experimental aesthetics, and scaling theory, as well as by investigators of various forms of choice behavior in animals. The *utility* variable has been of particular interest to decision theorists and

others on the borderline between psychology and other social sciences, such as economics. Recent neurophysiological work on "reward" or "pleasure" *centers in the brain* has opened up a new line of investigation, which promises to illuminate what has been yielded by the other lines. All these concepts, which have grown out of widely differing areas of research, seem to be closely related, but there is an obvious need to work out what they have in common and how they complement one another. Early investigators of "pleasure" were compelled to consider the factors that determine how pleasant or unpleasant something is. Some learning theorists and neurophysiologists have struggled with the problem of what makes some events rewarding, e.g., theories stressing reduction or increase of drive and, latterly, of arousal. Others have, however, studied the effects of events known to have reward value while neglecting this kind of question. Many of those who have studied "preference" or "utility" have concentrated on the methodological problems of scaling these variables, and on axioms governing them, but have not given much consideration to what they depend on. It is hoped that a symposium bringing together representatives of as many as possible of these different approaches will encourage much needed efforts towards synthesis.

The Editors of this volume, who were, respectively, the Director and Co-Director of the Symposium, consider themselves very fortunate indeed to have persuaded so many distinguished figures in contemporary behavioral science to act as main speakers. They are all busy men with many demands on their time. Their willingness to devote a few days to the discussion of our topic was highly gratifying. It strengthened our belief that the topic was signally important and timely. We were no less fortunate in the enrollment of participants other than main speakers. All NATO countries except Iceland and Luxembourg were represented. In all, there were people of 15 nationalities. Apart from psychologists specializing in various areas, both basic and applied, there were representatives of neighboring disciplines, including neurophysiology and psychiatry. There were even specialists in electronics and two distinguished contemporary painters, all of them actively interested in experimental psychology. It is very rare indeed nowadays to find such a varied assortment of interests and backgrounds represented at a small meeting of this sort. As science advances, researchers become more and more specialized, and their terminologies and ways of thinking diverge more and more, so that communication among them becomes difficult. Nevertheless, it was extremely encouraging to see how wholeheartedly our participants strove to collaborate with one another in attacking the problems we set for ourselves and to contribute their specialized knowledge fruitfully.

This book begins with an attempt at a historical perspective and review of the principal problems by D. E. Berlyne. Chapters by the six invited main speakers follow. They fulfill very well what was hoped of them, namely to present various facts, problems, and theoretical approaches that anybody who wishes to arrive at a comprehensive view of hedonic processes must think about very hard. These six chapters carry us all the way from neurophysiological research with animals to uniquely human, "cognitive" phenomena. After these comes a chapter by K. B. Madsen, providing a metascientific overview of possible attacks on the problems under discussion, including those exemplified by the authors of previous chapters. The book also contains three contributions by other participants, who report experiments illustrating three specialized, but fundamentally pertinent, lines of experimentation.

As we indicate both in this preface and in our own chapters, we think that the topic of this volume should be of concern to virtually all psychologists and other behavioral scientists. Yet, many of its aspects have of late been curiously neglected by experimenters and theorists. Such attention as it has received has taken the form of unduly isolated attacks on specific issues with much less intercommunication and theoretical integration than is needed. It is our hope that this book will play its part in remedying this state of affairs.

The main speakers will certainly all acknowledge how much they owe to the contributions of other participants, both when they broke up into small groups and when they reassembled for plenary discussion periods. We are pleased to record our appreciation of the help we received in planning and organizing the symposium from Dr. B. Bayraktar and his staff at the NATO Scientific Affairs Division office in Brussels, of the secretarial work of Mrs. J. Peters at the University of Toronto and of the secretarial staff at the Institute of General Psychology, Royal Danish School of Educational Studies, and of the cooperation we received from Miss J. Gynter and other staff members at the Klarskovgaard Training Institute.

CHAPTER 1

The Vicissitudes of Aplopathematic and Thelematoscopic Pneumatology (or The Hydrography of Hedonism)[1]

D. E. BERLYNE

University of Toronto

The Hedonistic Tradition

THREE KINDS OF MOTIVATION THEORY

Human beings have been pondering over their own and one another's behavior ever since the capacity to ponder evolved. And, from the very beginning, it must have been noticed that there are three ways to make the occurrence of a human action more intelligible. One is to examine events in the environment that the subject perceived just before acting as he did. The second is to look for evidence of events or processes that were going on inside the subject before the action took place. The third is to examine events following the action. So we find throughout the history of psychology three principal types of motivation theory, one relating behavior to *external stimuli,* one relating behavior to *internal factors,* and one relating behavior to *consequences.*

[1] The preparation of this paper was facilitated by research Grant A—73 from the National Research Council of Canada and research Grant S70–1570 from the Canada Council.

Theories seeking to account for behavior in terms of consequences have often attached importance to the attainment of specific goals, the fulfillment of specific purposes, the termination of specific irritations, and the avoidance of specific dangers. However, as soon as we ask what may be common to all the specific consequences that can influence behavior leading up to them, words like "pleasurable," "satisfying," "rewarding," and their opposites inevitably obtrude themselves.

In this volume, we are primarily concerned with explanations of behavior that lay stress on pleasant or unpleasant consequences, i.e., what are called hedonistic explanations. But it must be noted that the three kinds of theory have rarely appeared in pure forms. Most theories that have been offered actually represent compromises between them or combinations of them. For example, there is often a close correspondence between the pleasure accruing from what follows an action and internal motivational conditions preceding it. As Aristotle (*De Anima*) put it, ". . . where there is pleasure and pain, there is necessarily also desire . . . [4326]" and ". . . desire is an impulse towards what is pleasant [4146]." External stimuli commonly signal when pleasure and reward are available, or when pain may be incurred, through performance of particular acts. A truly satisfactory theory of behavior must surely incorporate all three kinds of explanation and give due recognition to the influence of external stimuli, internal factors, and consequences.

The hedonistic current in Western thought first becomes discernible in views put forward by Aristippus, Plato, Aristotle, and Epicurus. It surfaces again in the seventeenth and eighteenth centuries through the writings of Descartes, Hobbes, La Mettrie, and Helvétius, reaching full flood in the Utilitarian school of philosophy, psychology, economics, and politics founded by Bentham at the beginning of the nineteenth century. Bentham and his disciples, particularly the Mills, made hedonism into the more or less standard theory of motivation through most of the nineteenth century. Its imprint is clearly detectable, for example, in contemporary economics. It took a new turn of the utmost importance when Spencer (1870) linked it up with the Darwinian theory of evolution, contending that "pains are the correlatives of actions injurious to the organism, while pleasures are the correlatives of actions conducive to its welfare [Vol. I, p. 279]."

There is certainly much to say for Bentham's (1789) famous dictum that "Nature has placed mankind under the governance of two sovereign masters, *pain* and *pleasure*." Nevertheless, there were always some difficulties with the classical hedonistic theory. One was the tendency to blur the distinction between psychological hedonism and ethical hedonism: Factual questions concerning the role of pleasure and pain in determining behavior were commonly discussed in conjunction with normative questions regarding their role in the good life or in determining what is and is not moral conduct. This was characteristic of the early Cyrenaics and Epicureans as well as of the nineteenth–century Utilitarians. Some thinkers have been troubled by the apparent fact that, if we attribute the occurrence of an action to its consequences, we are invoking teleology or backward causality. But this uneasiness can readily be dispelled either by pointing out that the present action results from previous experiences of pleasure following the performance of similar actions or by invoking an anticipation or expectation of pleasure that precedes and prompts present action. Rather more serious is the abundance of heroic or stupid actions that seem to contradict the hedonistic principle. Hedonists maintained that those who perform these actions must have expected more pleasure or less pain than if they had refrained from them. But this shows how easily hedonistic theories can fall into circularity unless they are constructed with due attention to the requirement of testability.

At the start of the twentieth century, Freud (1911) was developing his highly original, and more complicated, brand of hedonism with its two distinct hedonistic principles, the "pleasure principle" and the "reality principle." Like Aristotle, he found close relations between pleasure and the satisfaction of desires or wishes. It is noteworthy that McDougall (1926), whose motivation theory had so much in common with Freud's, chided him for succumbing to the "fallacy known as psychological hedonism, the assumption that all human striving is fundamentally a striving for pleasure [p. 20]." He asserted that ". . . pleasure and pain are not in themselves springs of action, but at the most of undirected movements: they serve rather to modify instinctive processes, pleasure tending to sustain and prolong any mode of action, pain to cut it short . . . [1908, p. 43]." In other words, McDougall (cf. 1923, p. 70) acknowledged the crucial role of pleasure and pain in learning.

INTROSPECTIVE EXPERIMENTS

Meanwhile, the introspectionist pioneers of experimental psychology were using the "method of impression" to investigate determinants of "feeling," a kind of conscious experience varying along a pleasant–unpleasant dimension. Their investigations dissolved in an acrimonious flurry of disputation over such questions as whether feelings require other dimensions besides pleasantness–unpleasantness for their classification and whether they are distinct from sensations. This line of investigation had one outcome of considerable moment. It succeeded in discrediting pleasure and pain as explanatory concepts by stamping them so thoroughly as shadowy mental entities.

Curiously enough, both Watson and Titchener, who were poles apart in many ways, repudiated hedonism for essentially this reason. Watson (1914) undertook "to combat the idea that pleasure or pain has anything to do with habit formation . . . to call those stimuli pleasant to which the animal positively reacts, and unpleasant to which he negatively reacts is making a wholesale gratuitous assumption . . . [pp. 257–258]." Titchener (1910) denied that "pleasantness and unpleasantness are incentives to and deterrents from action [Vol. I, p. 467]." "We might ask," he wrote, "how it is that a mental process can incite or deter, 'stamp in' this and 'stamp out' that mode of reaction [Vol. I, p. 468]." Introspective evidence, he contended, indicates that "Movement follows on suggestion; and the conscious aspect of suggestion may be pleasurable, unpleasurable, or indifferent."

Thorndike (1933), the originator of the "law of effect," adopted the term "confirming reaction" to denote the "unknown reaction of neurons which is aroused by the satisfier and which strengthens connections upon which it impinges," i.e., what later came to be called "reinforcement." He also insisted that the "confirming reaction is independent of sensory pleasure," citing evidence (Tolman, Hall, & Bretnall, 1932) that it can sometimes be produced by painful stimulation.

After the Behaviorist Revolution

By the end of the 1920s, the influence of behaviorism and kindred movements in psychology, as well as of operationism and logical empiricism in philosophy of science, had deterred psychologists from interesting themselves in pleasure as a kind of conscious experience or an attribute of conscious experience, to be studied through descriptive introspection, and from placing great hopes in it as a means of illuminating behavior. Nevertheless, the irrefragable element of truth in the hedonistic current of thought precluded its drying up completely. It was simply diverted into new channels.

The new channels form, in fact, a bifurcation, breaking up into a delta (see Fig. 1-1). Deltas are typically fertile but muddy. This one is no exception. The various branches of the hedonistic delta have all contributed valuable theoretical notions and experimental data. But the divergence of so many heterogeneous lines of research from the hedonistic mainstream has impeded the formation of a satisfactory theory of motivation. The task of recombining them and synthesizing them must surely have a

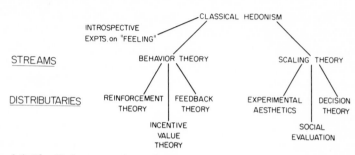

Fig. 1-1. The Hedonistic Delta. Offshoots of hedonism in psychological theory.

high priority both in this volume and in the research of the next few decades.

The bifurcation results from the two different ways in which experimental psychologists handle the problem of replacing mentalistic concepts derived either from experiments using descriptive introspection or from everyday language. Phenomenologists use a very different, and perhaps better thought-out, kind of introspection than the *Beschreibung* of Wundt and Titchener, but it is a kind practiced in the armchair rather than in the laboratory. Analytic philosophers of the ordinary–language school look for truths implicit in the turns of phrase that we use to discuss mental entities in nontechnical conversation. But experimental psychologists have two recourses. One is to adopt concepts rooted in observation of overt behavior. The other is to study "latent variables," "intervening variables" or "psychological magnitudes," derived from scaling techniques, i.e., from quantitative verbal (or quasi-verbal) judgments subjected to appropriate mathematical treatments. The two branches of our bifurcation can therefore be designated, respectively, as the *behavior-theory* stream and the *scaling-theory* stream. Both of them actually started some time before introspective structuralism petered out. But each of them has since split up into three main distributaries, which are worth considering in turn.

THE BEHAVIOR-THEORY STREAM

Representatives of the behavior-theory stream have taken either of two phenomena as their starting points. One is learning, i.e., a lasting change in the strength or probability of a response, or in the strength of a stimulus–response association, that results from certain conjunctions of stimuli or of stimuli and responses. The other is performance, i.e., the selection of one response among several alternatives that could be performed in a particular situation. Those concentrating on learning have hoped that their concepts and hypotheses will take care of the problems of performance, and vice versa.

Reinforcement. The experimental study of learning, especially in animals, has spawned the concept of "reinforcement." It can be traced back to Thorndike's (1898) research on trial-and-error learning (which had precursors in the writings of Spencer and of Bain), pointing to the "law of effect." The earliest version of this law (when it was still known as the "law of habit formation") is the most succinct: "Any act which in a given situation produces satisfaction becomes associated with that situation, so that, when the situation recurs, the act is more likely than before to recur also [Thorndike, 1903, p. 203]." However, Thorndike sought to preserve from circularity his statement about the role of satisfaction in learning by defining it in terms of performance: "By a satisfying state of affairs is meant one which the animal does nothing to avoid, often doing things which maintain or renew it [Thorndike, 1913, p. 2]."

Thorndike's term "satisfaction" soon gave way to a term appropriated, or rather misappropriated, from Pavlov, namely "reinforcement." I say "misappropriated," because Pavlov meant something rather different by it, and there is a need, which only this word can fulfill, for a term with a broader connotation (see Berlyne, 1967, 1969b). The kinds of reinforcement that apply to instrumental or operant conditioning, and promote the learning of responses on which they are consequent, are surely best called "rewards." Under whatever designation, the elucidation of this concept has consumed armies of experimental subjects and deluges of theoretical ink during the last half century. There has, however, been a curious and lamentable tendency to overlook the fact that reinforcement or reward, being something that manifests itself through learning, implies some durable change in behavior. This follows, in fact, from Thorndike's original statement of the law of effect. It is all too often forgotten that reward effects are liable to confusion with transient associative or motivational effects unless experimental designs incorporate appropriate precautions (Berlyne, 1967, 1969b, 1972c).

Incentive Value. According to a widespread alternative view, learned behavior is governed by expectations. This view holds, in a nutshell, that whether or not an animal or human being carries out a certain act depends on what consequences he expects or anticipates and on how he evaluates those consequences. "Incentive value" is probably the commonest, and on the whole the best, designation for this evaluation, although others have been used. For example, Tolman (1932, 1959) called it "demand," apparently influenced by Lewin's (1935) term *Aufforderungs-charakter*, which has been translated as "demand character" and as "valence."

Tolman's and Lewin's were the first influential theories centered on the concepts of expectation and incentive value. The former was offered as a neo-behavioristic account of animal learning, while the latter was associated with some of the earliest experimental attacks on human motivation. Since the work of these two pioneers, this kind of theory has won the allegiance of psychologists interested in social and personality aspects of motivation, particularly achievement motivation (e.g., Heckhausen, 1963; Atkinson, 1964). It has received new systematic treatments from Irwin (1971) and from Ryan (1971). It has spread to physiological psychology (e.g., Stein, 1964; Trowell, Panksepp, & Gandelman, 1969). Seward (1956) has even argued, with some justice, that the latest modifications of the Hull–Spence learning theory, long regarded as a bulwark of the reinforcement approach, turned it into something very close to an expectancy-incentive theory. The same could be said of the most recent version of Estes's (1971) mathematical theory of learning, which was originally built around the notion of a "reinforcing event."

Positive Feedback. The third distributary of the behavior-theory stream also takes performance as its criterion. It focuses on the accompaniments of a response. Certain conditions obtaining while an action is in progress promote the continuation and intensification of the action. Others bring about its attenuation and interruption.

These favorable and unfavorable accompaniments correspond to what the cyberneticians have taught us to call "positive feedback" and "negative feedback," respectively. Early in the history of cybernetics, these concepts were used to underpin objectivistic analyses of "purpose" and of "goal seeking" (Rosenblueth, Wiener, & Bigelow, 1943; Ashby, 1952). Mowrer (1956, 1960) and Smith and Smith (1966) have, in their different ways, suggested that the concept of "feedback" can account for most of the phenomena previously attributed to "reward" or "reinforcement." Closely related is Miller's (1963) notion of a "go mechanism," as well as the rather similar notion of a "go-to-it tendency" postulated much earlier by Razran (1939) in an analysis of instrumental conditioning.

It is worth noting that the reinforcement approach, the incentive-value approach, and the positive-feedback approach correspond precisely to Troland's (1928) "hedonism of the past," "hedonism of the future," and "hedonism of the present," respectively. This brings us to the first big problem with which, I suggest, we must concern ourselves:

Problem 1. *To what extent are theoretical approaches based on the concepts of "reinforcement (reward)," "incentive value," and "positive feedback" capable of accounting for the same phenomena? To the extent that they are, which approach is the most promising, or can some synthesis of them all be accomplished?*

The Scaling-Theory Stream

Experiments requiring human subjects to indicate which object, real or imaginary, they "prefer" or "like" more, to state how "pleasant" or "good" they find something, or to make other evaluative judgments, have been carried out with an immense assortment of stimulus material, with a rich arsenal of data-collecting procedures, and, as they became available, with more and more sophisticated techniques through which mathematical models could be built out of the data. In these experiments, a subject is faced with some form of what Coombs (1964) calls "Task A," requiring him to judge how near each stimulus comes to some point in a "psychological space" that represents his personal ideal.

The stimulus material has ranged from Russian female first names to occupations (see Zajonc, 1968). A compendious summary of relatively early research of this kind was provided by Beebe-Center (1932). Helson (1964) has incorporated evaluative judgments into his adaptation-level theory of perception, building on Beebe-Center's (1929) "law of affective equilibrium." This law states that the pleasantness or unpleasantness of a stimulus varies inversely with the pleasantness or unpleasantness of the stimuli that closely preceded it. Young (1959) and Pfaffman (1960) have, in default of verbal responses, derived "affective" or "hedonic" scales for edible and potable substances from animals' preferences, as revealed by frequencies of choice and amounts ingested.

However, most of the investigators within the scaling-theory stream have belonged to one or another of the following three approaches:

Experimental Aesthetics. The longest-lasting branch of the scaling-theory stream is experimental aesthetics. This, the second oldest area of experimental psychology, has been in existence continuously, though somewhat falteringly, since Fechner initiated it in the 1860s.

Until recently, experimental aesthetics consisted of asking subjects to state, in one form or another, how much they "liked" particular stimulus objects, which stimulus objects they "preferred," etc. Fechner introduced three methods of inquiry, two of which were adaptations of his psychophysical methods for the peculiar needs of aesthetics. Later refinements of scaling technique have been taken over by psychological aestheticians as they became available. Their stimulus material has sometimes consisted of genuine works of art (e.g., reproductions of paintings, musical excerpts), and sometimes of stimuli that might be found among the elements of a work of art (e.g., colors, shapes, musical chords and intervals).

Of late, experimental aesthetics has shown signs of revival, but a new phase that might appropriately be called "the new experimental aesthetics [Berlyne, 1971, 1972b]" is emerging. It differs from earlier phases by concentrating on the structural or "collative" variables that would seem to constitute the crux of aesthetic phenomena, in widening the range of verbal judgments that it elicits from subjects, and in supplementing verbal techniques with measures of psychophysiological reactions and of overt motor behavior.

Social-Attitude Scaling. Techniques for eliciting and analyzing evaluative judgments form a prominent part of the social psychologist's equipment. Measurement of evaluative attitudes toward ethnic groups was introduced by Bogardus (1925) with his social-distance scale. This led to the methodological contributions of Thurstone (1928) and Likert (1932), applicable to the measurement of attitudes toward social groups and toward opinions on matters of social importance. Moreno's (1934) sociometry introduced a rather different method for studying evaluations of individuals.

The general thrust of these lines of social–psychological research leads away from the fundamental concerns of hedonism. Nevertheless, the social psychologists have been more active than anybody else in devising sophisticated data-gathering and data-processing techniques that can be used for probing evaluative reactions to all kinds of stimuli, not only those of interest to social psychology.

Decision Theory. Researchers working in the frontier regions of psychology, economics, and statistics have, since World War II, been concerning themselves with how people ought to make decisions under uncertainty and risk if they are to be rational, with how people actually make decisions under uncertainty and risk, and with how far advisable decisions and actual decisions approximate each other. Rational behavior consists of acting in such a way as to maximize the expected value of the outcome. Expected value is the product of an outcome's probability and of the value placed in it, usually known as its "utility."

However, actual behavior can be guided only by subjective probabilities and subjective estimates of utility. So, a great deal of ingenuity has been expended on the search for ways of measuring subjective probabilities and subjective utilities, which raise special problems because the behavioral manifestations of the two are so closely intertwined. This problem was aired in the theoretical writings of Ramsey (1931), von

Neumann and Morgenstern (1944) and Savage (1951). These writers all suggested procedures requiring subjects to choose between alternative wagers. Procedures of this kind have been utilized by several experimenters, beginning with Mosteller and Nogee (1951), to measure subjective utility. There are, of course, other possible methods, such as simple rating or ranking. Economists have discussed indifference curves since the notion was originated by Edgeworth (1881). Thurstone (1931) introduced experimental procedures, requiring subjects to choose between combinations of commodities in different quantities, to identify these curves.

We therefore come to the second major problem facing us:

Problem 2. *To what extent are the scaling techniques used by the various currents of scaling theory to study evaluative judgments measuring the same variables?*

There is a fair amount of work (see Berlyne, 1971, 1972a) to suggest that judgments of how far stimulus objects are "pleasing," "pleasant," "beautiful," or "good" reflect a common underlying variable, related to Osgood's (Osgood, Suci, & Tannenbaum, 1957) evaluative dimension.

On the other hand, judgments of how "interesting" objects are seem to reflect a quite different kind of evaluation, related to the first kind in a complicated way. Experiments with visual and auditory patterns point, in fact, to two distinct kinds of evaluative judgments, one (interestingness) increasing with complexity over most of the range, while the other (pleasingness, etc.) reaches a peak at intermediate levels of complexity (Berlyne, 1971, 1972a).

Then comes the next problem:

Problem 3. *How much do the evaluative variables revealed by scaling techniques have in common with the evaluative concepts figuring in behavior-theory approaches, i.e., reward value, incentive value, and positive feedback?*

It is noteworthy that the theoretical models favored by decision theorists are very similar to those behavior theories that center around the concepts of "expectation" and "incentive value." This is one obvious and important link between the two streams.

Common experience suggests that instrumental learning is reinforced by many conditions that human subjects would, if asked, surely judge to be pleasant. They include opportunities to eat when hungry and termination of pain. There are no obvious counterexamples that come to mind readily, but, as it proceeds, research may very well reveal some. There have been a few experiments in which reward value, manifested through the learning of nonverbal responses, has shown correlations with evaluations as revealed by verbal judgments (see Berlyne, 1971, pp. 79–80; Witryol, 1971).

On the other hand, in at least some circumstances, the visual stimuli that human subjects choose to look at, and those they look at for a longer time, are ones that are judged more interesting rather than more pleasing (see Berlyne, 1971). Sometimes, in fact, exploration time and exploratory choice favor visual patterns that are judged less "pleasing" or "good" (Harrison, 1968; Berlyne, 1972a). The implication seems to be that reward value, incentive value, and positive feedback may not always increase with verbally revealed evaluations.

It is noteworthy that none of the distributaries we have reviewed, despite their common hedonistic ancestry, builds theories of behavior around the concept of "pleasure." For many people, pleasure is a subjective, conscious state. Now that the introspective techniques of Wundt, Titchener, and their contemporaries have been abandoned, those who think of it in this way must turn to the phenomenologist or to the post-Wittgenstein analytic philosopher for its elucidation. Pleasure can figure in the vocabulary of the modern experimental psychologist only as a term denoting an intervening variable, manifested or, as we say, expressed through verbal, facial, or postural responses. We may therefore appropriately extend Problem 3 to cover the relations between pleasure, in this sense, and the hedonic concepts of behavior theory and scaling theory.

Determinants of Hedonic Value

While awaiting the empirical data that alone can solve the three major problems we have noted, it will be convenient to use the term "hedonic value" to refer to all these hedonic variables collectively or, at least, to the highest common factor of their connotations.

We are therefore brought to the fourth major problem:

Problem 4. *What factors determine hedonic value?*

This problem will, of course, have to be examined separately for each of the hedonic variables to the extent that they turn out to be uncorrelated.

It is rather astonishing how little attention has been paid, especially in the last 20 years, to the question of what events do, and do not, have hedonic value and what gives them their hedonic value. A recent book

(Glaser, 1971) presents analyses of issues surrounding the concept of "reinforcement" by a fair number of distinguished contributors. But they have hardly anything to say on this particular matter. Investigators have concentrated on other questions; behavior theorists have been preoccupied with the scheduling, or distribution in time and space, of rewards or incentives, and decision theorists with the mathematical properties of preferences and utility scales. They have been content to confine their consideration to agents of proven positive hedonic value, such as food, water, relief from pain, and money. So, they have been led away from the question of what events actually have reward value, incentive value, or utility, and why.

Many writers have been deflected on to the curious pastime of asking whether learning can occur without reinforcement and trying to answer this question by finding out whether rats will learn mazes in the absence of food or water, whether children will learn to speak grammatically without parental browbeating, and whether verbal learning is improved by awards of points and money for successful recall. Some theoretical discussions have been equivalent to concluding that cars do not need sources of power because they will run without coal. Some experimental procedures have been equivalent to placing different quantities of coal in the petrol (gasoline) tank to see whether they determine how far a car will go before coming to a halt. Such observations do not, of course, tell us whether a car must have a source of power if it is to be mobile and whether its range depends on how much fuel it has. These questions can be answered in the affirmative by definition. A more profitable question is what substances can and cannot serve as sources of power for a car and why.

Stimuli or Responses

Some theorists have been inclined to define conditions of positive hedonic value, particularly reinforcing conditions, in terms of responses, whereas others have defined them in terms of stimuli. Those who think of pleasure or reward as dependent essentially on opportunities to perform certain kinds of actions have drawn encouragement from four directions. First, there is the observation that so many episodes of behavior, both unlearned and learned, lead up to, and terminate with, specific kinds of consummatory behavior. Second, there is the fact that the areas in the brain that produce the most pronounced rewarding effects when stimulated seem to coincide, in large measure, with the areas of the hypothalamus where stimulation has been found to elicit specific biological activities (Glickman & Schiff, 1967). Third, the latest phase of Hull–Spence theory (Spence, 1956) attributed effects of reward on learned responses to the "fractional-anticipatory-goal-response $(r_g\text{--}s_g)$" mechanism, i.e., the occurrence, in a conditioned anticipatory form, of some fragment of the behavior to be performed in the goal situation. Fourth, there is the imaginative theory advanced by Premack (1959, 1965), according to which a reinforcing situation is one that has a relatively high probability of evoking a response or evokes a particular kind of response for a relatively high proportion of the time.

There are, however, considerations to be set against these. The pleasurable or rewarding conditions to which human beings are susceptible seem to be too numerous and varied to correspond to specific kinds of response. Many of them, such as contemplation of works of art or absorption of interesting information in written or spoken form, do not seem to be associated with any characteristic overt action, unless the outward manifestations of the orientation reaction are regarded as such. It is noteworthy that Valenstein's (Valenstein, Cox, & Kakolewski, 1968; Valenstein 1970) recent findings cast doubt on the supposed fixed correlations between hypothalamic areas and specific drives or classes of activity. He and his collaborators have found that stimulation of one and the same point in the hypothalamus of the same animal can give rise to different behaviors, depending on which object is present. When, later on, the animal is confronted with several objects associated with different activities, what he does when stimulated is likely to depend on which objects have been presented singly in the past. The first of these observations is precisely what one would expect if hypothalamic stimulation produced something in the nature of a state of heightened general arousal (or general drive). There would be a markedly increased tendency to become active, with the precise form of activity determined by the external stimulus situation of the moment. The influence of the original experience with a single object on later behavior when confronted with several objects suggests that acting on a particular stimulus object when arousal is unusually high leads to reinforcement. Lastly, it is noteworthy that, in the most recent version of his theory, Premack (1971) sees fit to relate the probability of response, which is correlated with reinforcement value, to the "value" attaching to the corresponding stimulus situation.

There seems, therefore, much to be said for the alternative approach, the one that connects hedonic value with properties of stimuli. Within this approach, it is possible to discern some distinct positions. Troland (1928) spoke of "beneceptive" and "nociceptive sense channels" whose "normal excitation" produces pleasantness and unpleasantness, respectively. There seem indeed to be receptors that transmit predominantly agreeable or disagreeable sensations. But this can hardly be the kernel of the matter. Sensations coming from most, and conceivably all, of the sense organs can be pleasant, unpleasant, or indifferent at different times. Their hedonic value depends on parameters of stimulation and on the organism's state. Correspondences between stimuli and motivational states have, on the other hand, been viewed by other theorists as the bases of hedonic value. These are theorists who identify pleasantness and reward value with ability to satisfy wishes, wants, instincts, or drives.

As the scope of research on motivation spreads to more and more forms of human behavior, we are, in fact, driven to recognize that hedonic value can depend on a quite bewildering diversity of stimulus properties, interacting with various internal factors, including motivational conditions, traces left by other stimuli encountered in the last few minutes, and traces left by learning experiences stretching back over years. They include *psychophysical* properties, such as intensity, color, and rate of change, which are a matter of spatial and temporal distribution of energy. They include *ecological* factors, involving correlation with events that promote or threaten biological adaptation and consequently appropriateness to the motivational conditions of the moment. Finally, they include the *structural* or *collative* variables, such as familiarity–novelty, expectedness–surprisingness, simplicity–complexity, and clarity–ambiguity (Berlyne, 1960, 1963, 1965, 1966). These are bound up with relations of similarity or dissimilarity, concordance or discordance, among stimulus elements, whether perceived together or at different times.

The term *arousal potential* has been proposed (Berlyne, 1960) to cover all these stimulus properties. It represents the extent to which a stimulus is capable of raising *arousal*, a term to which we shall come in a moment. In other words, it represents something like overall power to excite the nervous system, to command attention, to influence behavior. Arousal potential includes everything that Walker (in Chapter 3) subsumes under "complexity." But broad as his use of this word is, it does not seem to include all the components (e.g., psychophysical and ecological properties) of arousal potential. Several other writers have sought to relate hedonic value to the information content of a stimulus (or of the environment as a whole). But it seems unlikely that informational measures encompass all the stimulus properties that can be of motivational importance. The total arousal potential of the environment (both external and internal) at a particular moment is identifiable with what Eysenck (in Chapter 6) calls *level of stimulation*.

Increases and Decreases in Arousal

The concept of "arousal" is the latest in a long line of concepts referring to the overall intensity of behavior, the degree to which the organism is mobilized and expending energy, level of excitation in the nervous system, or, in everyday language, level of excitement and alertness. Its immediate predecessor was "general drive level" (with the word "drive" in the singular, as distinct from "drives" in the plural), i.e., Hull's D. There has of late been some controversy over the value of the concept of "arousal." It is true that the many indices through which fluctuations in arousal are charted are imperfectly correlated with one another, and, in some circumstances, groups of them can vary with remarkable independence of one another. Nevertheless, as pointed out elsewhere (Berlyne, 1967), concepts presenting similar problems are familiar to students of personality and of human abilities, who nevertheless find them serviceable. The many tests of "intelligence" and "introversion" are intercorrelated significantly but not perfectly. They all presumably reflect some common underlying process or group of closely related processes, but, at the same time, each of them can be influenced by other processes peculiar to itself. Another analogy, which may appeal to those who are fortunate enough to be in closer touch with the portfolio analyst than with the factor analyst, is the stock-exchange index. It has its usefulness, even though the prices of individual shares and groups of shares may very well fall while it is rising, and vice versa.

There is, further, an ambiguity that has been responsible for some confusion, since many people are not aware of it. The term "arousal" usually means "arousal level," a variable that fluctuates from moment to moment both in response to external stimuli and in response to internal events. *Arousal*, in the sense of arousal level, must be carefully distinguished from degrees of *arousal increment* and *decrement*, which are the amounts by which arousal level goes up or down (i.e., if A is arousal level, arousal increment is ΔA). Some use the word "arousal" to signify not arousal level but arousal increment. Stimuli that produce larger arousal increments than others are commonly and naturally spoken of as more "arousing" stimuli, and it seems reasonable to conclude that more "arousal" is what more "arousing" stimuli produce. However, what actually results from them is a greater difference between arousal before they begin and arousal after they end.

Despite the hazards of basing speculations on existing neurophysiological knowledge, there are three kinds of evidence suggestive of close connections between hedonic value and changes in arousal, i.e., arousal increments and decrements. First, rewarding and pleasurable events commonly give rise to unmistakable changes in level of activity and excitement; sometimes they produce marked agitation, and sometimes they produce relaxation and quiescence. Second, all the properties of stimuli on which hedonic value seems to depend have been shown to influence one or other of the recognized indices of arousal. This does not imply that they necessarily exert their hedonic and other effects through changes in arousal, but it indicates that they might do so. Third, there are evidently plenty of overlaps and connections between the parts of the brain that govern changes in arousal and those that govern pleasure and reward.

As for our stress on upward and downward shifts in arousal level, it is worth noting how many recent theorists have been led from different starting points to the conclusion that hedonic value is dependent above all on changes in level of stimulation or level of activity. They include McClelland, Atkinson, Clark, and Lowell (1953), Premack (1959), Helson (1964), and Fowler (1971).

As just mentioned, common observation provides support both for the view that positive hedonic value results from conditions that raise arousal and for the contrary view that it results from conditions that reduce arousal. These opposite views found expression very early in the history of Western thought. Some time in the third or fourth century B.C., the Cyrenaic school, led by Aristippus, posited (according to Diogenes Laertius, II 86), "two states of passion, pain and pleasure, a gentle movement being pleasure and a violent movement being pain." Like so many later theorists, Aristippus recognized that highly disturbing stimuli are usually unpleasant, punishing, or aversive. He concluded therefore that hedonic value is nonmonotonically related to what we now call "arousal increment" or "magnitude of orientation reaction," a conclusion for which there is now a substantial amount of experimental evidence (Berlyne, 1967).

Aristippus's near contemporary, Plato (*Philebus*, 31D), contended, on the other hand, that "when the harmony in the organism is disturbed, there is at once a dissolution of the normal condition and simultaneously an origination of pain. On the other hand, when it is reconstituted and reverted to its normal condition pleasure is originated." His view resembles those of some motivation theorists of the last hundred years. Examples are Fechner (1873), who equated pleasure with conditions favoring stability, Freud (1915) in his middle period, when he held that "the nervous system is an apparatus having the function of abolishing stimuli which reach it, or of reducing excitation to the lowest possible level," Miller and Dollard (1941), who identified reward with "events producing reduction in . . . strength of stimulus," and many other twentieth-century writers using concepts like "homeostasis." Like these later writers, who believed that departures from homeostasis or disturbances due to stimulation are accompanied by drives impelling the organism toward corrective measures, Plato (41) referred to "desire for a state opposed to that present in the body." And finally, just as twentieth-century motivation theorists have felt compelled to supplement drive-reduction views with concepts like "cathexis" and "secondary reward (conditioned reinforcement)," Plato (32C) pointed to a second species of pleasures and pains, namely, "those aroused within the soul itself, independently of the body, by anticipation." He maintained (35), for example, that "pleasure due to memory and anticipation of repletion can accompany pain due to depletion."

THE AROUSAL-BOOST AND AROUSAL-REDUCTION MECHANISMS

Ever since these two early thinkers, what we may call arousal-increase and arousal-reduction theories of hedonic value have had their adherents and their arguments. It is admittedly dangerous, when told by one person that $2 + 2 = 4$ and by another that $2 + 2 = 6$, to conclude that the truth must be that $2 + 2 = 5$! Nevertheless, the persistence of these apparently opposite theoretical positions through the centuries certainly suggests that both have their elements of validity and that the ultimate answer will be found in some synthesis of them. A recent review of available evidence from several areas of research (Berlyne, 1967) reveals much support for the hypothesis that there are two mechanisms of positive hedonic value, one brought into play by moderate arousal increments, due to stimulation representing moderate levels of arousal potential, and the other activated by drops in arousal from aversive or unpleasant high levels. We may call these the "arousal-boost" and "arousal-reduction" mechanisms.

As far as the arousal-boost mechanism is concerned, the relations between hedonic value and arousal potential seem clearly enough to be nonmonotonic. They have often been represented by unimodal curves—the inverted U-shaped curve, the Wundt curve (Fig. 1-3), the butterfly curve (McClelland *et al.*, 1953) resembling two Wundt curves back to back—although curves with more than one peak have occasionally emerged.

The most obvious way in which such unimodal curves can arise is through the interaction of two antagonistic factors, one of which is predominant at lower values of the independent variable while the other predominates at higher values. A good example is provided by the first inverted U-shaped curve to appear in the history of science, namely the parabolic trajectory of the cannonball discussed by Galileo. Here, the succession of a rising phase followed by a falling phase results from the interaction of the upward component of the acceleration imparted by the explosive charge and the downward acceleration due to gravity.

So, it is interesting in this connection that several students of brain functions, of animal behavior, and of human behavior have been led to postulate two mutually counteracting systems, one productive of rewarding and pleasurable effects, approach movements, and positive feedback, whereas the other acts in the opposite directions. I counted nine of these the last time I tried to list them (Berlyne, 1971, p. 84), but it is more than likely that I missed some. One can make a few plausible assumptions about the way these two systems work, especially the assumption, for which a fair amount of evidence can be cited, that it takes more arousal potential to activate the negative or aversion system than the positive or reward system. These assumptions enable one to represent the degrees of activation of the two systems as functions of arousal potential by the two ogival curves in Fig. 1-2. The net hedonic values associated with different levels of arousal potential should then correspond to the algebraic sum of these two curves. If we subtract the ordinates of the aversion-system curve from the ordinates of the reward-system curve, we obtain the curve shown in Fig. 1-3, which has precisely the shape of the curve introduced by Wundt in 1874 to show how pleasantness and unpleasantness of sensations vary with stimulus intensity. Given our broader interpretation, this curve accounts tolerably well for a fair-sized body of experimental findings yielded by scaling and other techniques.[2]

The Wundt curve resulting from our present line of argument reveals three regions of importance. First, between the absolute threshold and the level of arousal potential corresponding to maximum hedonic value, we have a region (A) where stimulation is pleasurable and rewarding. Between this point and the point where the curve crosses the base line,

---

[2] Eysenck (in Chapter 6) suggests that the curve relating hedonic value to *level of stimulation* is more likely to have the shape of an inverted U than that of the Wundt curve. This point is well taken, because environments that are inordinately impoverished, like those that are overloaded with stimulation, are apt to be unpleasant, aversive, and punishing. However, the Wundt curve, as interpreted here, relates hedonic value to the *arousal potential* of a particular stimulus. This is likely to have a different shape from the curve discussed by Eysenck if only because, whereas an environment can be characterized by a relative lack of stimulation, a stimulus can hardly be characterized by its own absence!

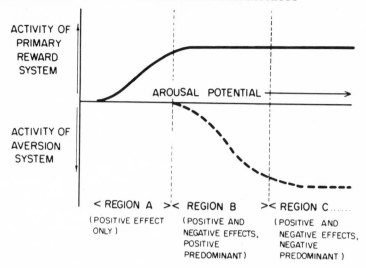

Fig. 1-2. Hypothetical curves representing degrees of activity in primary reward system and aversion system as functions of arousal potential.

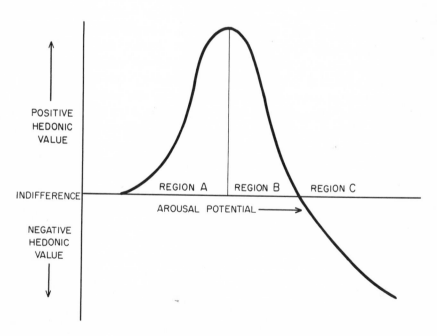

Fig. 1-3. The reinterpreted Wundt curve.

we have a region (B) where net hedonic value will be positive, but, since both reward and aversion systems are active to some extent, there should be an admixture of pleasant and unpleasant coloring or, in other words, both the onset and the termination of stimulation should be rewarding. There are reasons for believing that this paradoxical state of affairs is in fact realized in some circumstances (see Berlyne, 1971, Ch. 8). Finally, there is a region (C) corresponding to the highest values of arousal potential, where stimulation is predominantly unpleasant and punishing. This is the region where positive hedonic value will result from any agent that reduces arousal to a more tolerable level, which brings us to the second or arousal-reduction mechanism.

It must be strongly emphasized that this interpretation of the Wundt curve relates hedonic value to *arousal potential*, which, it will be remembered, means something like "stimulus strength" defined in terms of specifiable stimulus properties. With regard to the underlying physiology, the most plausible conjecture seems to be that arousal potential affects hedonic value by determining the extent of an *arousal increment*. So, the Wundt curve might represent hedonic value as a function of the degree by which arousal is momentarily raised by stimulation. What is involved is presumably something like the orientation reaction, which involves a short-lasting rise in arousal level followed, after a few seconds, by a return toward the initial level. This is quite different from the use of unimodal curves (Hebb, 1955; Fiske & Maddi, 1961) to represent hedonic value as a function of *arousal level*, implying that abnormally low levels, as well as abnormally high levels, are aversive.

There seem to be several arguments against this later view, popular as it has been. First, the distress occasioned by boredom (i.e., inordinately low arousal potential) seems to have more to do with the paradoxical rise in at least the autonomic and somatic indices of arousal that results from sensory deprivation. Second, everyday experience provides no reason for believing that low arousal (i.e., drowsiness) is necessarily uncomfortable. Fowler (1971, p. 178) argues, cogently enough, that it is contradictory to maintain that a state of low arousal can mean a high degree of motivation (i.e., to engage in stimulus-seeking activity).

Theories postulating two antagonistic systems in the brain are compatible with views that identify positive hedonic value with removal of distress. These include homeostatic theories from Plato to the twentieth century, the Hullian drive-reduction theory of reinforcement (Mowrer, 1938; Hull, 1943), and the newer drive-reduction theories of Konorski (1967), emphasizing reduction of specific drives, and Grastyán (Grastyán, Szabo, Molnar, & Kolta, 1968), stressing release from an inhibitory state.

It seems possible that the two groups of evaluative judgments that factor-analytic and other experiments have revealed (Berlyne, 1971, 1972a), namely those expressed through words like "pleasingness" and its nearsynonyms and those expressed through "interestingness," have something to do with these two hypothesized mechanisms of hedonic value. Interesting stimulus patterns may be those whose arousal potential is within the aversive range but permit relatively prompt arousal reduction through perceptual and intellectual processing. They presumably correspond to Region B and possibly Region C of the Wundt curve. There have been indications that patterns rated highly pleasing, etc., are ones productive of an arousal boost, which means that they belong either to Region A or Region B. This might explain why some patterns are judged to be both interesting and pleasing, whereas others are one without the other.

Olds and Olds (1965) have been led by their neurophysiological experiments to postulate three systems in the brain (see Fig. 1-4) governing hedonic processes. Their scheme fits in with our suggestion that positive

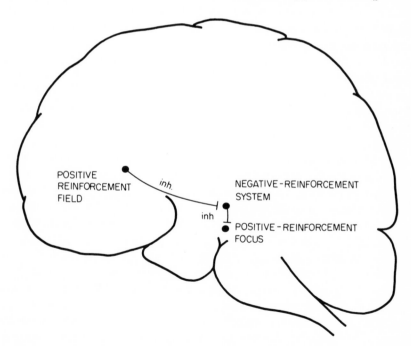

Fig. 1-4. Approximate location of three hedonic systems in the human brain according to Olds and Olds. [Adapted from diagram of rat brain in Olds & Olds, 1965).]

hedonic value can result either from removal of aversive conditions (arousal reduction) or from moderate stimulation (an arousal boost). The three systems are the "positive-reinforcement field" in the limbic system, which inhibits a "negative-reinforcement system" centered in the midbrain. This in its turn inhibits a "positive-reinforcement focus" located in the neighborhood of the lateral hypothalamus and medial forebrain bundle. Consequently, agents activating the positive-reinforcement field produce reward by attenuating unpleasantness and thus relieving the positive reinforcement focus from inhibition. We may surmise that this is how our supposed arousal-reduction mechanism works. On the other hand, some stimuli could conceivably act on the positive reinforcement focus directly, bypassing the other two systems. These would be stimuli productive of arousal boosts.

Since the Olds' provocative scheme first appeared, it has stirred up some debate. Valenstein and Campbell (1966) have shown that removal of large amounts of tissue from areas identified by Olds with the positive-reinforcement focus do not eliminate self-stimulation. This finding presumably casts doubt on Olds's anatomical mapping of these three systems rather than on the logical structure of his theory. Stein (1968) has interpreted recent neurophysiological findings as supportive of a two-system scheme, based on the assumption that, within the brain structures subserving hedonic value, traffic is mainly upward or rostrad, rather than downward or caudad as Olds maintained. We shall have to wait a resolution of these neurophysiological and neuroanatomical problems before we can judge their bearing on psychological problems in motivation theory.

One further difficulty comes from recent experiments (e.g., Kamiya, 1969) indicating that the EEG patterns, and associated emotional states, of human beings are subject to instrumental conditioning with feedback signals functioning as rewards. If changes in arousal level underlie reward value, could these changes themselves be subject to reinforcement by rewarding conditions? At one time (e.g., Dollard & Miller, 1950), learning theorists hypothesized that the onset of fear might be reinforced by subsequent fear reduction. Similarly, but in a different context, Premack (1971, p. 135) concludes from his own work that "goal responses" (i.e., responses occurring characteristically in reinforcing conditions) "are subject to reinforcement." Could changes in arousal be reinforced by subsequent changes in arousal? Or do these findings mean that whatever brain processes underlie reward value are separable from at least some manifestations of arousal? We shall presumably have to wait a little while for these questions also to be cleared up.

Hedonic Factors in Learning

Of all the hedonic words that we have reviewed, only "reinforcement" and "reward" (designating a special kind of reinforcement) are explicitly defined in terms of learning, i.e., lasting changes in behavior. Used in this way, these words correspond to concepts that are theoretically quite neutral. That rewarding and other reinforcing conditions, in our sense, influence learning is an incontrovertible fact. The question of how reinforcement works to produce learning is open to many different answers, and many have been proposed. How reward and reinforcement are related to the other hedonic concepts, which are defined in terms of performance or of verbal and other expressive responses, and what these other concepts may have to do with learning, are, it must be repeated, moot questions that have yet to be settled by empirical inquiry.

LEVELS OF LEARNING

The answers to these questions may very well be different for different kinds or levels of learning. It is significant that, in this volume, both Olds (Chapter 2) and Nuttin (Chapter 10), representatives of contrasting areas of research, differentiate a primitive level of "attentional learning" from a higher "cognitive" level. Olds, it is true, differentiates not only these two but other levels as well, all of them depending on distinct levels of the central nervous system and corresponding to successive evolutionary phases. The view that Olds has arrived at, after investigating the order in which various brain structures are implicated in the learning process, is strikingly in keeping with the view that Razran (1971) has derived from his comparative review of experiments on learning in different species. Razran concludes, with lavish documentation, that evolution has produced in turn no fewer than seven forms of learning whose governing principles are partly the same and partly different. As both Olds and Razran point out, the mechanism responsible for one form of learning is retained when a more advanced form appears on the scene. Nature is evidently like people who, after investing in a new color television set, relegate the old set to the basement rather than throwing it out. It remains in use, but its function changes.

EXPECTANCY LEARNING

The highest or "cognitive" level of learning evidently involves the phylogenetically newest brain structures in the neocortex (see Luria, 1973; Pribram, 1971). To this level belong the kinds of learning that give rise to, and make use of, rational processes—foresight, symbolic representation, reasoning (Berlyne, 1965). This is presumably the level where incentive value and expectation jointly hold sway. As we have seen, the kind of theory that centers on these two concepts (sometimes disguised by varying nomenclatures) has been applied to animal behavior by Tolman and by Spence and to human behavior by the decision theorists. As Walker reminds us (Chapter 3), he has compiled more recent evidence (1969) that, in animals, incentives, goals, pleasurable events—"rewards" in the everyday, as distinct from the technical, sense —do not determine what is learned so much as which piece of learning is utilized after acquisition. Learning requires no more than contiguity. Estes (1971) has mustered evidence from verbal-learning experiments in support of essentially the same points. Yet other findings cited by Bolles (1972) indicate that instrumental learning means acquisition of expectations rather than stimulus-response associations.

Theories holding that reinforcing events strengthen stimulus-response associations directly could compete for credence with expectancy theories as long as experimenters and theoreticians concentrated on simple instrumental conditioning. When a rat learns to obtain food by running to the goal box of a maze or by pressing a lever, the response that was followed by reward in the past and the response that can be expected to produce reward in the future are one and the same. Opportunities for crucial tests offer themselves when the behaviors that can be expected to produce maximal satisfaction at a particular time differ from those that have previously led to satisfaction.

Two areas in which this condition obtains, and voluminous research has shown that propitious new responses replace successful old responses, are exploratory behavior and achievement motivation. In these areas, the consequences of an act depend largely on novelty for their incentive value. Consequently, the act from which the most gratifying consequences can be expected is usually not the same as the act that was followed by gratification last time. And it is the former that invariably prevails. So, observations of this kind lend support to expectancy theory, and, more generally, to the view that hedonic value may control behavior as through the mediation of representational or "cognitive" processes. Other kinds of evidence are presented in this volume by Heckhausen (Chapter 9), Helson (Chapter 7), and Nuttin (Chapter 10).

LIMITATIONS OF EXISTING EXPECTANCY THEORIES

Despite the comfort that partisans of expectancy theory can draw from these conclusions, some reservations must be expressed about the expectancy theories that have appeared hitherto:

1. There has been a tendency to assume that the expectancy-incentive

mechanism applies to all learning, even the simplest. The evidence collected by Razran and by Olds warns against the belief that what holds for some forms of learning must hold for all of its forms. Expectations are intervening variables and, in accordance with Occam's razor, should be evoked only when there is no other practicable recourse. It is by no means clear that this condition is fulfilled with regard to the most primitive kinds of learning, e.g., instrumental conditioning in its most elementary forms, classical conditioning, and the predecessors of true classical conditioning that Razran discusses. In view of all this, we need to be told more than we have been told about how the relatively complex kinds of learning dependent on expectations are related to more primitive learning mechanisms and, in particular, how they might have grown out of these. The makings of answers to these questions may conceivably be found in the notion of a "transformation-selecting habit" that was introduced (Berlyne, 1965) to account for some peculiarities of directed thinking but may well be generalizable to motor behavior. Hull's (1931) theory of the "fractional anticipatory goal-response (r_G)" provides some inkling, however incomplete and imperfect, of how a stimulus-producing internal response may serve as a symbolic representation of an absent but desirable state of affairs. Through "configural conditioning" (Razran, 1939), or "positive patterning" (Hull, 1943), the combination of a present stimulus situation and a representation of a goal situation could become associated with, and therefore tend to evoke, a motor act capable of turning the one situation into the other. Similarly, a "transformation-applying habit" (Berlyne, 1965) could enable the organism to represent to itself the resulting goal situation when it is presented with an initial stimulus situation coupled with a representation of an act. Mechanisms of "stimulus–response generalization," which have still to receive adequate empirical investigation, would account for the appearance of novel transformational responses in novel situations in consequence of previous learning involving other responses in other situations.[3]

2. Defenders of expectancy theory have concentrated on recurrent contiguities between stimulus elements, or between stimuli and responses,

---

[3] Bolles (1972) argues that two kinds of expectation suffice to explain instrumental learning, namely the expectation of a particular kind of stimulus when another stimulus has occurred (S–S°) and the expectation of a particular kind of stimulus when a certain response has been performed (R–S°). His suggestion ignores, however, the fact that particular consequences can generally be expected after a particular response only if the response is performed in an appropriate stimulus situation. This fact receives recognition in Tolman's (1959) SR → S formula and in the notion (Berlyne, 1965) of a "transformation–applying habit" ($<u_1, \phi_1> \rightarrow u_2$).

as necessary and sufficient conditions for the formation of expectations. But, just as they ought to examine more thoroughly than they have done the links between the kinds of learning they are interested in and more primitive kinds, they need also to consider more complex kinds without overlooking either similarities or differences. In human beings, at least, contiguity is not a necessary condition for an expectation. In human life, most expectations are formed through the intervention of symbolic capacities, particularly through imitation (observational learning), verbal instruction, and reasoning.

3. We may, on the other hand, wonder whether, even when contiguities produce expectations, contiguity is a sufficient condition for learning. Do all combinations of stimuli that are repeatedly experienced together or in close succession give rise to learning? They certainly do not all give rise to learning of equal strength.

The arch-expectancy-theorist Tolman (Tolman, *et al.*, 1932) recognized this, when he introduced his "law of emphasis." He acknowledged that "an accent or emphasis (such as a bell or shock) upon the correct responses will tend to favor learning." There is now quite an assortment of evidence that the effectiveness of learning depends on the stimulus properties, including the collative properties, that govern arousal, the orientation reaction, and, to use a term with multiple meanings (see Berlyne, 1969a, 1970), attention.

As pointed out elsewhere (Berlyne, 1967), at least some of the processes denoted by the word "attention" turn out to be indistinguishable from reinforcement according to our usage. The reinforcing conditions that govern verbal and other symbolic forms of learning are likely, it was suggested, to be ones that everyday language would designate as conditions conducive to attention. But indications are accumulating that such conditions also affect more elementary kinds of learning. The informational value of a conditioned stimulus apparently influences classical conditioning (Rescorla, 1967; Kamin, 1968) and secondary reward (Egger & Miller, 1962). Classical conditioning is, more generally, affected by various factors that contribute to the arousal potential of a conditioned stimulus (Razran, 1957; Asratian, 1965). There is plenty of evidence for a critical role of the orientation reaction in classical conditioning and other kinds of learning (see Berlyne, 1967). Maltzman and Raskin (1965) conclude from their findings that "elicitation of an orienting reflex constitutes a reinforcing state of affairs." Collative properties have been found to influence the effectiveness of a reinforcing stimulus in instrumental conditioning (see Berlyne, 1969b) and the effectiveness of a cue stimulus in latent learning (Franken, 1967b) and discriminative learning (Franken, 1967a).

So, there are a fair number of findings in tune with Olds's suggestion that the most elementary forms of learning are essentially attentional learning and that attentional learning constitutes both a precursor and a constituent of higher forms of learning. This is where, according to Olds, Hull's reinforcement theory may come into its own. It would be ironic if the factors that act as "reinforcing states of affairs" according to Hull's usage, and thus qualify as "rewards" according to our definition, turned out not to be rewards in the usual sense of this word but rather events compelling attention, while rewards in the usual sense come into play, as Tolman maintained, when decisions about performance are made.

But things seem unlikely to be quite as simple as that. There are abundant signs that, even when they undergo the simplest kinds of learning, organisms learn a little more than simply what is worth attending to. They may learn to place certain kinds of stimuli, when they encounter them, in control of their behavior and to transmit information coming from them through the nervous system to the detriment of information from competing sources. But they seem also to learn whether a stimulus has positive or negative hedonic value, whether its significance is appetitive or aversive, whether it betokens something beneficial or noxious (cf. Fowler, Fago, Domber, & Hochhauser, 1973). Even the most primitive animals tend apparently to make this distinction on the basis of arousal potential, approaching moderate stimuli and shunning powerful ones in a manner related to the Wundt curve (Schneirla, 1959; Berlyne, 1967). Finally, there seem to be at least some primitive forms of classical conditioning in which a specific motor response becomes attached to a specific kind of stimulus.

Aplopathematic and Thelematoscopic Pneumatology?

There is one more question that will no doubt be raised, and that is what the terms appearing in the title of this chapter signify. They were actually introduced by Bentham (1816; see McReynolds, 1968).

"Pneumatology" was proposed as an alternative to "psychology." *Pneuma* was, of course, one of the words used by the ancient Greeks to denote "spirit" or "mind," another being *psykhe*. Both of these nouns come from verbs (*pnein* and *psykhein*) meaning to "blow" or "breathe." Nowadays, more and more of us are coming to feel that nothing could benefit psychology more than its dissociation from the name "psychology." For most members of the public, this word signifies quite different activities from those we are engaged in. Perhaps "pneumatology" is worth considering as a substitute.

The term "aplopathematic" came from the classical Greek *haploos*, meaning "simple," and *pathema*, meaning "sensation" or "feeling." Aplopathematic pneumatology, in Bentham's (1816) words, has for its subject "the aggregate of *Pleasures* and *Pains* of all kinds. . . ." He added, however, the reservation that it deals with pleasures and pains "considered apart from whatever influence, in the character of motives, the prospects of them may have upon the *will* or *volitional* faculty, and the acts, as well purely mental and internal, as corporeal and external, of which these prospects may become the causes [p. 86]." The questions excluded by this reservation belong to the province of "thelematoscopic pneumatology," this adjective coming from Greek roots that, when put together, mean "will-examining."

We thus find Bentham distinguishing two areas of research, concerning, respectively, the determinants of hedonic value and the role of hedonic value in the determination of behavior. A century and a half after he wrote, the charting of these areas is still fragmentary and calls for a new breed of adventurers. They must be intrepid enough to tear themselves away from the safe and well traveled public highways of research. They will have to pursue the various offshoots of the hedonistic delta, keeping in close touch with one another's progress, until they all debouch into the Ocean of Truth and Illumination.

References

Ashby, W. R. *Design for a brain.* London: Chapman & Hall, 1952.

Asratian, E. A. *Compensatory adaptations, reflex activity and the brain.* Oxford: Pergamon, 1965.

Atkinson, J. W. *An introduction to motivation.* Princeton, New Jersey: Van Nostrand-Reinhold, 1964.

Beebe-Center, J. G. The law of affective equilibrium. *American Journal of Psychology,* 1929, **41**, 54–69.

Beebe-Center, J. G. *The psychology of pleasantness and unpleasantness.* Princeton, New Jersey: Van Nostrand-Reinhold, 1932.

Bentham, J. *An introduction to the principles of morals and legislation.* London: Payne, 1789.

Bentham, J. Chrestomathia. In J. Bowring (Ed.), *The works of Jeremy Bentham,* Vol. VIII. Edinburgh: Tait, 1843. (Written, 1816).

Berlyne, D. E. *Conflict, arousal and curiosity.* New York: McGraw-Hill, 1960.

Berlyne, D. E. Motivational problems raised by exploratory and epistemic behavior. In S. Koch (Ed.), *Psychology—A study of a science,* Vol. 5. New York: McGraw-Hill, 1963.

Berlyne, D. E. *Structure and direction in thinking.* New York: Wiley, 1965.

Berlyne, D. E. Curiosity and exploration. *Science,* 1966, **153,** 25–33.

Berlyne, D. E. Arousal and reinforcement. In D. Levine (Ed.), *Nebraska symposium on motivation,* 1967. Lincoln: Univ. of Nebraska Press, 1967.

Berlyne, D. E. The development of the concept of attention in psychology. In C. R. Evans & T. Mulholland (Eds.), *Attention in neurophysiology.* London: Butterworth, 1969. (a)

Berlyne, D. E. The reward value of indifferent stimulation. In J. T. Tapp (Ed.), *Reinforcement and behavior.* New York: Academic Press, 1969. (b)

Berlyne, D. E. Attention as a problem in behavior theory. In D. Mostofsky (Ed.), *Attention: Contemporary theory and analysis.* New York: Appleton, 1970.

Berlyne, D. E. *Aesthetics and psychobiology.* New York: Appleton, 1971.

Berlyne, D. E. Ends and means of experimental aesthetics. *Canadian Journal of Psychology,* 1972, **26,**303–325. (a)

Berlyne, D. E. Experimental aesthetics. In P. C. Dodwell (Ed.), *New horizons in psychology 2.* Harmondsworth, London: Penguin, 1972. (b)

Berlyne, D. E. Reinforcement values of visual patterns compared through concurrent performances. *Journal of the Experimental Analysis of Behavior,* 1972, **18,** 281–285. (c)

Bogardus, E. S. Measuring social distance. *Journal of Applied Sociology,* 1925, **9,** 299–308.

Bolles, R. C. Reinforcement, expectancy and learning. *Psychological Review,* 1972, **79,** 394–409.

Coombs, C. H. *A theory of data.* New York: Wiley, 1964.

Dollard J., & Miller, N. E. *Personality and psychotherapy.* New York: McGraw-Hill, 1950.

Edgeworth, F. Y. *Mathematical psychics.* London: Kegan Paul, 1881.

Egger, M. D., & Miller, N. E. Secondary reinforcement in rats as a function of information value and reliability of stimulus. *Journal of Experimental Psychology,* 1962, **64,** 97–104.

Estes, W. K. Reward in human learning: Theoretical issues and strategic choice points. In R. Glaser (Ed.), *The nature of reinforcement.* New York: Academic Press, 1971.

Fechner, G. T. *Einige Ideen zur Schöpfungs- und Entwicklungsgeschichte der Organismen.* Leipzig: Breitkopf & Härtel, 1873.

Fiske, D. W., & Maddi, S. (Eds.) *Functions of varied experience.* Homewood, Illinois: Dorsey Press, 1961.

Fowler, H. Implications of sensory reinforcement. In R. Glaser (Ed.), *The nature of reinforcement.* New York: Academic Press, 1971.

Fowler, H., Fago, G. C., Domber, E. A., & Hockhauser, M. Signaling and affective functions in Pavlovian conditioning. *Animal Learning and Behavior,* 1973, **1,** 81–89.

Franken, R. E. Stimulus change, attention, and brightness discrimination learning. *Journal of Comparative and Physiological Psychology,* 1967, **64,** 499–501. (a)

Franken, R. E. Stimulus change, exploration, and latent learning. *Journal of Comparative and Physiological Psychology,* 1967, **64,** 301–307. (b)

Freud, S. Formulierungen über zwei Prinzipien des psychischen Geschehens. *Jahr-buch für Psychoanalyse und psychopathologische Forschung*, 1911, **3**, 1–8. [For-mulations regarding the two principles in mental functioning. In *Collected Papers*, Vol. IV. London: Hogarth, 1925.]

Freud, S. Triebe and Triebsschicksale. *Internationale Zeitschrift für ärztliche Psycho-analyse*, 1915, **3**, 84–100. [Instincts and their vicissitudes. In S. Freud, *Collected Papers*, Vol. IV. London: 1925.]

Glaser, R. (Ed.). *The nature of reinforcement*. New York: Academic Press, 1971.

Glickman, S. E., & Schiff, B. B. A biological theory of reinforcement. *Psychological Review*, 1967, **74**, 81–109.

Grastyán, E., Szabo, I., Molnar, P., & Kolta, P. Rebound, reinforcement and self-stimulation. *Communications in Behavioral Biology*, 1968, **2**, 235–266.

Harrison, A. A. Response competition, frequency, exploratory behavior and liking. *Journal of Personality and Social Psychology*, 1968, **9**, 363–368.

Hebb, D. O. Drives and the C.N.S. (conceptual nervous system). *Psychological Review*, 1955, **62**, 243–254.

Heckhausen, H. *Hoffnung und Furcht in der Leistungsmotivation*. Meisenheim: Hain, 1963. [*The anatomy of achievement motivation*. New York: Academic Press, 1967.]

Helson, H. *Adaptation-level theory*. New York: Harper, 1964.

Hull, C. L. Goal attraction and directing ideas conceived as habit phenomena. *Psychological Review*, 1931, **38**, 487–506.

Hull, C. L. *Principles of behavior*. New York: Appleton, 1943.

Irwin, F. W. *Intentional behavior and motivation: A cognitive theory*. Philadelphia, Pennsylvania: Lippincott, 1971.

Kamin, L. J. "Attention-like" processes in classical conditioning. In M. R. Jones (Ed.), *Miami symposium on the prediction of behavior*. Coral Gables, Florida: Univ. of Miami Press, 1968.

Kamiya, J. Operant control of the EEG alpha rhythm and some of its reported effects on consciousness. In C. Tart (Ed.), *Altered states of consciousness*. New York: Wiley, 1969.

Konorski, J. *Integrative action of the brain*. Chicago, Illinois: Univ. of Chicago Press, 1967.

Lewin, K. *Dynamic theory of personality*. New York: McGraw-Hill, 1935.

Likert, R. A technique for the measurement of attitudes. *Archives of Psychology*, 1932, No. 140.

Luria, A. R. *The working brain*. Harmondsworth: Penguin, 1973.

Maltzman, I., & Raskin, D. C. Effects of individual differences in the orienting reflex on conditioning and complex processes. *Journal of Experimental Research in Per-sonality*, 1965, **1**, 1–16.

McClelland, D. C., Atkinson, J. W., Clark, R. A., & Lowell, E. L. *The achievement motive*. New York: Appleton, 1953.

McDougall, W. *An introduction to social psychology*. London: Methuen, 1908.

McDougall, W. *Outline of psychology*. London: Methuen, 1923.

McDougall, W. *Outline of abnormal psychology*. London: Methuen, 1926.

McReynolds, P. The motivational psychology of Jeremy Bentham. *Journal of the History of the Behavioral Sciences*, 1968, **4**, 230–244; 349–364.

Miller, N. E. Some reflections on the law of effect produce a new alternative to drive reduction. In M. R. Jones (Ed.), *Nebraska symposium on motivation*, 1963. Lincoln: Univ. of Nebraska Press, 1963.

Miller, N. E., & Dollard, J. *Social learning and imitation*. New Haven, Connecticut: Yale Univ. Press, 1941.

Moreno, J. L. Who shall survive? *Nervous and mental Disease Monographs*, 1934, No. 58.

Mosteller, F., & Nogee, P. An experimental measure of utility. *Journal of Political Economy*, 1951, **59**, 371–404.

Mowrer, O. H. Preparatory set (expectancy): A determinant in motivation and learning. *Psychological Review*, 1938, **45**, 62–91.

Mowrer, O. H. Two-factor learning theory reconsidered with special reference to secondary reinforcement and the concept of habit. *Psychological Review*, 1956, **63**, 114–128.

Mowrer, O. H. *Learning theory and behavior*. New York: Wiley, 1960.

Neumann, J. von., & Morgenstern, O. *Theory of games and economic behavior*. Princeton, New Jersey: Princeton Univ. Press, 1944.

Olds, J., & Olds, M. Drives, rewards and the brain. In *New directions in Psychology II*. New York: Holt, 1965.

Osgood, C. E., Suci, G. J., & Tannenbaum, P. H. *The measurement of meaning*. Urbana, Illinois: Univ. of Illinois Press, 1957.

Pfaffman, C. The pleasures of sensation. *Psychological Review*, 1960, **67**, 253–268.

Premack, D. Toward empirical behavior laws: I. Positive reinforcement. *Psychological Review*, 1959, **66**, 219–233.

Premack, D. Reinforcement theory. In D. Levine (Ed.), *Nebraska symposium on motivation*, 1965. Lincoln: Univ. of Nebraska Press, 1965.

Premack, D. Catching up with common sense or two sides of a generalization: Reinforcement and punishment. In R. Glaser (Ed.), *The nature of reinforcement*. New York: Academic Press, 1971.

Pribram, K. H. *Languages of the brain*. Englewood Cliffs, New Jersey: Prentice-Hall, 1971.

Ramsey, F. P. Truth and probability. In *Foundations of mathematics and other logical essays*. London: Routledge & Kegan Paul, 1931.

Razran, G. The law of effect or the law of qualitative conditioning. *Psychological Review*, 1939, **46**, 445–463.

Razran, G. The dominance-contiguity theory of the acquisition of classical conditioning. *Psychological Review*, 1957, **54**, 1–46.

Razran, G. *Mind in evolution*. Boston: Houghton, 1971.

Rescorla, R. A. Pavlovian conditioning and its proper control procedures. *Psychological Review*, 1967, **74**, 71–80.

Rosenblueth, A., Wiener, N., & Bigelow, J. H. Behavior, purpose and teleology. *Philosophy of Science*, 1943, **10**, 18–24.

Ryan, T. A. *Intentional behavior*. New York: Ronald Press, 1971.

Savage, L. J. The theory of statistical decision. *Journal of the American Statistical Association*, 1951, **46**, 55–67.

Schneirla, T. C. An evolutionary and developmental theory of biphasic processes underlying approach and withdrawal. In M. R. Jones (Ed.), *Nebraska symposium on motivation, 1959.* Lincoln: Univ. of Nebraska Press, 1959.

Seward, J. P. Reinforcement and expectancy: Two theories in search of a controversy. *Psychological Review,* 1956, **63**, 105–113.

Smith, K. U., & Smith, M. F. *Cybernetic principles of learning and educational design.* New York: Holt, 1966.

Spence, K. W. *Behavior theory and conditioning.* New Haven, Connecticut: Yale Univ. Press, 1956.

Spencer, H. *Principles of psychology* (2nd ed.). London: Williams & Norgate, 1870.

Stein, L. Reciprocal action of reward and punishment mechanisms. In R. G. Heath (Ed.), *The role of pleasure in behavior.* New York: Harper, 1964.

Stein, L. Chemistry of reward and punishment. In D. Efran (Ed.), *Psychopharmacology.* Washington: U.S. Government Printing Office, 1968.

Thorndike, E. L. Animal intelligence. *Psychological Review Monograph Supplements,* 1898, **2**, No. 8.

Thorndike, E. L. *Educational psychology.* New York: Lemcke & Buechner, 1903.

Thorndike, E. L. *Educational psychology II. The psychology of learning.* New York: Teachers College, 1913.

Thorndike, E. L. The theory of the action of the after effects of a connection upon it. *Psychological Review,* 1933, **40**, 434–439.

Thurstone, L. L. The measurement of opinion. *Journal of Abnormal and Social Psychology,* 1928, **22**, 415–430.

Thurstone, L. L. The indifference function. *Journal of Social Psychology,* 1931, **2**, 139–167.

Titchener, E. B. *A text-book of psychology.* New York: Macmillan, 1910.

Tolman, E. C. *Purposive behavior in animals and men.* New York: Appleton, 1932.

Tolman, E. C. Principles of purposive behavior. In S. Koch (Ed.), *Psychology—A study of a science,* Vol. 2. New York: McGraw-Hill, 1959.

Tolman, E. C., Hall, C. S., & Bretnall, E. P. A disproof of the law of effect and a substitution of the laws of emphasis, motivation and disruption. *Journal of Experimental Psychology,* 1932, **15**, 601–614.

Troland, L. T. *Fundamentals of human motivation.* Princeton, New Jersey: Van Nostrand-Reinhold, 1928.

Trowell, J. A., Panksepp, J., & Gandelman, R. An incentive model of rewarding brain stimulation. *Psychological Review,* 1969, **76**, 264–281.

Valenstein, E. S. Stability and plasticity of motivation systems. In F. O. Schmitt (Ed.), *The neurosciences: Second study program.* New York: Rockefeller Univ. Press, 1970.

Valenstein, E. S., & Campbell, J. F. Medial forebrain bundle-lateral hypothalamic area and reinforcing brain stimulation. *American Journal of Physiology,* 1966, **210**, 270–274.

Valenstein, E. S., Cox, V. C., & Kakolewski, J. W. Modification of motivated behavior elicited by electrical stimulation of the hypothalamus. *Science,* 1968, **159**, 1119–1121.

Vinogradova, O. S. [The role of the orientation reflex in the process of establishing conditioned connections in man.] In E. N. Sokolov (Ed.), *Orientirovochny refleks i voprosy vysshei nervnoi deiatel'nosti v norme i patologii.* [*The orientation reflex and questions of higher nervous activity in normality and pathology.*] Moscow: Academy of Pedagogical Sciences, 1959.

Walker, E. L. Reinforcement—"The one ring." In J. T. Tapp (Ed.), *Reinforcement and behavior.* New York: Academic Press, 1969.

Watson, J. B. *Behavior: An introduction to comparative psychology.* New York: Holt, 1914.

Witryol, S. L. Incentives and learning in children. *Advances in Child Development and Behavior,* 1971, **6,** 1–61.

Wundt, W. *Grundzüge der physiologischen Psychologie.* Leipzig: Englemann, 1874.

Young, P. T. The role of affective processes in learning and motivation. *Psychological Review,* 1959, **66,** 104–125.

Zajonc, R. B. Attitudinal effects of mere exposure. *Journal of Personality and Social Psychology,* 1968, **9** (Monograph Supplement 2, Part 2).

CHAPTER 2

Brain Mechanisms of Reinforcement Learning

JAMES OLDS

California Institute of Technology

Will the brain experiments yet teach us anything about the way rewards and punishments act in learning to modify the behavior repertory?

Brain stimulation experiments (Olds, 1969) have demonstrated that there is a fairly large and anatomically coherent system in the brain (see Fig. 2-1), different from the primary sensory and motor systems, within which neuronal processes pathologically induced by direct electric stimulation cause the animal to behave as if it had been rewarded by a normal drive-relevant rewarding stimulus. Many experiments have made it possible to view this effect as evidence of an artificial activation of the brain's normal positive reinforcement mechanism. The experiments mapping this effect have led us to suppose that whenever an animal is rewarded by artificial or normal means, this entails the activation of particular fiber systems (see Fig. 2-2) which permeate the hypothalamus and the paleocortex. Except for connections of these fiber systems to chemical sensors of the olfactory bulb and the bloodstream on the afferent side, and connections to one another, very little is known about the sources of input to these neuronal mechanisms from the other, better known brain systems, such as the thalamus and the neocortex; and very little is known about the output pathways which mediate effects on behavior.

We are quite sure that rewarding brain stimuli have their effects by stimulating fibers, not by stimulating cell bodies. But we do not know where the critical fibers project to, in order to influence behavior.

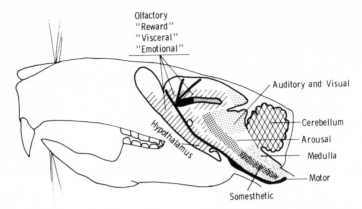

Fig. 2-1. Rat brain as it appears on the medial wall. The heavy black line running through the brain is the pyramidal motor system. The single hatched areas are the areas where pathologically induced neuronal processes cause the animal to behave as if rewarded.

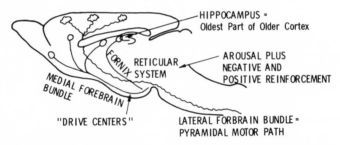

Fig. 2-2. Rat brain with medial forebrain bundle schematically portrayed as it runs along the base of the brain from the olfactory parts of the forebrain.

Because the consequences we observe consist in a modification of learned behavior repertoires, we believe there must be pathways from the reward points to the learning centers of the brain. This gives grounds for one of our best hopes of tracking down the sites of learning in the brain; for we believe that the learning phenomena which interest us occur one or two or three synaptic steps from our stimulation point.

Lesion experiments have been used in attempts to destroy the critical pathways from the stimulation point to the areas responsible for the learning and other behavioral consequences. Boyd and Gardner (1967) showed that when rewarding stimulation was applied in posterior hypothalamus (which is a very good place), three pathways in three different directions were all responsible for some part of the rewarding effect (see Fig. 2-3). One pathway was toward paleocortex, a second pathway was

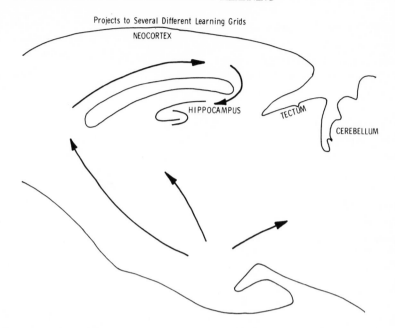

Fig. 2-3. Three different pathways from the "reward centers" that need to be cut to stop self-stimulation.

toward thalamus, and a third pathway was descending, pointing toward the midbrain, the cerebellum, and the spinal cord. Destruction of each of these three pathways separately caused a mitigation of the effect, that is the abolition of some part of it, but when only one pathway was destroyed, there was usually only a moderate slowing of the behavior.

The failure to find complete abolition of rewarding effects with any one set of lesions, and the corollary finding that many different pathways from the point of stimulation may be involved in mediating the effect, converged with a long string of findings stemming from Lashley suggesting that no unitary locus of learning would ever be found. Most neuropsychologists, myself included, persist in believing that the brain is differentiated with respect to learning. Giving up a single locus, we nevertheless believe that learning does not go on equally in all places, but rather that different forms of learning go on in different places, and that many of the well-organized structures of the brain may be involved in learning, and that some of the learning tests presented to animals can be solved more or less equally well by any one of the learning mechanisms taken separately. Therefore lesions which extirpate any one of the mechanisms leave several more to do the job. One view is that relatively primitive learning centers (involved in the learning of skills) are placed in lower parts of the brain, perhaps in the tectum of the midbrain or even in the cerebellum; that these are modulated or controlled by higher learning mechanisms perhaps involving paleocortex, and that these in their turn may be modulated or controlled by mechanisms of thalamus and neocortex. A common pluralistic view is that all of these mechanisms exist side by side, the higher mechanisms normally coming into play when problems become too complex for the lower systems. The systems could be relatively independent, and be engaged simultaneously. But because they pull in a common direction, the pluralistic control might go unnoticed. If this were so, we might seek to follow, by neurophysiological techniques, neuronal excitation channeled by different pathways from the reward point independently toward several different systems where it would have consequences.

In recent experiments of this type (see Fig. 2-4), Ito (Ito & Olds, 1971; Ito, 1972) has studied accelerations and decelerations in the firing rate of single neurons recorded by means of chronically implanted microelectrodes during free self-stimulation behavior. Stimulation along the whole brain floor from midbrain to preoptic area yielded self-stimulation; it was surprising to find that rewarding brain stimulation in the middle of this region caused inhibition of nearby neurons (see Figs. 2-4 and 2-5), and excitation of ones farther away. This raised an interesting question. Was it the local inhibition or the more distant excitation which was more important in yielding the positive reinforcing effect caused by brain stimulation?

More recent work of Marianne Olds and Ito (in press) has made some progress toward answering this question. Certain drugs were particularly effective in antagonizing self-stimulation behavior. Drugs which counteract catecholamine cause brain reward behavior to cease. Marianne Olds and Ito tested to find whether drugs countering self-stimulation would counteract either the distant excitations, or the proximal inhibitions caused by the rewarding stimulus. The catecholamine drugs, the ones that counteracted catecholamine systems and counteracted brain rewarding effects, were interesting. These were effective against the local inhibitions, but had little effect on the distant excitation. From the neuropsychological point of view these data suggest that the local inhibitions might be more importantly related to the brain reward than were the more distant excitatory actions.

The notion that positive reinforcement might be related in one way or another to the suppression of activity in a large family of neurons local to the medial forebrain bundle was also suggested by data from

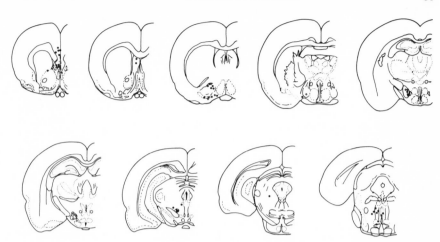

Fig. 2-4. Locations of excitation (solid circles) and inhibition (open circles) of unit responses caused by rewarding brain stimulation. The stimulus is applied at the location marked S (the S is difficult to see, it is in the left section of the second row). Units near the stimulus are inhibited; those farther removed are excited. All points tested were in the "reward pathway"; i.e. the medial forebrain bundle. [From Olds & Ito, in press.]

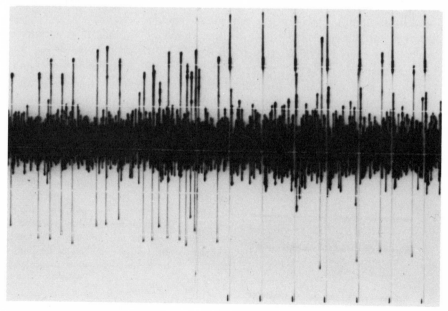

Fig. 2-5. Inhibition of local unit caused by brain "reward." The unit is active in the left half of the picture; it stops when the large spikes (which are artifacts of the brain shock) appear.

Hamburg (1971). This investigator set out to study the effects of feeding on neurons in the supposed feeding center of the lateral hypothalamus. He recorded from the same large lateral hypothalamic neurons that Ito studied during self-stimulation. When the animal was hungry and approaching food, these neurons were often highly activated. It was surprising, therefore, to find that when the animal actually engaged in consummatory behavior, these neurons were suppressed or totally silenced (see Fig. 2-6). Even though the animal was still equally hungry, and only consuming the first pellet or two, there was nevertheless a marked silencing of the large neurons in the supposed feeding center. Interestingly, it turned out that the termination of instrumental behavior was more important than the initiation of consummatory behavior. When the hungry animal was presented with a horde of food in a dish, the animal stationed itself with its forepaws inside the dish, and began feeding itself and eating in a more or less automatic fashion. You might say he looked like a plane on automatic pilot. The forepaws moved from the pellet dish to the mouth and back to the dish (these were small 45-mg food pellets and the animal could place whole pellets in the mouth at one time). If attempts were made at this point to remove the food dish, the animal would cling and pull back while continuing to consume the food in its mouth. During these periods of resumed striving, and overlap between instrumental and consummatory behavior, the neuronal activity which was silenced would return full-fledged. In the end, therefore, it seemed that when there was a state of no instrumental behavior (no striving) these neurons were turned off. When, however, there was an instrumental action these neurons were on. The actual consummatory

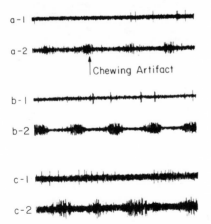

Fig. 2-6. Inhibition of units in feeding part of the "reward pathway" during feeding. On the first line of each pair, the units are active, and the animal is not chewing food. On the second line, in each pair, the animal is eating (muscle artifacts of feeding appear); at these times the units are relatively silent.

state, when it was a state of completely automated activity, fully driven, was accompanied by a quiescence of these neurons.

An interesting question poses itself. Here are neurons that are turned off by rewarding brain stimulation, and during normal feeding consummatory behavior they are also turned off. Agreeing with these suggestions that their suppression has something to do with reward, is the fact that drugs which keep them from being suppressed also keep the brain stimulation from being rewarding. But when both rewarding consummatory behavior, and instrumental striving behavior occur at the same time, they are activated by the instrumental behavior, rather than being suppressed by the reward. What are these neurons really doing? Are they drive neurons whose suppression is involved in reinforcement? Do they project from this hypothalamic stimulation point toward the real centers of reinforcement and learning? Or are they somehow local elements involved in energizing instrumental behaviors?

The question of what kind of function was performed by these local neurons went together in our minds with the other question of where in the brain reinforcing mechanisms and learning mechanisms intersected in such a fashion that reward could exercise its control over behavior repertories. One important supposition all along which has occurred not only to us but to others, I suppose, is that some important aspect of learning might occur not in other parts of the brain but locally. The question was whether we might not show that the important pathway from reward mechanisms to learning mechanisms was the medial forebrain bundle itself. If this were true, then its main targets might be importantly involved in learning. It is surprising, I suppose, that it took us so long to realize that the main targets of the medial forebrain bundle were the large neuronal elements which were recorded by means of probes located in this fiber bundle itself. A question therefore was whether we could devise a means whereby a special involvement of these neurons in learning processes might be demonstrated.

Lesion studies have regularly failed to give unambiguous answers to the question of where learning mechanisms reside. I have already suggested that this may be due to the extreme dispersion and redundancy of learning mechanisms. Brain stimulation studies have also failed to localize learning. This is mainly because it is unclear what kind of influence might be expected from stimulating a learning center. One obvious mode of procedure was to observe the neuronal activity in each of the supposed mechanisms during learning episodes. The crux of the problem lay in finding some characteristic of the observation that would give assurance that learning was being observed at the critical brain point where the brain change itself was occurring.

The Pavlovian conditioning experiment provides a method to start. It allows the investigator to observe unit spike accelerations caused by each application of the conditioned stimulus. And then, one looks not at all the accelerations caused by the conditioned stimulus, but only at the *new* accelerations, that is, those that developed during the course of the learning experiment.

The observation of new neuronal responses in the brain evoked by the conditioned stimulus after conditioning is by now an old procedure in neuropsychology. However, the observation of these new neuronal responses by itself does not offer any certification that the locus of learning is being observed. If every new biological response to the conditioned stimulus which developed during conditioning indicated a locus of conditioning, then Pavlov already discovered one of the prime locations, namely the salivary gland itself. The fact of the matter is that new responses may be secondary, tertiary, and even farther consequences of the critical change, rather than being at the site of the change itself. Many of the new neuronal responses observed in a freely behaving animal result in fact from the new overt responses and the consequent modification of proprioceptive and environment feedback. Other new neuronal responses consist in descending consequences of learned changes and are involved merely in mediating the effect of these critical changes on behavior, on overt behavior.

The question is then pressed upon us: How can we, from an enormous number of changes fed back upon changes in a confusing web of neuron behavior cycles and neuron–neuron epicycles, sort out the critical changes which come first, and being at the sites of learning, cause the others?

The answer fastened upon in our present series of investigations (Olds, Disterhoft, Segal, Kornblith, & Hirsh, 1972) is to take seriously the idea that the important changes are the ones that come first. Actually there are two important time series in which we may look to see whether a change comes first. One is the millisecond time series that intervenes between stimulus and response. The other is the trial-to-trial sequence of events that marks the course of learning starting from a time when the animal is naive and ending at a time when the animal is trained. By the simple rule that the cause must precede the effect, it is quite clear that nothing which comes first in either of these chains can be caused by something that comes later. Therefore the first things must be primary (providing that we can offer some sensible proof that they are first).

My argument is that the message started by the auditory signal takes one path into the brain prior to conditioning. After conditioning it takes this path to some degree but at several or many points it is now switched into new pathways and aimed thus toward the new behavioral responses. There are clearly several or many switching points. Our method is aimed to locate some of them. Because the arguments are complex and because some of you will trust me I will not go into the logical details, but will stipulate:

(1) after training is complete, the shortest latency "conditioned brain responses" are probably at switching points;
(2) during training, the first brain region to show signs of learning would be at a switching point; and
(3) if there are several clearly demarcated stages of conditioning, and if several different parts of the brain all start to reflect "learning" together at one particular stage, then within this stage-defined group, latency mapping would also show a switching point.

We have proceeded with studies aimed to attend carefully to these time series.

I shall not discuss the methodological details here. It is sufficient to say that these were carefully controlled experiments; many of the controls which we should have made we did make. The conditioned stimulus was a pure tone. The unconditioned stimulus was a food pellet discharged by an automatic food magazine which made a noise and caused the cage to vibrate when it was discharged. Recordings were made of spike rates, action potential rates, from individual neurons in different parts of the brain. The responses of these neurons to auditory stimulations consisted in accelerations or decelerations of background firing rate (see Fig. 2-7). The latency of the brain response was taken as the time between the onset of the tone and the onset of the acceleration or deceleration of spike rate. These onset times were gotten by averaging the responses to several hundred repetitions (presented over a period of many hours). The measure of behavior, and the measure of behavioral learning, was a measure of the gross behavioral movement of the animal. Prior to training, the more or less neutral auditory tones caused very little movement of the animal. After training the tone caused a large orienting movement followed by a preparatory response and movement toward the pellet dispenser. A movement-recording device which was very sensitive to even the smallest movements was attached to the animal, and the probability of a movement detection in any given 10-msec

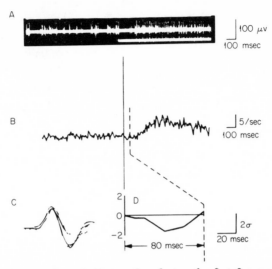

Fig. 2-7. Single unit data. A. Unit spikes during the first 2 sec of a trial photographed from the tube of a cathode ray oscilloscope. The white line below the tracing denotes the auditory signal which came on at the start of the 2nd second. It caused a brief deceleration and a later acceleration in this case. B. Pre- and poststimulus histogram indicating the average spike rate for each 10 msec time bin; individual trials (such as the one shown in A) were averaged to get this histogram. C. Tracing of individual spikes with time scale spread out (1 msec full scale) to show actual shape of these action potential spikes. D. Statistical treatment of the first 80 msec of the poststimulus period from B. The mean and standard deviation of the prestimulus tracing was derived, and then the points after the stimulus were converted to standard scores (indicating the number of standard deviations from the background mean). One such score was derived from the first poststimulus bin (up to 10 msec after the stimulus) and then such scores were also derived for two bin groups, 1 & 2 (up to 20 msec after the stimulus), 3 & 4 (20–40 msec after the stimulus), 5 & 6 (40–60 msec), and 7 & 8 (60–80 msec). For the two bin groups, standard scores of 1.55 or larger were significant beyond the .05 level.

period was measured. As I said, before training, the auditory signal caused no change in the background rate of movement detection. After training was completed, the onset of the tone was followed in about 100 to 200 msec by a great augmentation of movement detection (see Fig., 2-8).

Brain responses from most brain areas were quite similar to the movement responses (see Fig. 2-9). Before learning, the auditory tone caused very little change in the spiking rate of these neurons. After training was complete, each presentation of the tone was followed after a period of milliseconds usually by an augmentation of the firing rate of the recorded neurons. While there were some parts of the brain where new responses did not appear, it is fair to say that we were more surprised

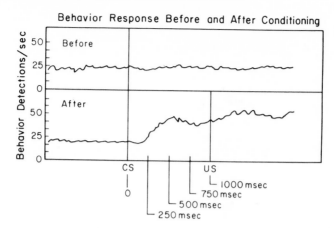

Fig. 2-8. Pre- and poststimulus "behavior-rate" histograms for one rat. The behavior rate was indicated by a very sensitive movement detector attached to the animal. This yielded a countable output at each slight movement or tremor. Changes in the base line rate of movement were caused by the stimulus after conditioning. No important changes were observed during the pseudoconditioning period. The latency of the behavior change was about 200 msec.

by the large number of cases where learning was reflected in neuronal activity, than we were impressed by the small number of cases which appeared to take an "I don't care" attitude toward the whole process. Furthermore, while there were some particular families of neurons that yielded decelerating or inhibitory responses to the conditioned stimulus after training, these were a small minority; by far the largest number of neurons observed yielded new excitatory responses to the conditioned stimulus after conditioning. I believe we have recorded from more than one thousand probes in these studies. No large system of brain structures has been omitted from these investigations. The data I will discuss, however, are taken from about the first 700 points.

While almost all brain areas yielded new responses, there were exceptions (see Fig. 2-10) and there were many differences in the intensity (that is the degree of change), there were also differences in the duration of the response, and there were differences in the latency of these new responses. I will discuss first the differences in latency.

The shortest latency learned responses were in neocortex [1] (see Fig. 2-11), where you might expect them to be. While these were the shortest latency new responses, they were by no means the most numerous. In cortex short latency new responses were few and far between (see Fig.

---

[1] By the time of going to press, a more refined time grid showed new responses with still shorter latencies along the input pathway from receptor to cortex at medial geniculate, inferior colliculus, and possibly even at the cochlear nucleus.

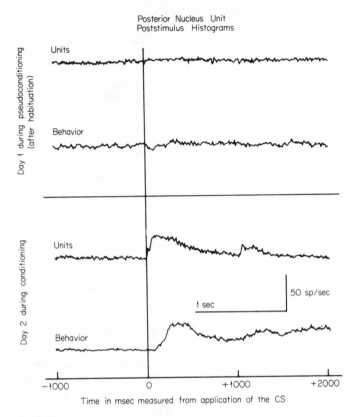

Fig. 2-9. Comparison of unit (upper tracing in each pair) and behavior (lower tracing) histograms in the same animal (animal 9227). During pseudoconditioning there is no sizable response in the unit (posterior thalamus) or in the behavior. Afterward, both show a response, behavior at about 100 msec, posterior thalamus at or before 20 msec.

2-12). The auditory centers of thalamus were far ahead when looked at for large numbers and large size of new responses with short latencies. It was actually not the primary auditory center of thalamus (the medial geniculate) but the secondary or association nuclei. In the case of the auditory system this is the posterior nucleus of the thalamus. In the posterior nucleus (see Fig. 2-13), a very large proportion of the neurons studied (amounting to considerably more than half) yielded very large short latency new responses (see Fig. 2-14) after conditioning (Olds *et al.*, 1972; Disterhoft and Olds, 1972). Various other features of these responses convinced us that the association nuclei of the thalamus play a very significant and important role in conditioning, and this find-

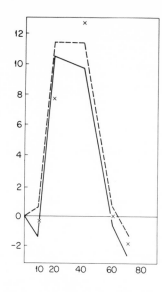

Fig. 2-10. Unchanged response in the midbrain auditory center (inferior colliculus). There is a large response with latency between 10 and 20 msec; it is of the same order before and after conditioning. [Abscissa: msec after stimulus onset; ordinate: standard deviations from base line; (———): CS + after conditioning; (– – –): CS + before conditioning; (xxx): CS − after conditioning.]

ing is importantly related to data provided by Professor Robert Thompson of Tulane University indicating that animals without this group of nuclei sometimes cannot learn at all.

Besides thalamus and cortex, there were other interesting locations with very short latency learned responses. I will not talk about all of them. But there were also short latency new responses in the reward system on the floor of the brain which concerns us (Linseman, 1972). This is the part of the brain that houses the large "feeding center"

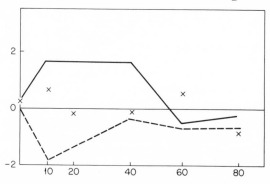

Fig. 2-11. Changed response in frontal cortex. A short latency inhibitory response is converted to a very definite excitatory response by conditioning. No similar response appears to the CS −. [Abscissa: msec after stimulus onset; ordinate: standard deviations from base line; (———): CS + after conditioning; (– – –): CS + before conditioning; (xxx): CS − after conditioning.]

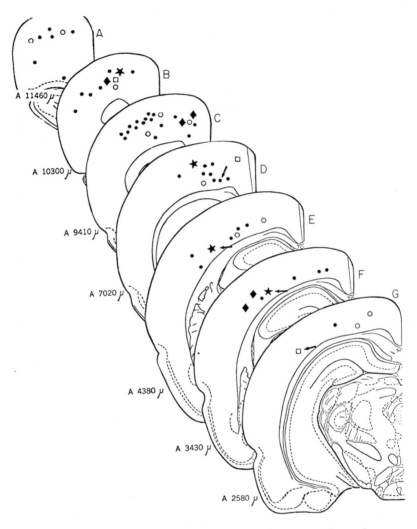

Fig. 2-12. Map of cortical points yielding short latency conditioned responses. Stars indicate 20 msec latency CR's, diamonds indicate 40 msec ones, squares indicate 60 and open circles 80 msec latency CR's. Filled circles indicate points tested that did not yield CR's with latency of 80 msec or less.

neurons, and the other large neurons in the path of the medial forebrain bundle. The thing to say about the short latency responses in these reward centers is that they were unspectacular so far as the latency tests were concerned. The shortest latencies were in the cortex; the largest proportion of short-latency responses were in the thalamus. Some

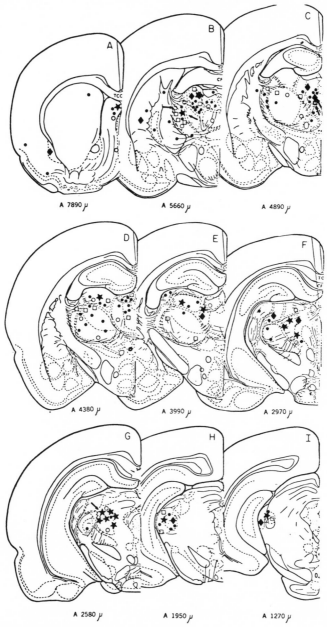

Fig. 2-13. Map of thalamus points yielding short latency conditioned responses. There is a large number of stars concentrated in the lower left section of the map; this is the posterior nucleus of the thalamus.

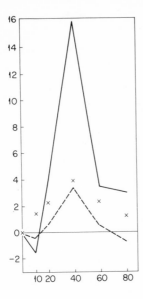

Fg. 2-14. Changed response in the posterior nucleus of the thalamus. The response on the first day is relatively small. The "learned reponse" in posterior nucleus has a latency between 10 and 20 msec (the same as the unlearned response in the inferior colliculus). [Abscissa: msec after stimulus onset; ordinate: standard deviations from base line; (————): CS + after conditioning; (– – –): CS + before conditioning; (xxx): CS − after conditioning.]

neurons on the floor of the brain had responses with very short latencies (possibly even as short as those in cortex), but they were clearly not shorter. New responses with reasonably short latencies were possibly even quite numerous; but they were clearly not as numerous as those in the posterior nucleus of the thalamus. It was, I would say, a second rate showing; but it raised a question in our minds whether we might show some special feature or aspect of learning that occurred in these regions especially near to or bordering on or in the path of the fibers whose stimulation yielded rewarding effects.

The second stage of our experiment Disterhoft & Olds, 1972; Linseman, 1972; Segal & Olds, 1972; Kornblith, 1972) was aimed originally at the question of whether the cortical neurons that had claim to priority by their very short latencies might be prior to and responsible for the large number of short latency new responses in thalamus. The second method of sorting was pressed into service. The question was whether new responses would appear in cortex very early in the trial series, early enough so that they might be viewed as responsible for responses in the thalamus. Actually the primary responses in cortex did not fare very well in this test.

In order to talk about the "learning times" of different brain systems, it is necessary to demarcate the stages in behavioral learning. The change from the condition when the auditory tone caused no behavioral effect at all, to the condition when it caused a dramatic behavioral effect within 100 to 200 msec did not come about all at once. It took about 20 trials before there was any apparent effect of the conditioning or training procedure on this measure of behavior at all. This long time course before the learning curve even began is partly because our rats were not bright, I suppose, but it was also due to the fact that there was a prior day of pseudoconditioning and habituation, and this caused the animals to learn not to respond to the auditory tone, but only to respond to the noise of the pellet dispenser. The course of this learning-not-to-respond can be documented by plotting the amount of movement caused by the conditioned stimulus during the first day's experiment (see Fig. 2-15). This declined steadily all during the course of the first day's pseudoconditioning or sensitization test. Also during this period, there was a gradual decrement in movement caused by all other sources. This could be seen by looking at the background movement (the movement that occurred before the application of the auditory tone).

Because of the slow onset of learning, and the slow progression of learning after it began, five stages of learning were readily apparent in behavioral conditioning (see Fig. 2-16). First, there was a stage after conditioning had started but before there was any apparent behavioral change (these were trials 1 through 20). Second, there was a stage when new behavior was clearly observed; however it was poorly executed and it was dubious whether it had any purposive character (these were trials

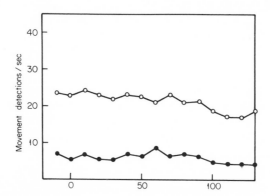

Fig. 2-15. Behavioral activity (gross activity) changes during the pseudoconditioning day (16 hours). The upper trace indicates random behavior rates. The lower trace indicates the excess of behavior (above background rates) caused during the one sec immediately following the auditory signal (the tone which would be the CS + next day). The curve appears to be below the background rate because background has been subtracted; in other words this is just the surplus of behavior caused by the signal. [(●——●): Rate changes caused by CS; (○——○): background rates.]

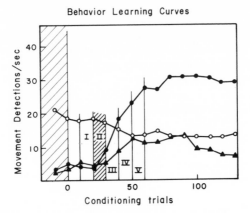

Fig. 2-16. Behavioral learning curves for CS + and CS − (with background behavior rate also). This again is the excess of behavior caused by the auditory signals. The first two points indicate two 10 trial groups of pseudoconditioning. The next points indicate 10 trial groups of conditioning. These are averages for 72 rats. Behavioral learning did not appear during the first or second 10 trial group. In the third group (trials 20–30) there was some rise above pseudoconditioning response levels (observation during this period showed mainly gross behavior); in the fourth group there was a substantial rise in activity caused by the signal and purposive behavior caused by the tone appeared. The absolute values of this measure are not so important as the relative values: At the start, the excess of movement over background levels caused by the auditory signal amounted to only about 10–20% of the background rate. At the end of conditioning, the background rate was more than tripled by the positive auditory signal (and almost doubled by the negative signal). [(●——●): Rate increases caused by CS +; (○——○): background rates; (▲——▲): rate increase caused by CS −.]

20 to 30). Third, there was a stage when behavior improved and purposive behavior clearly appeared (these were trials 30 to 40). Fourth, there was a period of purposive behavior improvement, increasing skill (these were trials 40 to 50). Fifth, there was a period after behavior improvement could no longer be measured (these were trials 50 through 70). Brain structures were divided into groups depending on the stages at which "conditioned brain responses" appeared in these areas.

In the neocortex where the shortest latency learned responses were recorded when conditioning was completed, signs of learned responding appeared in the 40- to 50-trial time interval (see Table 2-1). At that time also these signs appeared in the medial geniculate (that is at the thalamic station of the primary sensory system). Also at this time new responses appeared in other highly organized brain structures, namely cerebellum and hippocampus. This was the period between trial 40 and trial 50,

TABLE 2–1

Parts of the Brain that Did Not Evidence Learning Until Stage Four of Behavior Learning [a]

1. Posterior cortex (or stage III)	$(N = 12)$ [b]
2. Medial geniculate	$(N = 9)$
3. Lateral nucleus (or stage III)	$(N = 13)$
4. Middle cortex (or stage II)	$(N = 28)$
5. Anterior pons (to cerebellum)	$(N = 14)$
6. CA–3 (hippocampus)	$(N = 38)$

[a] Stage IV = Learning at 40–50 trials.
[b] N = Number of cases tested.

during which the purposive behavior of the animal became highly skilled. This was a point in the conditioning sequence, long after the gross conditioned response appeared, and considerably after the purposive pellet taking behavior also appeared in response to the conditioned stimulus.

These data suggested that a considerable number of important processes were learned, and were capable of controlling behaviors, before the organized and layered cortical structures entered the picture. The data from other sectors of the brain bear out this supposition. Neurons in the extrapyramidal motor system showed signs of the conditioned response during the 30 to 40 trial interval (see Table 2-2). At this time, or earlier, new responses also appeared in the posterior nucleus of the thalamus.

Prior to this period of purposive learning, there was the period from 20 to 30 trials after the beginning of conditioning when gross behavioral learning (arousal conditioning you might call it) appeared in the behavior of the animal. Together with this first behavioral sign of

TABLE 2–2

Parts of the Brain That Evidenced Learning at Stage Three of Behavior Learning [a]

1. Posterior nucleus (or stage II)	$(N = 11)$ [b]
2. Preoptic (excitatory)	$(N = 11)$
3. Anterior midbrain	$(N = 4)$
4. Caudate	$(N = 8)$
5. Globus pallidus	$(N = 16)$
6. ?Lateral nucleus? [c]	$(N = 13)$
7. ?Posterior cortex? [c]	$(N = 13)$

[a] Stage III = Learning at 30–40 trials.
[b] N = Number of cases tested.
[c] ? = Questionable evidence at this stage.

TABLE 2–3

Parts of the Brain That Evidenced Learning at Stage Two (at the same time as behavioral signs of learning appeared) [a]

1. Nonspecific thalamus	$(N = 28)$ [b]
2. Posterior diencephalon	$(N = 11)$
3. Central midbrain	$(N = 17)$
4. Ventral nucleus	$(N = 22)$
5. Dentate gyrus	$(N = 35)$
6. Internal capsule	$(N = 40)$
7. ?Middle cortex? [c]	$(N = 28)$
8. ?Posterior nucleus? [c]	$(N = 11)$

[a] Stage II = Learning at 20–30 trials.
[b] N = Number of cases tested.
[c] ? = Questionable evidence at this stage.

conditioning, a number of brain motor centers showed signs of learning (see Table 2-3). The ventral nucleus of thalamus, some parts of motor cortex, some neurons in the descending reticular formation, all showed signs of learning at this time concurrent with the first behavioral signs of conditioning.

An important and interesting question was left. Were there any centers of the brain where signs of conditioning appeared before it had any effect in the overt behavior of the animal? The answer is yes!

All of the neurons that showed signs of learning before any behavioral signs emerged, all of these were in or on the boundaries of the medial forebrain bundle path (Kornblith, 1972; Linseman, 1972), that is the fiber system whose stimulation causes as its most marked effect the positive reinforcement of behavior (see Table 2-4).

TABLE 2–4

Parts of the Brain That Evidenced Learning at Stage One (trials 10–20, prior to the appearance of behavior signs of learning) [a]

1. Hypothalamus	$(N = 17)$
2. Posterior pons	$(N = 7)$
3. Posterior midbrain	$(N = 9)$
4. Central pons	$(N = 10)$
5. Pyriform-amygdala	$(N = 5)$
6. Preoptic (inhibitory)	$(N = 8)$

[a] Stage I = Learning within 20 trials.
[b] N = Number of cases tested.

New responses appeared clearly in the hypothalamus during the 10 to 20 trial interval, during which there was absolutely no sign of conditioning in the overt behavior of the animal (see Fig. 2-17). It seems

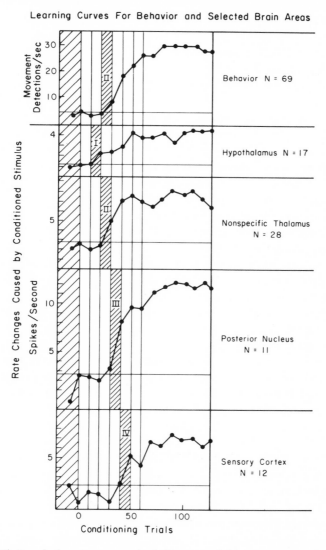

Fig. 2-17. Sample learning curves for behavior, and for representative brain areas from each of the learning groups. At the top, behavior learning appears first between trials 20 and 30. Hypothalamic "learning" appears between trials 10 and 20, non-specific thalamus shows learning between trials 20 and 30, posterior nucleus shows learning between trials 30 and 40, specific cortex between trials 40 and 50.

suggested, at least, by these data that targets of the reward path, either direct or one step removed, may very likely be the main centers involved in this prior (before-the-beginning) kind of learning. Stimuli seemed to need access to these neurons before they could get started in behavioral conditioning. Studies on the neurons in hypothalamus have now been done extensively by Dr. Marianne Olds and repeatedly we find changes appearing at 10–20 pairings before there is any sign of conditioning in overt behavior (see Fig. 2-18).

I would like to discuss briefly the type of learning that might go on somewhere in these nether regions. It seems to me that the problem we gave our rats was extraordinary and not really fair. Whoever introduces a stimulus on day 1, carefully teaches the animal to ignore it, and then suddenly reverses all the significances? Nature would never plan it that way, and no animal (except perhaps the white rat) needs to be prepared for such a game. What do you suppose these neurons were prepared for? I suppose they were prepared for what I call reinforcement learning. It is called by Skinnerians "chaining" and it is related to the problem named "secondary reinforcement." You all know about it better than I.

It seems to me that in reinforcement learning (i.e., the kind of learning where the trace or engram is called into existence not by prior attention, but is rather created by the application of a relatively unexpected rewarding stimulus after the fact), there are special problems.

In the learning of behavioral skills, something like this (but slightly different) happens. I imagine that there is somewhere a grid with axons carrying sensory codes forming the warp, and dendrites representing behaviors forming the woof. Simultaneous activation of the two must set up some sort of very temporary connection which deteriorates rapidly in a brief period of time. If reinforcement is then conveyed this must cause the temporary connection to be rejuvenated, or at least to be prolonged so that it lasts, and possibly grows more firm with repeated reinforcements of this type. To my mind a machine like this requires a three-cross grid, sensory warp, motor woof, and a third wire at all synapses representing the reward. For this kind of reinforcement learning, I believe the cerebellum is well suited by its obvious "three-wire" arrangement (see Fig. 2-19), and I feel the suggestion of the Englishman Marr (Bloomfield & Marr, 1970) that this may serve in the learning of skills has merit.

The chaining of meaningful actions after the prior learning of skills is different. I suppose that higher brain centers are usually involved in man. I would guess cortex plays a role in this kind of learning. But here I imagine that engrams are induced not by application or rewards but instead by prior attention. Reinforcement would be involved in the trig-

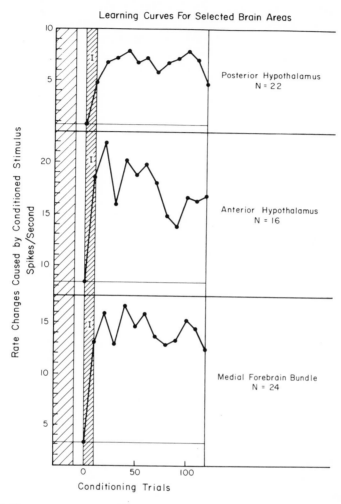

Fig. 2-18. Learning curves for different parts of hypothalamus from a different experiment. All three groups show evidence of signs of learning during the 10–20 trial period.

gering of later performance but not directly in causing engrams to be formed.

Between this higher attention learning in cortex and the lower learning of skills, it seems to me there must be an in-between kind of learning, and it is the mechanism of this learning that I would like to speculate on.

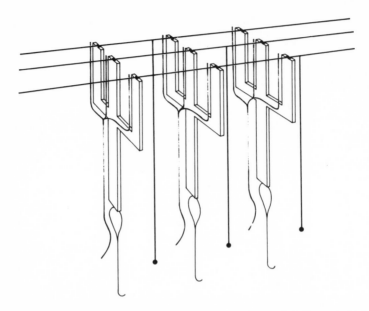

Fig. 2-19. Cerebellum. Schematic portrayal showing parallel fibers (which carry information from stimulations), crossing through the dendrites of Purkinje cells (which control behavior) and climbing fibers which ascend the dendrite trees and are juxtaposed to all of the parallel-Purkinje synapses.

It would be possible to have a set of neurons that would have relatively specific receptive fields at any particular point in time, but that would change their receptive fields from time to time as interest dictates. This would be something like the way the accumulator of a computer has rather specific contents at any point in time but changes rapidly from moment to moment. The question is how we might imagine a machine with these highly labile neurons working.

One possibility would be that a family of memory elements (non-dedicated sensory-motor links) would probe with their dendrites a rather large array of sensory input codes, and would probe with their axons a rather large array of motor output codes (see Fig. 2-20). If this kind of neuron existed in hypothalamus, they would get sensory messages from descending branches of the secondary sensory systems which clearly enter this region from the optic system on the one end and from the inferior colliculus on the other. They would send their axons toward the extrapyramidal systems. Each element would have perhaps as many as 10,000 afferent synapses, and 10,000 efferent. At any given time, only a

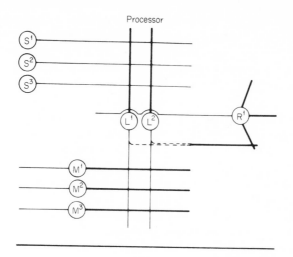

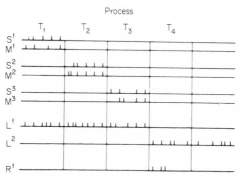

Fig. 2-20. Theory of reinforcement learning in diencephalon. Sensory elements are labeled S; memory-link elements are labeled L; motor elements are labeled M; reinforcement ones are labeled R. Successive times are labeled T. In the lower frame, the horizontal lines represent schematically the activity (as vertical marks) or silence of the elements. In the upper frame, sensory fibers pass through the dendrites of memory-link cells; the axons of the memory-links pass through the extrapyramidal motor dendrites. A memory-link group (e.g., L¹ constitutes a "push down" store, "hooking-up" to each sensory-motor configuration that occurs, and then dropping those connections, and "hooking-up" to the next. When a reinforcement occurs, this stops this repeated reconnection, so that the L group retains its last connection before reinforcement. Also at this time, it gains control over reinforcement elements so that when fired next time it will act as a reinforcer. At this point a second L group is called into play. An L group "fixed" by reinforcement will hold its connections for a period of minutes or maybe even hours or days but by no means forever. It will later be pressed into service again when all other L groups have had their turn. Thus, memory in this "store" does not last for very long.

small fraction, say 100, of these would be in a switched-in and ready-to-use condition, and the elements would therefore function as rather specific sensory–motor links. One possibility would be that the whole family of nondedicated links would be divided into a number of teams or sets. At each sensory–motor moment, a team would form temporary connections between the sensory and motor events, and then, barring a reinforcement, they would drop these connections and take on a new set at the next moment. This would continue until the application of a reinforcement. At that point, they would retain their connections, and the teams or sets would be changed. The team taken out would then hold for some longer moment the sensory–motor links and would be transformed at the same time into a set of reinforcing elements in its own right. When fired next time by the newly transcribed sensory pattern, they would not only link these patterns to the previously coactive motor responses, but would also act as reinforcers. This would serve to carry on the chaining of behavior one step farther. There would be several tens or hundreds (or thousands) of these "teams" and they would thus be in a position to hold temporary inscriptions of a rather large number of sensory–motor configurations. While holding these they would function as sensory–motor cross links. But after several times around, their turn to take on new inscriptions would come and the old information would be overwritten by new.

In any event, it seems to me that a mechanism of this type might play a role in unconscious learning, learning which would be retrospective, caused by surprise. The animal would have to look back to see what were the events leading up to the surprising positive state. The state would be held for a moment in this nondedicated neuronal family and would still be there as a "set of notes" which would then be caused to be held still longer by the reward.

By a slight logical gyration, this kind of an explanation engendered by me (and possibly by Nature) to account for behavioral chaining, might be amended so it would serve to extend the significance of habituated auditory signals. I will not go into the details.

In any event, it is clear and interesting that the neurons in the medial forebrain bundle pathway, neurons whose activity is inhibited briefly by rewarding input, and by rewarding brain stimulation, appear to play some role in a special kind of learning. This may be the role of modifying significances, extending traces, when this needs to be done prior to the expression of conditioning in overt behavior. It is almost as if we could say, in this kind of experiment, the *reward* systems learn first, certain *arousal* systems related to gross motor responses learn second, the *association nuclei* of thalamus and the *extrapyramidal systems* learn third, the *primary sensory systems* learn fourth. Actually there is a set of systems including frontal cortex and its correlated parts of thalamus that learns still later.

In answer to the original question of what the neurons of the reward pathway might be doing, it seems that they might be involved in some special kind of learning. They could be involved in an operant behavior chaining device. And in answer to the question of where the reward bundle is carrying its "reward message," one answer might be, to the path neurons which themselves participate in some important way in the learning process. The difficulty with lesions which needed to be extensive to disrupt self-stimulation would be well explained because, *unlike path fibers*, the axons of these path neurons exit from hypothalamus in all direction (possibly being directed toward the variety of different extrapyramidal systems that lie on its borders).

Theories of Reinforcement

I should like to conclude by appending a comment on the present status of drive reduction versus "hedonic increment" theories. Some years ago (Olds and Olds, 1965), I had imagined a three-step inhibitory chain:

(1) The first mediated rewards and inhibited the second.
(2) The second mediated aversive behavior and inhibited the third.
(3) The third mediated the two behind it and exercised control over behavior.

The data for this involved brain stimulation and behavior. Stimulation at point 1 was rewarding; stimulation at point 2 was aversive; and stimulation at point 3 was rewarding. When the animal was escaping from stimulation at 2, the experimenter could halt this by stimulation at 1; this led to the concept of 1-to-2 inhibition. When the animal was self-stimulating through a probe in 3, the experimenter could halt this by stimulating at 2; thus there was evidence for 2-to-3 inhibition. It was surprising that inhibition did not work back in the other direction. When the animal was escaping from stimulation at 2, the experimenter could *not* halt this by stimulating at 3; in fact, 3-stimulation caused the escape behavior to be accelerated. This acceleration suggested that the escape behavior might be supported by activity at 3. We guessed it might be supported by a "3-rebound" when inhibition from 2 was withdrawn. We also guessed that the rewardingness of 1 might be mediated by its stopping 2 and causing the same "3-rebound." These speculations were to some degree supported by data showing that lesions at 3 caused both 1-self-stimulation, and 2-escape to be depressed or abolished. These lesions also blocked other purposive behaviors caused by more normal stimulations.

Our view at that time was that an acceleration of neurons at 3 was the final "reinforcing" step in this 1-2-3 pathway. Direct recording of neuronal activity in this region has caused second thoughts. Neurons at 3 are usually slowed or stopped during consummatory behaviors (Hamburg, 1971) and they are momentarily silenced by each pulse in a train of rewarding brain stimulation (Ito, 1972). Conversely, they are excessively active during instrumental activity and they are "turned-on" by a conditioned stimulus which triggers instrumental activity.

These data leave some paradoxes to be cleared up. First, why does the stimulus silence most of the closest recordable neurons? The answer is that we stimulate fibers and record from cell bodies, and quite often the fibers are carrying inhibitory messages. Another question is raised by the fact that the brain stimulus is at one time both a reward and a drive inducer (an inducer of instrumental behaviors). Why does it cause instrumental behaviors yet silence the large neurons that are ordinarily correlated with such behaviors? The answer to this question is first that the paradox is there to begin with: Why does the stimulus both reward and drive at the same time (like food and food-deprivation being administered at the same time)? Brain stimulation is like that; applied in a system with prominent inhibitory connections it will of course trigger contradictory messages.

As things stand, it seems to me that we should give serious consideration to a four-step chain. For clarity, I list below the candidates for the four steps along with the properties which I, hypothetically, impute to them.

Step 1. Cell bodies are in paleocortex and in septal and amygdaloid nuclei. Input is from the environment, abstracted as to positive motivational properties. Output toward next step would be inhibitory.

Step 2. Cell bodies are in midline hypothalamus, thalamus, and midbrain. Input from the environment is abstracted as to negative motivational properties, but also there is inhibition from 1. Output toward the next step would be inhibitory.

Step 3. Cell bodies are in locations unknown; possibly aminergic neurons in midbrain and other parts of brain stem, but also possibly some neurons in lateral hypothalamus and preoptic area. Input would be inhibitory from step 2 and possibly excitatory from step 1. Output toward the next step would be neither excitatory nor inhibitory but "reinforcing."

Step 4. Cell bodies would be the path neurons in the medial fore-brain bundle. There would be labile connections to sensory systems on the input side, and labile connections to motor systems in the extra-pyramidal system on the output side. The "reinforcing" input from step 3 would cause these neurons to be "turned-off" but to become temporarily connected to the sensory and motor systems with which they were coactive.

References

Bloomfield, S., & Marr, D. How the cerebellum may be used. *Nature,* 1970, **227,** 1224–1228.

Boyd, E. S., & Gardner, L. Effect of some brain lesions on intracranial self-stimulation in the rat. *American Journal of Physiology,* 1967, **213,** 1044–1052.

Disterhoft, J., & Olds, J. Differential development of conditioned unit changes in thalamus and cortex of rat. *Journal of Neurophysiology,* 1972, **35,** 665–679.

Hamburg, M. D. Hypothalamic unit activity and eating behavior. *American Journal of Physiology,* 1971, **220,** 980–985.

Ito, M. The excitability of medial forebrain bundle neurons during self-stimulation behavior. *Journal of Neurophysiology,* 1972, **35,** 652–664.

Ito, M., & Olds, J. Unit activity during self-stimulation behavior. *Journal of Neurophysiology,* 1971, 34: 263–273.

Kornblith, C. L. Conditioned responses in the reticular formation. Ph.D. Thesis submitted to Division of Biology, California Institute of Technology, Pasadena, California, 1972.

Linseman, M. A. Unit activity in the hypothalamus and striatum of the rat during learning. Ph.D. Thesis submitted to the Division of Biology, California Institute of Technology, Pasadena, California, 1972.

Olds, J. The central nervous system and the reinforcement of behavior. *American Psychologist,* 1969, **24,** 707–719.

Olds, J. & Olds, M. E. Drive rewards and the brain. In: *New Directions in Psychology II,* T. M. Newcomb (ed.) New York: Holt, 1965. Pp. 327–404.

Olds, M. E. and Ito, M. Noradrenergic and cholinergic action on neuronal activity during self-stimulation behavior in the rat. *Neuropharmacology* (in press).

Olds, J., Disterhoft, J. F., Segal, M., Kornblith, C. L., & Hirsh, R. Learning centers of rat brain mapped by measuring latencies of conditioned unit responses. *Journal of Neurophysiology,* 1972, **35,** 202–219.

Segal, M., & Olds, J. The behavior of units in the hippocampal circuit of the rat during learning. *Journal of Neurophysiology,* 1972, **35,** 680–690.

CHAPTER 3

Psychological Complexity and Preference: A Hedgehog Theory of Behavior [1]

EDWARD LEWIS WALKER

University of Michigan

I should like to present a very simple theory of motivation and learning. It is simple in the sense that it consist of a very small set of definitions, principles, or postulates. Yet, I think it offers some potential for dealing with a very large number of psychological phenomena including a great many with more complicated and elaborate explanations.

Why a Hedgehog?

I have chosen to refer to the theory of *Psychological Complexity and Preference* as a hedgehog theory of behavior. The hedgehog, as you probably know, is an Old World insectivorous mammal with spines

[1] Complexity and Preference Theory is to some extent in the same position as an old fashioned bride. It is wearing "something old, something new, something borrowed, and something true." Much of the theory is borrowed from Daniel Berlyne (1960) and from William Dember and Robert Earl (1957) as well as from a long list of teachers disguised as students whom I have enjoyed over the years.

This paper is a severely reduced version of a longer paper which is in the process of growing into a book to be completed in 1973.

The time to carry out the research and to prepare this paper has been provided by the National Institute of Mental Health through grant number K6-MH-21, 868.

65

pointing in almost every direction. The most remarkable thing about a hedgehog is that while he doesn't do very much of anything, what he does do, he does exceedingly well. If a hedgehog is tired, he simply rolls up into a ball. If he is frightened, he rolls up into a ball. In fact, it doesn't seem to matter much what happens, there he is rolled up into a ball again. This limited talent has earned the hedgehog a place in literature and possibly even a degree of grudging admiration (see Fig. 3-1).

Archilocus in the seventh century B.C. said something which was paraphrased by Erasmus in about A.D. 1500 as,

> *The fox has many tricks.*
> *The hedgehog only one,*
> *But that is the best of all.*

The fox, for his part, is a very clever animal. He has a very large repertory of tricks. One might say that the fox is a kind of animal who has more solutions than he has problems.

Psychological theories can be categorized into hedgehog theories and fox theories. Guthrie had a hedgehog theory because of his single-minded employment of stimulus–response contiguity. Because of the imputed holy power of the reinforcement principle, Skinner might also be categorized as a hedgehog theorist. Hull would be classified as a fox theorist because his theory probably had more postulates than predictions. Tolman was a fox, as was Freud. Both could predict the same thing several different ways. Psychological complexity and preference theory is a hedgehog theory because it has only one trick, and it attempts to meet a large variety of situations and problems both successfully and simply without additional tools or weapons.

In psychological complexity theory, man is a creature fated to be quickly bored with whatever he is doing now and thus be forced to seek a more interesting activity. The most predictable aspects of the stream of human behavior are that whatever psychological event is occurring at one moment in time will be replaced by a different event in the next

Awoke   **Asleep and Otherwise**

Fig. 3-1. Hypothetical Hedgehog.

moment, and that succeeding events will be remarkably similar in their levels of complexity.

Psychological Complexity and Preference Theory

I should like to discuss some aspects of psychological complexity and preference theory (Walker, 1964, 1969, 1970) to provide a general context, to differentiate aspects which might not be shared by others in this volume, and to provide a basis for the discussion of some empirical research by some of my colleagues. The hedgehog is a very simple piece of theoretical machinery, involving a very small set of definitions and principles.

THE PSYCHOLOGICAL EVENT

A psychological event is a theoretical concept. It is conceived as a unit of psychological activity of limited and somewhat arbitrary duration. A practical minimum duration is probably about 500σ and is similar in character to what has been called a *psychological moment*. Psychological events terminate abruptly and automatically. Behavior requiring a longer time span constitutes a string or sequence of psychological events and can reflect the stream of thought or the stream of behavior. A psychological event may or may not be accompanied by overt behavior, may or may not be correlated with conscious experience, but very probably cannot occur without corresponding neural activity.

PSYCHOLOGICAL COMPLEXITY

I should like to reserve this term to refer to the complexity of a psychological event. It is a theoretical variable within the hedgehog which should be related to but not necessarily be identical with the complexity of an overt response, the complexity of a conscious experience, or the complexity of the underlying neurophysiological activity. It is to be distinguished from *stimulus complexity, a priori complexity, consensual complexity,* and *subjective complexity.* These terms refer to physical properties of the stimulus, assumed properties of the stimulus, mean reference group ratings, and individual ratings of an event or a stimulus.

OPTIMAL COMPLEXITY LEVEL

There is a point on the psychological complexity dimension which is optimal. In a situation in which there are a number of potential events which could occur, that event which is nearest optimum will have priority and will tend to occur with a high probability. Potential events which are either more or less complex will have a lower probability of occurrence. Optimal complexity level is assumed to be a relatively fixed characteristic of the organism, similar or related to information processing capacity or channel capacity. There are individual differences in optimal complexity level. Within the individual there are at least two major variations. There are developmental changes. Optimal complexity level is assumed to rise from birth to midadolescence, to remain fairly stable through the middle years, and to decline in senescence. There are also assumed to be diurnal variations. The optimal complexity level is high in an awake organism and low in an organism which is asleep or in a comparable resting state.

All preference functions are to be derived from optimal complexity level. Preference is perfectly correlated with the probability of the occurrence of an event. In a completely free responding situation, whichever event is closest to optimal complexity level will occur. When there are constraints and the organism may choose only between two or more alternatives which are somewhat removed from optimum, the choice will be that event which is closest to optimum, regardless of whether it is more or less complex than the optimum. Preference should be related to but not necessarily identical with verbal evaluation in terms of pleasure and pain or to overt approach and avoidance behavior.

There are at least three very different appearing functions obtained when an evaluative variable, such as preference, is plotted against a structural variable, such as psychological complexity. They are:

1. A monotonically increasing function.
2. An inverted U-shaped function.
3. A double invested U-shaped function.

I have portrayed these three in Fig. 3-2. It is my thesis that the primary function is the inverted U-shaped function, and the other two are derived from it only under specific and special circumstances.

The basic inverted U-shaped function should occur whenever a subject is asked for his preference among samples from a dimension of complexity ranging from very high to very low and when the choice is made in terms of the intrinsic properties of the stimuli. Thus, if a subject is presented with an array of paintings that vary in complexity, and he is asked to make a judgment of how well he likes the paintings relative to each other, an inverted U-shaped function should be the result.

If I have a scale composed of piles of money ranging from a very

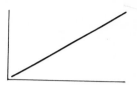

Fig. 3-2. Possible relations between complexity and preference.

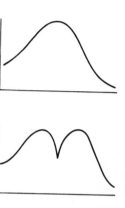

small pile to a very large pile, one can predict that a subject will consistently choose the larger of any two piles, and given a completely free choice of any pile he wants, he will choose the largest. This monotonically increasing function can occur whenever the choice is not in terms of the intrinsic qualities of the stimuli, but in terms of the instrumental role of the stimuli in reducing the complexities of other complex psychological events. Each of us would experience a major reduction in a number of complexities imposed by external social constraints that would be brought nearer to optimum if we possessed large amounts of money. Thus the preference function for piles or amounts of money is a monotonically increasing function in the service of an inverted U-shaped function.

The double inverted U-shaped function characterizes adaptation level theory, such as that of Helson (Chapter 7), and discrepancy theories of affect such as that of McClelland (1963). It should be obtained in any situation in which adaptation level theory is applicable. With psychological complexity and preference theory, adaptation results in a gross temporary reduction in the complexity of an event and a correlated reduction in preference.

Habituation

Operationally, habituation is produced by the repeated elicitation of the same psychological event by applying the same inducing stimulus a number of times with very short intervals between elicitations. Unfortunately, the effects of repeated activations of the same event are complex and varied. They differ markedly depending on the particular class of event being elicited and upon the time parameters involved.

The most typical effect of habituation operations is a progressive reduction in the response magnitude. Jane Mackworth (1969) has compiled almost a catalog of responses which show an orderly, exponential reduction. She lists such responses as attentional deployment, psychomotor and mental tracking tasks, motion aftereffects, reaction time, and a rather large group of sensory thresholds.

There are organismic responses which do not appear to undergo habituation. Sparrows are reported not to habituate to an owl or to a model of an owl even in hand-reared specimens (Nice & ter Pelkwyk, 1941). Dewsbury (1966), reported in more detail in Walker (1969) made extraordinary efforts to induce a decrease in the frequency of the electrical response of the weak electric knife fish *Gymnotus carapo* to several stimuli including the introduction of a metallic object into the water. Intense massing of the stimulus presentations failed to produce any decrement in the response and thus no evidence of habituation. There are very little data in the literature concerning the rate of recovery from habituation. It may be that this class of responses recovers so rapidly from the effects of elicitation that no one has elicited them rapidly enough to demonstrate the effects of habituation.

The intensity of some responses increase or potentiate, at least through a number of repetitions, before beginning to show decremental effects. One of the most obvious is the primary sexual response which appears to increase or to undergo potentiation through a number of stimulus induced events until orgasm is reached, after which there is a decrement in intensity from further stimulation. Some very elegant experimental work (and logical analysis) has been applied to this problem by Groves and Thompson (1970). They chose to do experimental work with the much less titillating hindleg flexion response in the spinal cat and the startle response in the intact rat. They report a number of curves showing that with repeated activation, the magnitude of the response may rise through a number of elicitations and then begin to drop to a level far below the amplitude of the initial or control response.

They have presented a very persuasive theory to account for habituation curves which first rise and then fall. They postulate a dual process involving a decremental process, *habituation*, and an incremental process, *sensitization*. They say that every stimulus that evokes a response has two properties: It elicits a response and it influences the "state" of the organism. Habituation is assumed to be a process which occurs in the primary specific pathway involved in making the response. It is an inferred decremental process which is exponential in form and thus approaches an asymptote. Within a given S–R pathway, the amount and rate of development of habituation are directly related to frequency and inversely related to intensity.

Frequency has a strong effect and intensity a weak effect on habituation. They assert that habituation decays spontaneously after cessation of stimulation. Sensitization is the product of the state of the organism which is described as the general level of excitation, arousal, activation, tendency to respond, etc. During habituation procedures, sensitization is said first to grow and then to decay. Sensitization is directly related to stimulus intensity with little or no sensitization occurring at low intensities. Sensitization is expected to decay spontaneously with cessation of the stimulus which produced it.

In the Groves and Thompson dual process theory, habituation and sensitization occur and develop independently of one another, yet they interact to yield the final response output function. The result of repeated stimulation, when the stimulation produced an increase followed by a decrease in the arousal level of the organism would be similar to that seen in Fig. 3-3.

One of the major virtues of the Groves and Thompson theory is that it provides an explanation of discrepant results and offers both the possibility of independent manipulation of the two effects, as they have done, but it also offers the possibility of independent measurements of the two processes. State changes, as they conceive them, are precisely those which have been subject to extensive manipulation and measurement in pursuit of indices of arousal.

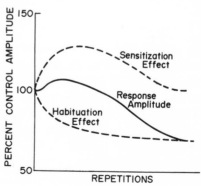

Fig. 3-3. Interaction of sensitization and habituation.

AROUSAL

[margin note: not necessarily / depends on / novelty / effect.]

Arousal is an organismic state which serves to modulate the psychological complexity of a psychological event. An event that occurs when the organism is in a high arousal state will be more complex than a similar event occurring during a state of low arousal. A special property of arousal is that it endures and can transcend the event which induced it. It is otherwise reducible to psychological complexity. Thus, sensitization is a special case of arousal increase. Stimuli which induce increases in response magnitude during habituation operations, are stimuli with arousal properties.

It should be noted in passing, because it will not be an issue elsewhere in this chapter, that arousal level has a second special property. There are intraindividual variations in optimal complexity level. The most pronounced are diurnal variations. Optimal complexity level in a sleeping organism is lower than in the awake and alert organism. The fact that wounds are reported not to be painful in the heat of battle indicates that the 'heat of battle' must refer as well to a temporarily elevated optimal complexity level.

[margin note: in other words, optimal level of complexity complements (is independent) homeostatic (primary) drive) system.]

INCENTIVES

Incentives are stimuli or potential events which are closer to optimum than the ongoing event. Incentives are also stimuli or events which produce increases in the arousal level, and thus the complexity level, of an event through a change in the state of the organism. Thus incentive properties of stimuli also become special cases of arousal increase. Stimuli with acquired incentive property have simply acquired arousal properties, thus increased complexity through association with another event that has arousal or incentive properties.

[margin note: or of more novelty than others.]

THE SEMIPERMANENT EFFECTS OF EXPERIENCE

In psychological complexity and preference theory, all learning is to be accounted for by changes in the complexity levels of psychological events, and all performance is to be accounted for in terms of the distances between the complexity levels of events and optimal complexity level. The hedgehog character of the theory is nowhere more apparent than in its intended simplicity and universality in the complex field of learning and performance.

[margin note: overly simplistic]

When a psychological event occurs repeatedly with an interval between occurrences of sufficient length that habituation effects are not a significant factor, the complexity of that event will usually undergo a

novelty

progressive reduction in level as an exponential function of the frequency of occurrence. A reasonable mathematical description of this change in complexity is the following:

$$C = kC_u(10^{-aN}) + C_u,$$

where C is the psychological complexity, C_u is the ultimate or unreducible psychological complexity, k a constant, a a constant controlling rate of reduction in complexity, and N the frequency of occurrence of the event.

The suggested equation is an empirically derived equation which fits many learning curves. The choice of this equation has, however, several interesting theoretical consequences. Figure 3-4 is an idealized plot of changes in the psychological complexity levels of seven events which differ primarily in the value of C_u, the ultimate or asymptotic complexity levels. They are arranged in quite reasonable relations to optimal complexity level and thus to the associated preference function drawn in a superimposed position on the right side of the figure.

Some of the interesting implications are these. If I know the psychological complexity values of a range of stimuli, I can choose a set composed only of stimuli above optimum. I can then have them rated for complexity and preference and obtain a monotonically decreasing curve relating preference to complexity. I can as easily choose a set which will give me an inverted U-shaped function, or, if I select very simple stimuli, I can obtain a monotonically increasing function. Thus the question of curve shape is not critical without some independent assessment of psychological complexity and optimal complexity level.

The effects of repeated experience on preference are equally varied. I can choose a complex stimulus as might be represented by the upper curves and obtain a preference function with experience which verfies Zajonc's (1968) variant of the old saw, "familiarity breeds content." I could

Fig. 3-4. Basic psychological complexity and preference theory.

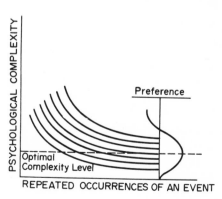

PSYCHOLOGICAL COMPLEXITY

Preference

Optimal Complexity Level

REPEATED OCCURRENCES OF AN EVENT

74   EDWARD LEWIS WALKER

as well choose a stimulus slightly above optimal complexity level and
obtain a preference curve with experience which confirmed an inverted
U-shaped pattern. I could also choose a stimulus that was so simple that
repeated experience produced a progressive decrease in preference.
Again, meaningful predictions require independent assessment of psychological complexity and optimal complexity level.

PERTURBATIONS IN THE LEARNING CURVE

A learning curve is not always a simple, smooth exponential change.
Both sudden increases and decreases can occur. Suppose I ask you to
participate in a rote learning experiment in which you are to learn to
reproduce a sequence of numbers such as the following,

8 4 0 2 4 2 0 1 2 1 5 6 5 2 8 2 1 4 6 2 3 6 1 8 4.

This sequence is obviously beyond your immediate memory span, and
mine. The learning process you might undergo might be represented by
the curve for $C_u = 20$ in Fig. 3-5. In the figure a set of curves has been
calculated with arbitrary asymptotic values ranging from 1 to 20. It
probably would require many trials for you to master such a list, especially if you obeyed the instructions to learn it by rote.

Suppose, however, that you had inadvertently disobeyed instructions.
After a number of trials, you notice that the end of the sequence has a
regularity about it when examined in reverse order. You would hardly
notice this regularity before you would become aware that the very complicated, very difficult 25-digit sequence you have been learning by rote,

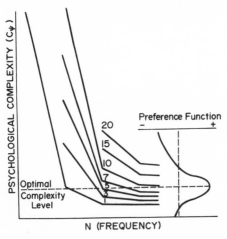

Fig. 3-5. Effect of learning on preference.

is, in fact, a very simple, very easy 10-number sequence when seen in reverse. Thus, when it is reversed, the sequence becomes:

4 8 16 32 64 128 256 512 1024 2048.

This sudden shift in complexity level of the task, as seen by you, the subject, would be represented by a sudden change in the C_u value from 20 to perhaps 1. This sudden shift is portrayed in Fig. 3-6, where the changes in complexity with further occurrences of the event is represented as a broken line after the point at which insight had occurred.

The figure also portrays an example of the reverse kind of perturbation. Some psychological events have the potential of undergoing elaboration or complication, an increase in the ultimate complexity level, with repeated experience. Two patterns of complication are drawn in the figure. In one, the curve for $C_u = 1$ suddenly rises to match the curve for $C_u = 15$. I have been unable to think of a realistic example of such a sudden rise without external input to accomplish the change in complexity level. Such a change might occur in the study of a simple organism when a microscope suddenly became available. Through the microscope, the seemingly simple organism might become a very complex one. A much more realistic picture is that portrayed by the curve that rises in a number of smaller steps. Such a curve might represent changes that occur in one's reactions to a game such as bridge or chess which might at first appear relatively simple but undergo successive increases in the complexity level as more and more of the games' complexities come into the awareness of the player.

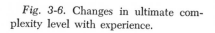

Fig. 3-6. Changes in ultimate complexity level with experience.

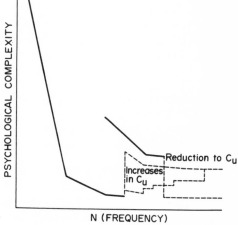

SUMMARY OF THEORETICAL EFFECTS OF REPEATED EXPERIENCE OF PSYCHOLOGICAL EVENTS

The effects of experience should be divided into temporary and semi-permanent effects. There are two temporary effects, habituation and sensitization. Habituation is a temporary decrement in the intensity and complexity of the event. Sensitization is the temporary increment in the arousal level of the organism. Habituation and sensitization interact to produce either a progressive decrement in the event or an increment followed by a decrement in the intensity and thus complexity of the event when the same event is repeated at intervals close enough in time that the temporary effects of one occurrence of the event are not dissipated before the subsequent occurrence of the event.

Learning consists in semipermanent changes in the complexity level of psychological events. The most common change is an exponential decrease in the complexity of the event. Sudden changes in the complexity levels of events can occur without additional input as the result of either sudden insight that what had appeared to be a complex event was in fact a simple one, or when what had appeared as a simple event undergoes sudden increases in complexity level when possibly subtle complexities are perceived for the first time.

THE SIMPLICITY OF THE HEDGEHOG

While it has been necessary to deal with a number of psychological terms such as arousal, incentive habituation, and sensitization, the essence of psychological complexity and preference theory is much simpler. There is one concept, the *psychological event,* one dimension, *psychological complexity,* one nodal point, *optimal complexity level,* and one dynamic principle, an *exponential simplification of the event with experience.* Thus the theory is a truly simple machine—a true hedgehog.

Experimental Studies of Complexity and Preference

EFFECTS OF REPEATED EXPOSURE ON THE PSYCHOLOGICAL COMPLEXITY AND LIKING FOR MUSICAL COMPOSITIONS

A theory of psychological complexity and preference should be applicable to the aesthetic response to musical compositions both in terms of our preferences on first hearing them and upon the effects of repeated experience of them. If we have an array of compositions representing a sufficient range of complexity levels, we should obtain an inverted

U-shaped function of complexity and preference. If we listen to the same short piece repeatedly without a sufficient interval between presentations, we might expect the result to be pure habituation and thus either a simple decrease in the liking for all such pieces or possibly a rise and fall in the liking for all. If there is a sufficient interval between presentations to permit recovery from habituation, then we would expect very complex pieces to be liked better with repeated experience and very simple pieces to be liked less with repeated experience.

There have been a number of studies to which this set of propositions should be applicable, but I find many of them difficult to interpret because of a number of complex problems relating to the nature of the stimuli, the experimental procedures, and the absence of relevant evaluations on the part of experimental subjects. Given the problem of the different effects to be expected from habituation and from longer term simplification, it is exceedingly easy to construct a noncritical or uninterpretable experiment.

Heyduk (1972) has made a beginning on some of these problems in a series of experiments conducted at the University of Michigan. He began by constructing four musical compositions. The four had a number of common properties. Each lasted 30 sec. Each consisted of three parts: an original statement consisting of seven chord changes played with both hands and lasting four bars (10 sec); an interlude of six bars with five chord changes and some melody in the right hand (15 sec); and a resolution of two bars with three chord changes played with both hands (5 sec). An attempt was made to vary the complexity levels of the four compositions in two ways: the chord structure and the amount and kind of syncopation. The four compositions can be labeled A, B, C, and D, with A intended to be the least complex and D the most. Composition A had only two chords, both of which were major chords (100%). Composition B had four different chords, three of which (75%) were major chords. Composition C had eight different chords, four of which were major chords (50%). Composition D had 12 different chords, four of which were major chords (33%). In addition, A was played with no syncopation. Composition B was played with left–right coordinated syncopation. Composition C had syncopation in the left hand and no coordination. Composition D had different syncopations in the two hands.

The four compositions, when played on the piano, are reasonably musical and they cover a perceptible span of the complexity dimension even to the unmusical ear.

Heyduk has carried out several studies, one of which I should like to discuss in some detail. The basic experimental plan was to play a tape of the four compositions twice each for a subject or group of subjects and ask them to rate each composition the second time it was heard for *how much you like* each selection on a scale ranging from 1 to 13, from *dislike very much* to *like very much*. Then each was rated for how complex it sounds on another 1 to 13 scale ranging from *extremely simple* to *extremely complex*.

Following the initial ratings of all four compositions, a given subject heard one of the compositions 16 times in succession, rating it for liking and complexity after each exposure.

Finally, each of the four compositions was played a second (or 19th) time and subjected to a final rating of liking and complexity.

Basically, the theory of psychological complexity and preference is a theory of process within the individual. It should therefore hold true for the choices of individual subjects. There are a number of ways of testing whether the preference ratings of a given subject agree with the theory or disagree. One way is to use a variety of Coombs (1964) unfolding technique for ordered data.

To apply the technique the ratings given by the subjects are reduced to rankings under the conservative assumption that the rating scale values are not on an equal-interval scale. The *preference order* supplied by the subject can then be compared to any one of several measures of the relative complexity of the stimuli. One measure of complexity is the a priori complexity ordering based on the manipulations employed in constructing the stimuli. In this case, the complexity ordering is D > C > B > A, indicating that composition D is the most complex and composition A the least. A second measure of complexity could be what I have called *consensual complexity*. This would be an ordering based on the mean complexity rating (or ranking) assigned by a reference group. In Heyduk's study, he had constructed his stimuli well, and *a priori complexity* and *consensual complexity* yield the same ordering of the four stimuli. Still another possible basis for ordering the four stimuli for complexity could be the ratings supplied by the subject. The individual subject might or might not agree with the group on the relative complexities of the four stimuli. We shall refer to this ordering of the complexity of the stimuli as the *subjective complexity* ordering. Thus we have a choice of several ways of ordering complexity of the stimuli. Since *a priori complexity* and *consensual complexity* ordering agree in Heyduk's data, we are left with a choice of two.

The preference order (how much each was liked relative to the others) can then be matched with the complexity orderings. To illustrate, let us use the consensual complexity ordering, D > C > B > A. The subject could have ordered his preference (or liking) for these stimuli in 24 different orders. Since his optimal complexity level could be in any position along the complexity scale, 8 of the 24 possible orderings would agree with the theory and 16 would not. The 8 which would agree, if complexity and preference are plotted together, would form the one possible monotonically increasing function, the one possible monotonically decreasing function, and the six possible inverted U-shaped functions. The 16 orderings which would controvert the theory would all form U-shaped and other nonmonotonic functions.

Using this technique, the preference order provided by each subject on each occasion can be examined to determine whether it agrees with the theory. Then the number of such agreements can be compared with the number expected by chance to determine the extent to which the theory holds in these data. The result of this analysis of individual protocols is presented in Table 3-1. It will be noted that the Expected proportion of supporting protocols varies slightly from a p of .333. These differences arise because the probability of a supporting protocol arising by chance is smaller if either D or A are rated as the most preferred, and larger if B or C are so rated. In the table, the actual frequencies of each choice are taken into account. It is apparent from the table that the

TABLE 3-1

Psychological Complexity and Liking: Individual Protocol Analysis [a]

Alternative bases for ordering liking	Observed number of supporting protocols	Expected number of supporting protocols	Expected proportion of supporting protocols	χ^2	p
Initial ratings					
Consensual complexity	85	42.7	.356	64.0	<.001
Subjective complexity	73	36.4	.303	51.4	<.001
Final ratings					
Consensual complexity	91	41.3	.344	89.4	<.001
Subjective complexity	83	35.6	.297	87.8	<.001

[a] $N = 120$.

theory can be used to predict preference order from the complexity of the stimuli much better than chance. Theoretically, *subjective complexity* should be a better basis for prediction than *consensual complexity*, but it is not. My guess is that this difference is attributable to the fact that when *subjective complexity* is used, both orderings, preference order and complexity order, are subject to error. When *consensual complexity* is used, since it agrees with the a priori ordering, it is the same for all subjects and is not subject to error.

An additional aspect of this analysis should be mentioned. Examination of the protocols which do not agree with the theory indicates that they generally depart from the expectations of the theory in minor ways and are not distributed equally among the 16 other possible orderings.

The analysis of individual protocols reveals what might be hidden under the highly regular looking relationships between complexity and preference in a group analysis. Figure 3-7 is a plot of mean complexity and mean liking ratings for these stimuli for 120 subjects the first time they heard the four selections. *Consensual complexity* is clearly a simple linear increasing function of *a priori complexity*. The mean liking rating shows the classical inverted U-shaped function with a group optimal complexity level somewhere around the complexity of composition C.

It is to be noted that the number of observed supporting protocols indicated in Table 3-1 increased from the initial to the final rating. This increase could easily be attributable to the order effect during the initial ratings. If so, then the final ratings might be considered the more representative.

The major effect of experience is to be seen in the ratings of the same musical composition heard 19 times in close succession. Figure 3-8 shows

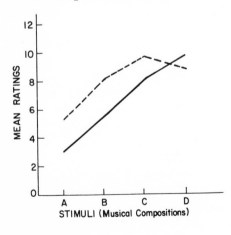

Fig. 3-7. Psychological complexity and preference for musical compositions.

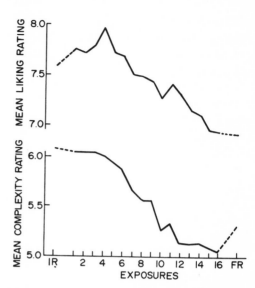

Fig. 3-8. Effect of repeated experience on ratings.

that the general effect of experience on rated complexity was a gradual decrease in rating. Liking ratings appear to rise over the first few repetitions and then to fall.

Since little or nothing is known concerning the time course of recovery from habituation, there is no external basis for deciding whether the observed effects are attributable to habituation or to long term changes in the psychological complexity and preference for the musical compositions.

Heyduk performed a revealing analysis on the individual protocols of the change with experience data to reveal the degree of agreement with three theories of expected change. Psychological complexity theory makes different predictions depending on the location of the optimal complexity level of the individual. Optimal complexity level can be determined for an individual from his original preference ratings of the four stimuli. If he originally prefers D, then his optimal complexity level must be nearer to D than to C. If he originally prefers C, then his optimal complexity level must be nearer to C than to either B or D, etc. Thus the original ratings can be used to determine the optimal complexity level for an individual, and knowledge of his optimal complexity level can be used to predict the direction of long term change in liking. What Heyduk calls Satiation Theory predicts that all ratings will be downward, regardless of the original preference rating. Mere exposure theory (Zajonc, 1968) predicts that any increase in familiarity will lead to an increase in liking.

TABLE 3-2

Effects of Repeated Experience: Individual Protocol Analysis

Theory of effect of repeated exposure	Observed number of supporting protocols	Expected number of supporting protocols	Expected proportion of supporting protocols	x^2	p
Psychological complexity theory	71	50.2	.418	14.1	$< .001$
Satiation theory	51	39.6	.330	4.5	$< .05$
Mere exposure theory	21	39.6	.330		n.s.

Table 3-2 contains the results of this analysis. Psychological complexity theory succeeds in predicting the direction of change in 71 of 120 instances, a success rate that is significantly better than chance. Satiation theory (which does not differ in its prediction from the expected effects of habituation, making the reasonable assumption that sensitization, if any, has disappeared by the 16th trial) is successful in 51 instances, significant beyond the .05 level. Mere exposure theory is correct in only 21 instances, less than the number expected by chance. The fact that psychological complexity theory predicts better than satiation (or habituation) theory appears to indicate that the long term effects of experience are predominant in these data.

Heyduk's studies serve to verify the predicted relationship between psychological complexity and preference and do so both on the basis of the appropriate individual protocol analysis and the more typical group analyses. His studies also provide primary information in the area of the effects of repeated experience.

REDUCING PSYCHOLOGICAL COMPLEXITY THROUGH CHUNKING

Complex material can be made simpler through the process of chunking. G. A. Miller's (1956) concept of a chunk refers to the organization of items into a *Gestalt* or unit of cognitive organization. A chunk is simpler, in terms of psychological complexity, than a set of items which has not been organized into a chunk. For the most part, it is probably more complex than would be a single item. Thus chunking is a means of making complex material simpler through a process of cognitive organization. If a sequence of items is formed into cognitive chunks, the sequence is probably less complex psychologically than if it was not organized into chunks, but how much simpler is it? If a sequence of 15 tones is organized into 5 chunks of 3 tones each or a sequence of 3 chunks of 5 tones each, how much simpler are the chunked sequences and which of the two patterns or organization is the simpler?

Arkes (1971) has taken at least one step toward a solution to this problem. He began with seven square-wave tones ranging over two octaves from 511.8 to 2049.2 Hz. Each tone was given a duration of .167 sec with a normal interval between tones also of .167 sec duration. A sequence of tones was chunked in two ways. Chunks of 3, 4, 5, or 6 tones were formed by increasing the duration of the interval between tones to 1.167 sec at appropriate positions in the sequence. In addition, each chunk consisted of a run (abcd), a trill (abab) or a repetition (aaaa). He then formed sequences of 5, 8, 10, 12, or 15 chunks, with the chunk size constant within any given sequence. The initial note of each chunk was randomly determined, and the sequence composition in terms of runs, trills, and repetitions was generally random except that some constraint was imposed to achieve balance. Each subject heard two representatives of each possible combination of chunk length and chunk number. Fourteen subjects rated the sequences for complexity and 14 rated them for how much they liked each.

The results are shown in Figs. 3-9 and 3-10 where they are plotted in terms of the average number of tones produced by the various combinations of numbers of tones within chunks (3, 4, 5, or 6) × 10 (the average number of sequences) or the number of sequences (5, 8, 10, 12, or 15) × 4.5 (the average number of tones in a sequence).

The only result that is statistically significant is the increase in complexity rating with an increase in the number of chunks and thus the length of the sequence. It is remarkable that doubling the size of a chunk from three to six tones did not lead to an increase in rated complexity. Thus Arkes has provided us with an instance of an answer to our original question. Given his procedures, he could double the number of tones by adding to chunk length without a significant increase in the psychological complexity of the response, but doubling the number of tones by doubling the number of chunks leads to a substantial increase in psychological complexity.

Chunking also occurs in rote serial learning problems. When an organism has to deal with a task that is too complex for immediate channel capacity and is thus considerably above the optimal complexity level, the

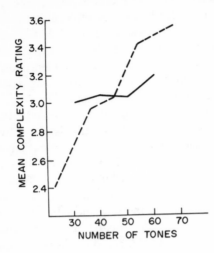

Fig. 3-9. Psychological complexity and preference for tones varying in chunk size and number of chunks. [Means of manipulation: (———): tones in chunks; (– – – –): number of chunks.]

Fig. 3-10. Psychological complexity and preferences for tones varying in chunk size and number of chunks. [Means of manipulation: (———): tones in chunks; (– – –): number of chunks.]

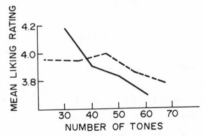

most common response, perhaps, is to organize subsets of the task into chunks. Thus, a 10-digit telephone number is usually chunked into three subsets consisting of a 3-digit area code, a 3-digit exchange code, and a 4-digit address within the exchange. In a great many of the serial learning tasks employed by psychologists since the time of Ebbinghaus, the task is made a learning task by deliberately constructing a task that is above complexity level. If it was at or below optimal level, the material could be reproduced in a single trial and no learning process would be apparent in the data. Since the optimal level is approximately 7 ± 2, according to George Miller (1956), the typical list to be learned contains 10 to 20 items. Such lists are sufficiently long to require more than one trial for mastery and sufficiently short that the patience of neither the subject nor the experimenter is strained unduly by the length of the learning process.

While most learning curves which represent the learning process in such tasks appear to represent a smooth and gradual accretion of correctly reproduced material, it seems likely that within the individual subject, the learning process consists in the formation of one or more, usually more, chunks, and a coalescence of these chunks into larger chunks until the whole set of 14 digits can be repeated without error. A plot of individual learning might therefore tend to consist of fits and starts, large jumps and regressions as the subject struggles to organize the material into a simpler pattern than that presented to him by the experimenter.

Arkes (1971) has made an initial effort to examine the learning process in the light of psychological complexity theory by looking at the chunking process within individual learning protocols. He presented 10 undergraduates with a number of 14-digit strings to be learned. The strings were constructed from random number tables with the constraint that there should be no successive repetitions and no more than three digits in serial order. Each subject learned to a criterion of two successive correct repetitions, five different strings which were presented to him on a memory drum with the entire string visible on each trial for 6 sec and with 14 sec for recall. Thus he obtained 50 instances of the mastery of a 14-digit list which was approximately twice the optimal complexity level of his subjects.

The identification of a cognitive chunk within the subject can only be approximated. Arkes, in his studies, actually employed a number of identification procedures including analyses of interresponse times. However, I shall discuss results using only a crude but defensible measure. A chunk can be defined as any two or more consecutive items that are correctly repeated in the correct position and separated from other correct items by at least one incorrect item.[2]

By this criterion, it is obvious that when a subject reached criterion, he had organized all 14 items into a single chunk. But what about the first trial? In 49 of the 50 instances there were one or more chunks present in the output of the subjects. In 38 instances there was one chunk present, and in 11 instances there were two chunks. Was there any advantage to the two-chunk organization over the one-chunk organization in terms of the number of items reproduced on the first trial? In these protocols, the answer is in the negative. Instances in which there was only one chunk contained a mean of 6.26 items. When there were

---

[2] During the first two presentations of each of the five strings, Arkes divided the 14-digit strings into 7 chunks of 2 digits each separating such pairs by fine red lines on the tape.

two chunks, there were 6.27 correct items, or 3.13 per chunk. Thus, on the first trial the magic number 7 ± 2 holds whether there is one chunk or two.

Yet, at criterion, every subject on every list has 14 items in a single chunk. What happens to the numbers of chunks and average chunk size during the acquisition process? Figure 3-11 is a plot of two manifestations of the chunking process. In each case, the value that is plotted is mean chunk size calculated by dividing the number of items within the chunks by the number of chunks. There are two manifestations because of the well known dilemma of how to deal with the fact that trials to criterion is a variable, in this case ranging from 3 to 18. One alternative is to retain all criterion performances until all subjects have learned each task to criterion. Using this procedure, the mean number of chunks rises from about 1.2 to about 1.35 by the fifth trial and then quickly subsides to a small fraction over 1.0. In this instance, mean chunk size is a very smooth function which does not look very different from the standard learning curve representing total items correct. However, there is another procedure. One can drop any instance from further consideration after the last trial before criterion. Such a plot represents a decreasing N ranging from 50 on the 1st trial to an N of 1 on the 18th. This procedure creates a sampling problem, of course, but the results are interesting. I have drawn the curve to rise from about six items to approximately seven as the most conservative curve I could draw by eye through the data. I resisted the temptation to draw it as a horizontal line representing a mean chunk size of about 6.25 items. The dots in the figure represent means of all instances remaining below criterion. It is also true that the mean chunk size on the trial before criterion in all 50 instances varies quite closely around 6 to 7 items.

What are we to make of all of this? From the standpoint of psychological complexity theory, we have presented subjects with a task that is

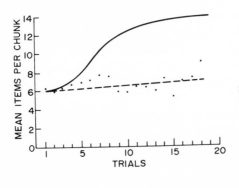

Fig. 3-11. Chunk size during learning of digits. [(———): All subjects; (– – –); criterion Ss removed.]

nearly double (in terms of number of items) optimal complexity level. Instead of the smooth process of acquisition which is usually plotted as a learning curve, acquisition of a 14-digit list is seen as a process of simultaneous organization of items into more than one chunk and a gradual coalescence of smaller chunks into larger chunks, a process that is much more discontinuous than we are ordinarily led to believe concerning the learning process. Nowhere, perhaps, is this discontinuity more apparent than in the fact that the mean gain in number of correct items from the last error trial to the first criterion trial is 3.84 items, while the mean rise on a single trial in the group curve where it is rising fastest is about one item. Another pair of meaningful numbers is the algebraic average of all *changes* in number correct prior to criterion, .627 items, and the average of all *gains* (mean of items gained only on trials on which there was a gain) prior to achieving the criterion, 3.13 items. Thus achieving criterion represents a giant leap forward, the biggest leap of all, saving the initial response. The process of chunking to reduce supraoptimal complexity is all but hidden in the traditional learning curve.

There is one more way we can look at items and chunks. The fact that the number of items was the same on the first trial whether in one chunk or two meant that there was no gain in simplification at that point deriving from the incorporation of items into chunks. When the criterion was reached, if the items are now regarded as belonging to one cognitive chunk, then the complexity of a single item had been reduced to about 44.6% (6.25/14) of its complexity at the outset of the learning process. This is probably an overestimation of the amount of reduction in psychological complexity, since some subjects may still have been using more than one chunk that was not revealed by this crude criterion. Interresponse times or some other index of organization may have revealed more than one chunk. Both Melton (1963) and Miller (1956) argue, in effect, that if practice is continued felicitously and indefinitely, the ultimate result would be a chunk containing 14 items that is essentially no more complex than a single unincorporated digit.

PROBLEM SOLVING AND PSYCHOLOGICAL COMPLEXITY

The simplification of a psychological event with experience need not be gradual. When the event in question has a hidden structure which is not apparent at first but which can become suddenly apparent, a very complex, supraoptimal event can suddenly become vary simple and at or below optimum. An example would be any classic problem in which a solution becomes suddenly apparent. A simple problem is above optimal complexity level until it is solved, and a difficult problem is far above optimal complexity level. After they are solved, they may not differ at all from each other and they are probably usually below optimal complexity level or one would undertake to solve the same problem over and over again.

An explicit relation can be stated between level of psychological complexity and the difficulty of problems. The more difficult a problem seems to be, the greater the psychological complexity of the event which is attempted solution to the problem.

Boykin (1972) has studied the relation between problem difficulty, psychological complexity, interestingness, and pleasantness. He chose an anagram task in which the subject was to solve the problem presented by unscrambling scrambled words. Table 3-3 contains some illustrative examples. Problem difficulty was manipulated by varying the length of the word to be unscrambled, and he used words of length 3, 4, 5, 7, and a longer set of words which was either 10 or 11 letters in length.

The words were presented in sets of four, of equal length within the set, and the subject was required to choose that one of the four which was the name of an animal and then indicate, on a three-point scale, how confident he was of his choice. This procedure was employed in order to control the time variables precisely. Each set was exposed for about 30 sec, and 5 sec was allowed for the indication of choice and confidence. A response was regarded as having been correct only when it was actually correct and one of the two higher levels of confidence of the correctness was indicated by the subject. It will be noted that this

TABLE 3–3

Examples of Anagram Task Employed by Boykin (1972) in a Study of Preference and Problem Difficulty (as a manifestation of complexity)

Number of letters	Scrambled version	Unscrambled
3	IGP	PIG
3	BRI	RIB
4	GTAO	GOAT
4	MGAR	GRAM
5	SRAKH	SHARK
5	CUHGO	COUGH
7	RLUEVTU	VULTURE
7	OVRTYCI	VICTORY
10/11	ODKGBICMRIN	MOCKINGBIRD
10/11	AERAOLIZITN	REALIZATION

procedure virtually eliminates the counting of responses which are correct by chance.

Each subject attempted to solve 10 blocks of problems and each block contained one set of each word length. In addition to recording the choice on each trial and the confidence level, an individual subject was asked to rate either the *complexity* of the task for each word length, the *interestingness* of it, or the *pleasantness* of each difficulty of task.[3] Each scale ranged from 1 to 13. Three different groups of subjects were used, and each group rated the tasks for only one of the scale dimensions—*complexity* ($N = 20$), *interestingness* ($N = 40$), or *pleasantness* ($N = 40$).

The length of the word in an anagram task represents an a priori scale of problem difficulty. Short words represent easy tasks and long words represent difficult tasks.. The group of subjects which evaluated the five word lengths for psychological complexity provide an estimate of the extent to which problem difficulty and psychological complexity are related. Figure 3-12 is a plot of that relationship. The relationship is a monotonically increasing function and appears to be approximately exponential. Thus each addition of a letter to the length of the word makes a smaller addition to the psychological complexity of the problem. Additional evidence for the correspondence of problem difficulty and psychological complexity comes from the comparison of the ratings of the most

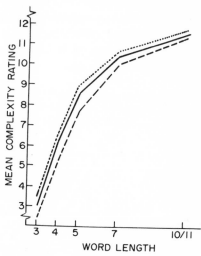

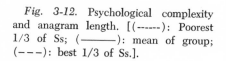

Fig. 3-12. Psychological complexity and anagram length. [(------): Poorest 1/3 of Ss; (———): mean of group; (– – –): best 1/3 of Ss.].

and least successful problem solvers in this group. Those who solved the smallest number of problems rated the task as more complex than the average, and those who solved the greatest number of problems rated it as less complex than the average for the group.

The curvilinear relationship in Fig. 3-12 justifies plotting subsequent graphs against mean psychological complexity ratings, a psychological scale as opposed to a physical scale.

Figure 3-13 lends additional support to this decision. The relationship between per cent correct and mean *complexity* rating is approximately linear until the lower asymptote is reached. The mean *complexity* ratings derived from Experiment I, in which the subjects rated the tasks for *complexity* is used on the abscissa, while the per cent correct for each of the three groups is plotted against this scale. It is probably an accident of sampling that the 80 subjects in Experiment II were slightly better problem solvers than the subjects of Experiment I.

Figure 3-14 is a plot of mean pleasantness rating derived from one group of 40 subjects and mean interestingness rating derived from a second group of 40 subjects in Experiment II. These results are not at all what one would be led to expect from previous comparisons of the relations between *interestingness* and *pleasantness* and *complexity*. The typical finding is that *pleasantness* shows an inverted U-shaped relationship to *complexity*, while interestingness is a monotonically increasing function of *complexity*.

One possible interpretation of this finding is that the dimensions of *pleasantness* and *interestingness* are qualitatively the same except that the difficulty threshold is higher for the *interestingness* dimension than for the *pleasantness* dimension. That is, as one proceeds from easy prob-

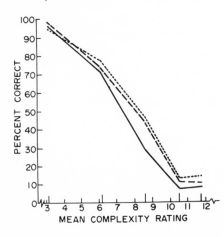

Fig. 3-13. Effect of problem difficulty on ratings. [(————): Exp. I, complexity; (– – –): Exp. II, pleasantness; (------): Exp. II, interestingness.]

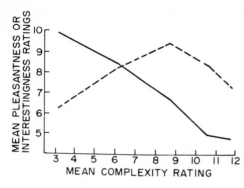

Fig. 3-14. Effect of psychological complexity on ratings of "interestingness" and "pleasantness". [(——): Pleasantness; (– – –): interestingness.]

lems to more and more difficult ones, the problems will be rated more interesting and more pleasant, but as the problems continue to be more difficult, there will come a level at which interest is sustained even though the problems are seen as progressively less pleasant. However, the *interestingness* relationship is also an inverted U-shaped function of *difficulty* but with a higher inflection point.

Boykin's studies demonstrate the efficacy of conceiving of problem solution as a decrease in the psychological complexity of the event represented by the problem. While psychological complexity does not exhaust the parameters of problem solving as a psychological field, it can be argued that the major parameter is psychological complexity and that it is reasonable to regard the easy–difficult dimension of problems to be solved as equivalent to a dimension of psychological complexity.

Context for and Some Implication of the Hedgehog

I should like to leave the details of the theory of psychological complexity and preference long enough to provide some of the broader context I see for the theory. I should like to discuss three problems briefly, learning, motivation, and the stream of psychological events.

LEARNING

At least three different patterns of change in the stream of behavior can be and have been referred to as learning.

1. A progressive increase (learning) or a decrease (extinction) in the degree of uniformity of behavior.

2. The acquisition of an association between two psychological events.

3. A progressive change in the character of behavior on succeeding occurrences.

An enormous amount of time, energy, money, and space in psychological journals has been devoted to the exploration of the principles and procedures which will induce uniformity in behavior. If one makes a particular psychological event stand in a contingent relationship to an incentive, the frequency of that event can be increased and the frequencies of other events which originally occurred in that situation can be reduced. The obsession with uniformity in behavior leads many psychologists to ignore any changes in the character of the behavior should any occur. A lever press is a lever press is a lever press. Experimental extinction is rarely viewed as an *increase* in the variability of psychological events, but only as a decrease in the uniformity or rate of the lever pressing response.

Association between psychological events can result in apparent learning of S–S, S–R, or R–R types. In each case, no change in the character of an S or an R is noted, only connections between them.

Learning can also be defined as a progressive change in the character of quality of a response, either motor or cognitive, with repeated occurrences. Such changes are tracked quantitatively in skill learning and sometimes in concept learning and attainment studies.

I would argue that while the first kind of learning is intrinsically interesting and easy to deal with, from the standpoint of ordinary human values, it is trivial and nearly pointless. The second, association, is more interesting, but emphasizes the less interesting aspect of change. Almost all learning that has human social value is of the third type. It is a progressive change in the character and quality of psychological events. The first and second seem (only seem) to suppress freedom and human dignity. The third kind of learning makes freedom and human dignity figural.

MOTIVATION

It should be made clear, if it is not already clear, that the hedgehog contains a complete theory of motivation. Moments of habituation followed by compelled choice of the next available event nearest optimum is the necessary and sufficient cause of behavior. Preference for the event nearest optimum is a complete basis of choice among available events. No other motivational principle is needed. Biological and social motives are both to be accounted for by derivation from the basic cycle of habituation and compelled choice.

Appetitive biological motives such as hunger and thirst involve growing afferent input with increasing deprivation. The afferent input arising from a hunger state, for example, is massive and highly complex. It induces persistent (repeated) psychological events we refer to as hunger. These events can be reduced in complexity by food ingestion. Thus the easiest way for an organism to escape from the supraoptimal complexity of the hunger state is to eat.

Pain is a product of supraoptimal complexity. Tissue damage probably disorganizes afferent input and the disorganization alone is probably an adequate input for pain.

A social motive, such as need for achievement, is often described as being based on the association of a variety of cues with achievement situations. Thus, when a person with a history which has produced such associations, steps into a classroom, for example, the achievement cues induce a series of psychological events which are more complex than optimal. The person who is high in need for achievement has little choice but to perform a task which leads to the appearance of success cues which must inhibit or suppress achievement cues.

Note that the hedgehog reverses the usual strategy of motivational analysis. Motivational theory, at least in the broad sense, has the task of categorizing all behavior in terms of need-goal relationships. A representative set might include such biological motives as hunger, thirst, sex, fear, and such psychological motives as need for affiliation, achievement, and need for power. Suppose we extend the two sets until we have 15 or 20 discriminable motives. Now let us collect a substantial tabulation of overt behaviors such as that collected by Barker and Wright (1951) and reported in *One boy's day*. Now let us categorize each bit of behavior in this day long record under one or another of our 15 to 20 biological and social motives. It becomes apparent very quickly that a very small number can be placed with confidence under any of them. The largest number, perhaps 90% or more, seem essentially pointless in terms of their role in achieving any of the goals in our list. One is reduced to using such terms as play, curiosity, exploration, or recreation, and none of these can be fit comfortably into a system in which there must first be a need state, then an instrumental act, which then reduces the need state. Where is the need that produces curiosity behavior or exploratory behavior or play behavior? Thus, this approach, the differentiation of need–goal relationships to account for specifiable categories of behavior, while productive, does not permit an account of a psychologically significant proportion of all of the behavior that occurs.

The hedgehog, on the other hand, offers the potential of accounting for *all* behavior. Play, or what Berlyne (1960) calls ludic behavior, is the most fundamental reflection of human (and animal) motivation. Curiosity, exploration, recreation, and others are loose descriptive terms which categorize the stream of behavior. Biological and social motives provide terms to describe subclasses of the cycle of habituation and compelled choice.

The terms *habituation* and *compelled* choice are technically accurate descriptive terms, but they do not have an appealing literary ring. At risk of implying more than is intended, one could use other descriptive terms. The hedgehog could be described as undergoing oscillations of boredom and excitement although they both imply more intensity or greater swings in intensity than is necessary. Tedium and titillation could also substitute for habituation and compelled choice, but again there is surplus meaning.

THE STREAM OF BEHAVIOR

All of the important pieces of the hedgehog are now in place, and the little beast is off and running. He will continue to run automatically as long as he lives. Figure 3-15 is a diagram of a short segment of the stream of behavior. It shows *Event a* occurring at the left, the subsequent choice of *Event b*, followed by *Event d*, then a repetition of *Event c*, and subsequent choices of *Events e* and *a*.

Many of the important characteristics of the hedgehog should now be apparent (see Fig. 3-16).

The hedgehog is fully autonomous. An event occurs. It is the nature of the beast that no matter how pleasurable the event, it promptly, inevitably, and automatically comes to a halt. There is no way an event can be sustained. At best it can be repeated a few times. Probably the

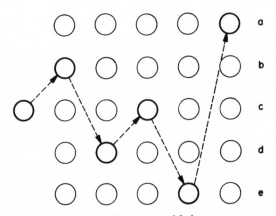

Fig. 3-15. The stream of behavior.

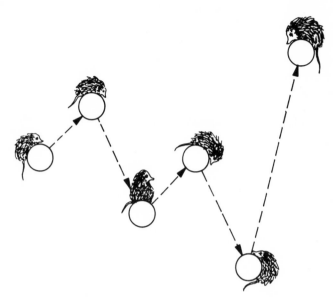

Fig. 3-16. Hedgehog choosing.

most predictable characteristic of organismic behavior is the fact that events, whatever their characters, do not survive a psychological moment. The automatic termination of psychological events is the basic dynamic principle of *boredom.* Organisms are first of all creatures subject to boredom.

Free responding organisms are in constant search for events of optimal complexity level. The hedgehog samples available events at a distance, sniffs them, if you will. From among those available, he chooses to activate that event nearest optimum. His sniffing and his choice, however, are fully automatic responses, and a machine could be built, or a computer could be programmed to behave in a similar manner. Most of the time, an organism is free to choose among a large variety of events close to optimum. In such a period, his state alternates from the boredom of the interval between events to the satisfaction of the occurrence of events. If complex events are imposed on the hedghog from external sources, then he reacts to their complexity levels with signs of low preference, feelings of unpleasantness, and possibly avoidance behavior.

The second most predictable characteristic of the stream of behavior is that in a situation in which the organism is free to choose events without external constraint, *events are all at about the same level of complexity.* The stream of behavior is somewhat like a string of beads in which the beads are all about the same size, but differ one from another in slight differences in shape and color.

The steps in the stream of behavior could be likened to Sisyphus where the choice of an event is a push up the hill, while the habituation phase is the sliding back down to the starting point. The imagery would be fine if Sisyphus had had a choice of hills to try in succession, but he did not. We shall have to settle then for a perky little hedgehog meandering his vagulous, protean way through the stream of consciousness and behavior—sometimes through both at once.

I have made some rather strong claims for the hedgehog. I believe they are justified. However, I occasionally entertain an image of this rather stupid little beast as Thomas Hood (1798–1845) pictured him in the poem "Her Dream."

> *Here lies a hedgehog rolled up the wrong way*
> *Tormenting himself with his prickles.*

Fig. 3-17.

References

Arkes, H. R. The relationship between repetition and organization and the role of organization in psychological complexity. Doctoral dissertation, University of Michigan, 1971.

Barker, R. G. & Wright, H. F. *One boy's day.* New York: Harper, 1951.

Berlyne, D. E. *Conflict, arousal and curiosity.* New York: McGraw-Hill, 1960.

Boykin, A. W., Jr. Verbally expressed preference and complexity judgments as they relate to levels of performance in a problem-solving situation. Doctoral dissertation, University of Michigan, 1972.

Coombs, C. H. *A theory of data.* New York: Wiley, 1964.

Dember, W. N., & Earl, R. W. Analysis of exploratory, manipulatory, and curiosity behavior. *Psychological Review,* 1957, **64**, 91–96.

Dewsbury, D. A. Stimulus-produced changes in discharge rate of an electric fish and their relation to arousal. *Psychological Record,* 1966, **16**, 495–504.

Groves, P. M. & Thompson, R. F. Habituation: a dual process theory. *Psychological Review,* 1970, **77**, 419–450.

Heyduk, R. Static and dynamic aspects of rated and exploratory preference for musical compositions. Doctoral dissertation, University of Michigan, 1972.

Mackworth, Jane F. *Vigilance and habituation.* Harmondsworth, England: Penguin Books, 1969.

McClelland, D. C. & Clark, R. A. Antecedent conditions for affective arousal. In D. C. McClelland, J. W. Atkinson, R. A. Clark & E. L. Lowell (Eds.), *The achievement motive.* New York: Appleton, 1963.

Melton, A. W. Implications of short term memory for a general theory of memory. *Journal of Verbal Learning and Verbal Behavior,* 1963, **2**,1–21.

Miller, G. A. The magic number seven, plus or minus two: Some limits on our capacity for processing information. *Psychological Review,* 1956, **63**, 81–97.

Nice, M. M. & Pelkwyk, J. J. ter Enemy recognition by song sparrow. Auk., 1941, **58**, 195–214. (Cited in Maier, R. A. & Maier, B. M. *Comparative animal behavior.* Belmont, California: Brooks, Cole, 1970.)

Walker, E. L. Psychological complexity as a basis for a theory of motivation and choice. *Nebraska Symposium on Motivation,* 1964, **13**, 47–95.

Walker, E. L. Stimulus-produced arousal patterns and learning. Final Report, HD 00904 (1–8), University of Michigan, Ann Arbor, Department of Psychology, 1969.

Walker, E. L. Complexity and preference in animals and men. *Annals of the New York Academy of Science,* 1970, **169**, 619–652.

Zajonc, R. B. Attitudinal effects of mere exposure. *Journal of Personality and Social Psychology Monograph Supplement,* 1968, 9, No. 2, Part 2.

CHAPTER 4

Meaning of Perceptual Complexity

E. LEEUWENBERG

University of Nijmegen

Meaning of Perceptual Complexity

The study of preference is often and without much questioning related to the study of subjective complexity. The exact relationship between these two qualities, however, remains mysterious and subject to
controversy. While listening to an interesting piece of music, or even
while digesting a theory on aesthetics, one may at the same moment
feel inclined to exclaim, "How clear and simple!" and, "How complicated!"

Here both complexity and simplicity are involved. Are these located
on the extremes of one dimension, or are there in fact two different
qualities each of which may be determined in its own fashion? There
is no doubt that in art, and generally in all objects capable of attracting
attention, that both the element of surprise and the fact that reduction
is possible form a necessary part in an indissoluble relationship (Berlyne,
1971). A first attempt to obtain clarity in this matter was undertaken by
Birkhoff (1933). He proposed: $M = O/C$, in which M is aesthetic value,
O is order, and C is complexity. Eysenck (1968), on the other hand,
suggested $M = O \times C$. In either way, order (or unity or redundancy)
is here distinguished from complexity. It seems possible, however, that
without providing much clarity with respect to aesthetic value, Birkhoff
stressed the "pleasantness" dimension, whereas Eysenck emphasized the

"interest" dimension. Indeed, as has been pointed out by Berlyne (1971), in the case of patterns exceeding a certain degree of complexity, the pleasantness value shows a sharp decline, in contrast to the interestingness ratings.

In the majority of these experiments, however, subjective complexity measures have been employed. Since subjective complexity is negatively determined by redundancy (Götz, 1968), the distinction between order (lawfulness) and a complexity value which is not dependent on it, namely, information, is virtually ruled out. To the extent that redundancy and information are distinguished in stimuli, it appears that not only "pleasantness" but also the "interestingness" rating above a certain degree of complexity can be determined positively by order and redundancy (Mindus, 1968). It becomes increasingly obvious that the distinction between order and information value must be made in the analysis of the factors determining interest. Before 1968, however, cases in which measures of order and complexity, based on the theory of selective information, displayed perceptual relevance, are very rare. Indeed, before the dimensions and descriptive categories (logons) of patterns have been specified, the application of information theory is pointless; it would be an arbitrary affair (MacKay, 1950). Systems of coding rules for describing the structure of patterns in terms of these descriptive categories have been developed by Simon (1972), Restle (1970), Vitz (1969), and Leeuwenberg (1969, 1971). These systems will not be dealt with here. We refer to them, however, in order to gain a grip on aspects of subjective complexity basing ourselves on a priori determined structural information values of patterns.

The present chapter consists of three parts.

(a) First, a way is proposed in which selective *information* is built in the structural information of 25 patterns, in order to derive a prediction concerning the relative preferences for these patterns.

(b) Then, *hierarchical order* in patterns is studied. A certain kind of hierarchy opens the possibility for simplicity and complexity to be present simultaneously within a single pattern.

(c) A nonhierarchical form of order is dealt with, which appears only in the *interaction* between properties of the pattern, and which cannot therefore be determined directly from outside. This type of order causes—exactly opposite to hierarchical order—a high degree of reconstruction complexity and, paradoxically, also a high degree of assimilation simplicity.

Information Theory

A demonstration of the arbitrariness of the notion of redundancy as an explanatory concept was provided by S. Evans in 1967. A similar criticism concerning the use of information theory was given by Ruyer in 1954, who questioned which of the two following structures contained more information: x, p, s, k, a, m, y, r or q, q, q, q, q, q, q, q. To this criticism no more than partial answers have been given. We shall look at the answers briefly.

In order to demonstrate Ruyer's analysis more clearly, we have first translated the preceding examples with letters into dot figures. Twenty-six photographs were taken of different patterns of balls on a billiard table. The number of balls varied from 3 to 12. Sixty subjects rated the likelihood that these patterns could be obtained by chance. The ratings showed consistent variations with differences in "orderliness." Since, however, the objective probability of a specific orderly structure is equal to that of a structure lacking orderliness, we must presume that subjects regard a structure as a representative of a whole class of patterns. Now, if this classification were determined by the relative amount of selective information of the figure, and this, again, by its likelihood, then we have made a full turn and are back to what we set out to explain. In 1950, D. MacKay introduced the concept of structural information. This kind of information is determined by the dimensions (logons) of the structures—or, more freely translated, by their descriptive categories. (In the next section, we shall discuss a simple example of a structural logon analysis.)

The amount of structural information (I) was determined for these dot patterns according to the specification given by the present author (Leeuwenberg 1969, 1971; Simon 1972). In brief, in this coding method, a pattern is described as a sequence of the following types of hierarchical transformations: symmetry, repetition, integration, and interruption Subsequently, the proportion of the amount of structural information (I) to the maximum amount of information in S "dots" is specified. The maximum amount of information is $2 \cdot (S) - 4$, for in the case of random patterns each dot has two coordinates : $2 \cdot (S)$; four transformations are perceptually irrelevant, and may therefore be omitted (height, width, angle, and scale). The relative entropy . $I/(2S - 4)$ thus determined showed a correlation of .89 with the empirically obtained scale values of the likelihood ratings. This result is entirely in agreement with that of the experiments by Handel and Garner (1966) on the relation between redundancy and "goodness" of patterns.

Thus far, we have not yet provided an answer to the question put by Ruyer. We have only made dot patterns of different degrees of orderliness amenable to selective information determination. In a further experiment we used 25 patterns, each comprising S = 44 dots, but with structural information varying between 5 and 84 (see Fig. 4-1). As in the preceding experiment, this pattern series runs from a high to a low degree of orderliness. How then can we determine a priori the selective information of each of these structures? We have seen that this cannot be done without determining the structural information. Indeed, differences in rated likelihoods and therefore differences in size of the categories into which the patterns are classified, require a structural description. What, then, is the size of the class to which a figure with I units of structural information belongs? There are I hierarchically ordered transformations involved, building upon each other. Each of these I transformations is independent of the others. Assume that they have each been chosen independently from K possible transformations. The class of figures with I units of information then comprises K^I patterns. The selective information (H) of such a pattern is, when chunking somewhat more roughly than binarily:

$$H = \log_K(K^I) = I.$$

In other words, selective and structural information thus boil down to the same thing. However, the present deduction is in flagrant contradiction to a form of information determination proposed by Brillouin in 1954. The latter approach is concerned with the value of experimental observations or of communications. His measure determines the con-

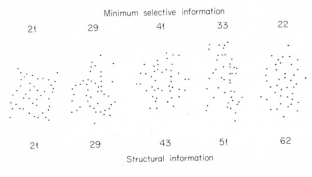

Minimum selective information

21   29   41   33   22

21   29   43   51   62

Structural information

Fig. 4-1.

straint imposed by the communication on the possible expectations without this communication. This interpretation of information not only has a great deal of face validity for the area it covers, but also seems to cover our dot patterns. The total number of possible expectations for our structures is

$$\sum_{i=1}^{2S-4} K^i.$$

Seeing K is extremely large, we may state that

$$\sum_{I=1}^{2S-4} K^i \approx K^{2S-4}.$$

Brillouin's form, then, reads

$$H = \log_K \frac{K^{2S-4}}{K^I} = 2S - 4 - I.$$

In a different notation, the question put by Ruyer is now: Which measure should we choose:

$H_1 = I$ or $H_2 = 2S - 4 - I$ (See Fig. 4–2)?

Our answer, based on our proposition concerning the efficiency of the human functions, is "the smaller one of H_1 and H_2."

This implies that the most informative structure for which $I = 2S - 4 - I$ holds, i.e., H max is then found at $I = S - 2$, in our case at 42. In order to obtain some empirical evidence for this, we might have had the 25 patterns rated for "complexity." However, this concept will, especially in this ambiguous context, correspond less well to information than the concept of "interestingness" which is more closely related to expressiveness or communicative power. The patterns were classified according to structural information in such a way that class 0 contained patterns where $0 < I < 5$, class 1 patterns with $5 < I < 15$, class 2 patterns with $15 < I < 25$, etc. Five sets of five figures were selected such that set 1 comprised classes 0 through 4, set 2 classes 1 through 5, etc.

Fig. 4-2.

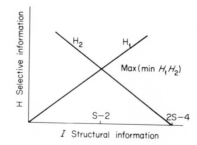

Each set was presented to different groups of 15 subjects, so that a total of 75 subjects took part. Each subject was given the task of selecting the most exciting or most interesting figure from the five figures of a set. This choice was scored in terms of the information class. The means of these preferred classes over the 15 subjects of each set are shown in Table 4-1. Each subject was presented with only one set in order to prevent central tendencies (Helson, 1964) from playing an important role. It appeared, in the first place, that at significance level of 01, the means within the sets declined in the direction of class 4. Furthermore, the total mean was $I = 41.2$, whereas the theoretical point of maximum information is located at 42.

In order to evaluate the significance of this outcome, it is necessary to give a brief description of how these patterns were constructed. (Later we shall enter into this construction a little further.) First, a simple figure is constructed (e.g., a square of 44 dots) and its information is determined. Then a sheet of paper is placed on top of this pattern, which is traced with the exception of one variation. The information of this variation is again determined and added to that of the preceding pattern. One should take care that these variations relate to all the points, or in other words that it corresponds to a rule, e.g., shift the left half of the figure downward and then rotate its right half several degrees, etc. In this context, we use the concept rule in the sense of a property of more than one element, such that, based on this property, a description of a group of elements is shorter than a description which does not employ this property. A rule presupposes, therefore, different levels of description. In the following section we shall explore this matter in greater detail.

TABLE 4-1

Number of subjects	Set	Classified information					Mean	Experimental mean
15	1	0	1	2	3	4	2	<3.1
15	2	1	2	3	4	5	3	<3.6
15	3	2	3	4	5	6	④	≈3.8
15	4	3	4	5	6	7	5	>4.3
15	5	4	5	6	7	8	6	>5.8
75		Total mean:					4.20	4.12

Discussion and Conclusions

From the experiment it may seem that to the extent that subjective complexity is determined by information, complexity is determined by the number of rules and the redundancy in their occurrence. The optimum is located at the maximum number of rules, each predicting the same amount of information as had to be invested for the adoption of these rules. It may also be said that a "rule" is not a rule if confirmation (redundancy) of that "rule" is lacking, so that complexity is thus determined by the number of rules. For $I < S\text{-}2$ information is determined by the deviations or unexpected rules, but for $I > S\text{-}2$, the surprise is determined by precisely what is expected. Subjects who are not inclined to discover new rules above $I = S\text{-}2$ should not be presumed stupid or lazy, but rather regarded as not finding it worthwhile. We shall return to this point later.

From the present experiment, it can be seen that there is not a fixed amount of information above which man cannot cope. Also in patterns consisting of 20 dots, the optimum is not situated at 42 but near $S\text{-}2 = 18$. For a fixed number of points, it is true that interestingness has an inverted-U relationship with structural information. However, subjective complexity does not increase with structural information but with selective information, which is a reasonable modification of structural information. Indeed, selective information is specified by the minimum of Uncertainty 1 (H_1) and Uncertainty 2 (H_2); (see Fig. 4-2).

If complexity is determined only in part by information content, it is important to note that interestingness constitutes a response indicator of information content that should not be disregarded. It therefore seems meaningful to study the creation of art with a view to obtaining insight into the process of information transmission. A good portrait is characterized by: (1) clarity and lack of ambiguity; (2) soberness; and (3) a varied classification of general human traits, among other things. These characteristics do not deviate substantially from those that we could deduce from our experiment.

Hierarchy

We have hitherto dealt with the question of how information content is related to judged complexity. Besides information content, however, there are certain other factors which determine complexity to a perhaps much greater extent. We saw that the perceiver looks for regularities. But the question of how these regularities are interconnected in the coding of figures has remained unanswered. In this connectedness we shall search for the other, very important factors determining complexity.

The first kind of connection that we shall discuss is of a hierarchical type. It is present where a rule has a different rule as argument. Let R denote a reversal of the elements a, b.

Thus, $R(a, b) = a, b, b, a$, and let $2 \cdot (a, b) = a, b, a, b,$

then the following example will demonstrate that a different hierarchical order between R and 2 does not yield identical results:

$$R(2(a, b)) = R(a, b, a, b) = ababbaba,$$
$$2 \cdot (R(a, b)) = 2 \cdot (a, b, b, a) = abbaabba.$$

This kind of hierarchy, for which no further examples need be given, because coding rules are not introduced here, may already lead to completely obscure structures with as few as seven rules. For such structures complexity does not arise from the information content but in the amount of energy needed to discover the rules. Once the rule structure is discovered, there is a low degree of complexity.

Another kind of hierarchy (No. 2) may be distinguished. This gives rise to different perceptual abstraction levels and which is of great importance for judged complexity tasks. We shall illustrate Hierarchy No. 2 with an example. Assume that the description of a pattern such as Figure 4-5 has the following preliminary structure in the brain:

$$\int (R(2(\int (R(2(\int (R(2(a, b))))))))).$$

For the moment we shall not discuss the question what this structure would look like, or what $\int$ stands for. Now a superhomunculus can be imagined looking at the latter structure and regarding the transformation $\int$, R, 2 as elements themselves, and arriving at the idea that the formula may be summed up as: 3 $\{\int, R, 2\}$, (a,b). In Fig. 4-3e the series ($\int$, R 2) is symbolized by Q. This superhomunculus does something quite different from the homunculus designed to perform in hierarchy No. 1. The latter dealt with values or quantitative relationships between values as the object of his analysis.

Five such perceptual levels may be clearly distinguished in perception on the basis of the hierarchy No. 2 type. We shall outline these levels only roughly:

(1) Grouping takes place of what, roughly speaking, lies in close proximity or in line. Studies of this perceptual level have been made by Zahn (1971), and Verstralen (1972). In Fig. 4-3a the obscuring power of

this level with respect to a higher level is represented. The figure comprises a cross of little crosses, and is, as such, again very simple.

2. Complexity is determined by *quantities*. Figure 4-3b is not identical to Fig. 4-3c. There is therefore complexity in the difference between the two figures.

3. The figures are, as far as "structure" goes, again identical, just as the two's in Fig. 4-3d. The formulas, built up on the underlying coding system are identical for these two's, if the actual numerical values appearing in the formulas are replaced by letters symbolizing those quantities. At this level we are concerned with *transformations*.

4. Transformations are made of transformations in the same manner as described previously. Figure 4-3e turns out, after a little study, to be simple. At this level Fig. 4-3e is not equal to Fig. 4-3f because, even though the basic transformations are disregarded, there still remain differences in values which transformations of transformations may assume.

5. The latter difference is discarded, and the Figs. 4-3e and 4-3f are thus made equal (see Fig. 4-3). Complexity has a different meaning at each level. But in this rather informal context we shall not enter into a precise quantification. One might call the levels abstraction levels.

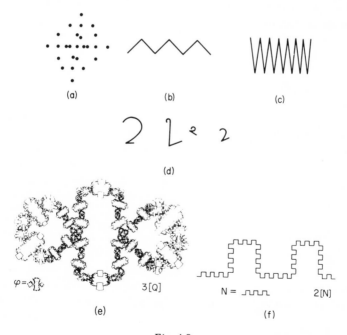

Fig. 4-3.

However, the abstractions require the processing of all the lower levels. It should also be emphasized that the abstraction at, e.g., level 2 is not always easy, seeing that the higher levels must be left out of consideration. At a further stage we shall discuss another form of abstraction.

The hierarchical form No. 1 has been recognized by Neisser in focal attention, where information processing takes place sequentially. Also in the "E.P.A.M." model of Simon and Feigenbaum this form of hierarchy is present. In Selfridge's (1966) Pandemonium model, hierarchy No. 2 is present, as also in the build up of a living creature from molecules to proteins to amino acids to cells and tissues. Simon (1969) demonstrates the efficiency of this construction by referring to the working method of a watchmaker. In conclusion, we can say that every level within a figure has its own complexity. Because of this, it is possible, among other things, for simplicity and complexity to occur simultaneously within one figure. This discrepancy corresponds to an ordering; let this be order No. 2, which constitutes an important attention determining factor.

Within each abstraction level, too there is a possibility of order: order No. 1. This order has two aspects: an aspect of intensity and an aspect of quality. The former may be determined by means of redundancy: $O = (I_{max} - I)/I_{max}$; the latter $O = r/I$, where r stands for the number of rules. This latter measure is the only usable measure for regularity at any rate for contiguous figures (Leeuwenberg, 1971).

Until now, it has been emphasized that hierarchy is efficient for construction, whereas for recognition it sometimes implies insurmountable difficulties. This is not necessarily the case so long as the redundancy of the rules is sufficiently great. If the latter condition is met, it does not at all imply as we have argued in the first section on information theory, that complexity level is thereby lowered. For complexity is determined, on the one hand, by the effort of discovering, but on the other hand by the nature of the information. In other words, even though a structure is clear, it can yet be called complex. If we study Rembrandt's painting *The Night Watch*, we see that the structure is clearly presented; yet the painting makes a complex impression. It is interesting to note how redundancy is divided over the structure. The large superstructure has subdivisions comprising about ⅓ of the total length. These parts are made up of subdivisions forming ⅓ to ¼ of the superparts. These subdivisions carry on in this fashion, their proportions becoming more and more redundant. Repetition is most frequent in details. However, in light patches, the redundancy is weaker than in dark parts within one and the same hierarchical level. The result of this is that equal requirements on analysis energy are made at all levels.

Interaction

In contrast to the patterns discussed under the heading "Hierarchy," the patterns that we shall now consider are such that the analysis of their structures is relatively easy; but their construction is difficult. The reason for their contrast will become clear later. For the moment, one might suspect that the hierarchy of analysis and that of reconstruction play a part here. However, it must be noted that a hierarchy of analysis and a hierarchy of reconstruction do indeed exist, but that virtually nothing is known about them: These hierarchies are not only the most interesting but also the most urgent issues in the study of pattern perception. Perhaps all that can be said so far is that it seems that these two forms of hierarchy sometimes work in opposite directions. A second remark to be made is that we are not, in fact, concerned with these forms of hierarchy. The forms of hierarchy discussed in the preceding section are related to the static coding of patterns and not to dynamic processes such as analysis and reconstruction.

Now let us return to our patterns and consider in some detail the perceptual coding of the pattern of Fig. 4a. Assume that the pattern is scanned point by point and that the difference between the angles, expressed in degrees are noted successively as they occur. The resulting series of numerals may then be rewritten such that hierarchy is maximally present, analogous to the way in which 0, 1, 1, 0, 0, 1, 1, 0 was written in $2 \cdot (R(0, 1))$ Leeuwenberg (1971).

Let us imagine that such a code is built up in the brain when the pattern is perceived. When looking at this code it appears that it does not do justice to the symmetry at all, and that the spherical properties are only in part represented. Apparently it is necessary to propose a different code in which not only sources of redundancy due to symmetrical and spherical features are dealt with, but in which the perceptually obvious aspects of pear shape (A) and zigzag structure (B) are also contained (see Fig. 4-4). This is possible by means of [A] ⋒ [B]. The exact technical meaning of this formulation does not need to be explained in the present context. The coding comprises:

1. the angle sequence formula of A;
2. the angle sequence formula of B;

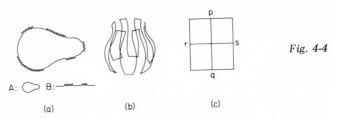

Fig. 4-4

A: ⬭   B: ∿∿∿

(a)   (b)   (c)

3. after these, the reconstruction of the pear shape A in its concrete, two-dimensional form,
4. and only subsequent to 3 the application of the zigzag structure (B) upon the pear shape.

Thus, B can only be related to A not when A's explicit angle sequence has become apparent, but when its implicit relationships are exposed, as they appear in A's concrete two-dimensional form. In other words, the direction of B is altered point-by-point by the shape of A. How this alteration is brought about at any one moment has not been laid down in an a priori rule, but rather in the form of a conditional rule between A and B. The distinction made here between an a priori rule and a conditional rule may be clarified by means of the following examples: "A circle is a sequence of points in which a certain angle is formed between adjacent pairs of points" is a formulation corresponding to a rule that can be generated a priori. "A circle is a set of points located such that their distance to a certain point is identical" is a formulation of the conditional type. A similar procedure applies also to the description of two-dimensional patterns imposed on three-dimensional structures such as in Fig. 4-4b. In these cases its necessity is even more cogent.

What follows from this form of coding for which we have decided?

First, we must assume a working space in which two- and three-dimensional structures are represented in a manner isomorphic with their real shapes. This provides the possibility for many aspects to be admissible simultaneously, which, in turn leads to the fact that, as a result of the accompanying potential redundancy, three-dimensional shapes can be easily remembered themselves and even that they may serve as a support in memory for material which is difficult to retain.

A second point which is more important in the present context, is that in the code [A] $\cap_*$ [B], there is no strictly hierarchical relationship between the A and B structures. This will, in general, be beneficial to the ease of their analysis. Another example in which coding is practically not determined by a priori hierarchical relationships, but by constraints of a conditional type, is provided by tree structures which may therefore be described fairly well by generative grammars (Hogeweg & Hesse 1971). Classification of trees is a task that can be performed with relative ease. However, the exact construction of a tree from memory is almost impossible. A very striking example is formed by the collar of Willem van Ruytenburch, the person in a bright yellow costume on Rembrandt's *The Night Watch*. A minimum amount of time is sufficient to see what that painted object represents. However, even the copying of that collar is extremely tiresome.

At each brush stroke one must simultaneously take into account

1. The substructures, hexagon-like patterns.
2. Every detail of these patterns is not fixed, but is biased, with a certain probability distribution in a certain direction.
3. The shadow of these hexagons themselves.
4. The overall distribution of light and shadow.
5. The color of the object itself.
6. The increased color contrast due to the shadow, resulting in decreased need for dark application because color contrast in part replaces brightness contrast.

In these examples the rules have not been linked together in a completely determined fashion. Thus, there is in this code in fact a juxtaposition of rules with a low degree of assimiliation complexity as a side phenomenon. However, the question arises why one selects exactly these complicated conditional relationships between rules. Juxtaposition is indeed also found among perceptual dimensions (height–width, color–brightness, movement–form). Surely the amount of transmitted information grows with the number of perceptual dimensions. Patterns composed according to these principles may be examples of a low degree of assimilation complexity.

The latter property however, has a trivial meaning in the case of the patterns with many perceptual dimensions without interaction, since each of these patterns may be regarded as a set of structures. Due to the lack of unity, though, the memory complexity will be high. *Complexity is only of importance if in a certain respect there is a high degree of complexity and in another respect there is unity.*

What determines unity? This question requires the introduction of a distinction between information and exformation (Visser, 1970). Let us look at Fig. 4-4c. If the pattern is "understood" by a perceiver, he may apprehend it as a square of squares. If, however the subject were to construct the pattern, and if he were to draw four squares in the attempt, it would appear that he had not understood that there are four squares in one. This would sooner have been the case if he had used that information, drawn a large square, and subsequently connected p with q and r with s. The limitations of the expression, exformation, are not contained in the information. There are, thus, exformation dimensions and information dimensions which show only a partial overlap. (An analogous distinction may be made between procedure and theory). In this framework we wish to show the structures with high exformation and low information levels, or in other words, where the interaction between exformation dimensions corresponds to a single information unit. If the exformation dimensions used in these structures are themselves also information dimensions, then the degree of assimilation complexity is surprisingly low, the memory complexity is also low due to the low information content, and the expression complexity high due to the interaction among exformation dimensions.

Let us give an example, in which pitch and duration are exformation dimensions and the underlying information of music has to be computed from the interaction between melody and rhythm. Melody can be expressed as a pitch sequence and rhythm as a sequence of durations. If we analyze either of these two sequences separately and if we determine the information content of each, and subsequently add the amounts of information found in order to obtain the total information content, we would be seriously wrong. We should, in contrast, note the sequence of pitch differences in such a way that, e.g., a doubling of the temporal duration of a certain tone has to be indicated by a double notation of that tone. Thus a sequence of numerals is obtained for pitch differences in which rhythm is also represented. When this whole is analyzed, in general a lower information content is found than with the procedure indicated earlier, because now interaction information, or rather interaction redundancy, is accounted for in the specification of information. We see here that a source of simultaneous complexity and simplicity is based on the distinction between exformation and information.

Summary

We set out to investigate the relationship between subjective complexity and information. In order to determine the selective information of a pattern it is necessary first to ascertain its structural information. It appeared that two kinds of selective information, which are partly opposed, play a role of equal importance. If the maximal minimum of both forms of selective information is worked out for 25 patterns, it appears that the value obtained very closely approximates the scale value of maximal interestedness. In other words, interestingness increases with selective information and therefore presumably also with subjective complexity, as has been argued by Berlyne (1971). However interestingness has an inverse relation with structural information. It can be deduced that interest is directed toward information in the form of rules that are 50% redundant. One may not therefore propose that the human perceiver has a certain optimal level of complexity.

Furthermore, we studied the significance of the *kind* of information for subjective complexity. Two kinds of structural information may be distinguished: (1) rules that may be generated a priori; (2) rules of a conditional type. The first type of information admits kinds of hierarchy which may be regarded as the most important source of a high subjective assimilation complexity and a low reconstruction complexity. Again, two types of hierarchy may be distinguished: One occurs where coding requires operational sequential transformations, the second generates different levels of abstraction, which are all characterized by their own measure of similarity.

Structures whose description requires conditional constraints do not possess a static coding hierarchy; as opposed to the structures already discussed, they are easy to assimilate, but difficult to generate. The latter is due to interaction among exformation dimensions. These show only partial overlap with information dimensions. The interaction mentioned above refers to a nonoverlapping information dimension.

By way of conclusion to the last two sections about hierarchy and interaction, it can be said that simultaneous simplicity and complexity in one figure are, in general, based on differences in peripheral and central codes of the figure. More specifically, complexity is at the side of low hierarchy versus high hierarchy; at the side of a low abstraction level versus high levels of abstraction; at the side of the imagination representation versus the procedural central coding; at the side of the exformation versus information.

References

Berlyne, D. E. *Aesthetics and psychobiology.* New York: Appleton, 1971.
Birkhoff, G. D. *Aesthetic measure.* Cambridge, Massachusetts: Harvard Univ. Press, 1933.
Brillouin, L. *Scientific uncertainty and observation.* New York: Academic Press, 1954.
Evans, S. Redundancy as a variable in pattern perception. *Psychological Bulletin,* 1967, **67**, 104–113.
Eysenck, H. J. An experimental study of aesthetic preference of polygonal figures. *Journal of General Psychology,* 1968, **79**, 3–17.

Götz, K. O. Möglichkeiten und Grenzen der informationstheorie bei der exakten bild-beschreibung. In H. Ronge (Ed.) *Kunst und Kybernetik,* Cologne: Du Mont Schauburg 1968.

Handel, S. & Garner, W. R. The structure of visual pattern associates and pattern goodness. *Perception and Psychophysics,* 1966, **1**, 33–38.

Helson, H. *Adaptation level theory.* New York: Harper, 1964.

Hogeweg, P. & Hesser, B. An heuristic study of the morphalogical variability of algo-rithmically generated branching patterns. University paper, central Interfaculty, University of Utrecht, 1971.

Leeuwenberg, E. L. J. *Structural information of visual patterns.* The Hague: Mouton Press, 1968.

Leeuwenberg, E. L. J. Quantitative specification of information in sequential patterns. *Psychological Review,* 1969, **76**, 216–220.

Leeuwenberg, E. A general coding system, simulating human classification of pat-terns. *De Ingenieur,* **40**, Oct. 1971. (a)

Leeuwenberg, E. A perceptual coding language for visual and auditory patterns. *American Journal of Psychology,* 1971, **84**, (3) 307–349. (b)

Mackay, D. M. Quantal aspects of scientific information. *Philosophical Magazine,* 1950, **41**, 289–301.

Mindus, L. *The role of redundancy and complexity in the perception of tone pat-terns.* Unpublished M.A. thesis, Clark University, 1968.

Restle, F. Theory of serial pattern learning: Structural trees. *Psychological Review,* 1970, **77**, 481–495.

Ruyer, R. *La cybernétique et l'origine de l'information.* Paris: Flammarion, 1954.

Selfridge, O. G. Pandemonium: A paradigm for learning. In Uhr, L. (Ed): *Pattern Recognition.* New York: Wiley, 1966.

Simon, A. H. *The sciences of the ortificial.* Cambridge, Massachusetts: M.I.T. Press, 1969.

Simon, A. H. Complexity and the representation of patterned sequences of symbols. *Psychological Review,* 1971, Sept.

Simon, H. A. & Feigenbaum, E. A. An information processing theory of some effects of similarity, familiarization and meaningfulness in verbal learning. *Journal of verbal learning and verbal behavior,* 1964, **3**, 385–396.

Verstralen, H. Experimental computer simulation of the perceptual clustering of point-figures by means of orientation sensitive filters. University paper. 1972, Feb-ruary, University of Nijmegen.

Visser, R. *Over het natekenen van de figuur van Rey.* Amsterdam: Swets & Zeit-linger, 1970.

Vitz, P. C. & Todd, T. C. A coded element model of the perceptual processing of sequential stimuli. *Psychological Review,* 1969, **76**, 433–449.

Zahn, C. T. Graph-theoretical methods of detecting and describing Gestalt Clusters, I.E.E. *Transactions on computers,* Vol. C–20, **1**, January, 1971.

CHAPTER 5

Exploratory Choice and Verbal Judgment[1]

SUITBERT ERTEL

Institute of Psychology
Göttingen, W. Germany

The general question guiding research on exploratory behavior can briefly be phrased as follows: What are the environmental factors that determine the preferences in perceptual behavior of an individual who is not looking for anything special? This alone, however, is enough to cause dissension among researchers. They do not agree on what is to be understood by environmental factors and hence what the independent variables governing exploratory behavior are. Many researchers feel it necessary to have a physically defined stimulus as an objective reference. They are trying to control the independent variable in terms of the measurable amount, intensity, and variability of stimulation. So long as one deals only with parameters of this kind the objective approach seems to work. However, difficulties arise as soon as one tries to handle the arrangement of stimuli, i.e., structural organization, objectively. This problem is crucial since structural properties are undeniably very important factors underlying exploratory behavior.

In everyday language, one is not so cautious. The naive perceiver gives verbal descriptions of different stimulus configurations such as: "That looks orderly, that is complex, pregnant, incongruous, harmonious,

---

[1] This article is based partly on a paper read at the 27th Congress of the German Psychological Association at Kiel, 1970.

confused, simple, monotonous, strained etc." But these terms are not considered as acceptable to tough-minded psychologists on the grounds that they are not immediately related to what is physically real. They try to solve the problem by using algorithms from information theory in order to generate graded degrees of structure in line patterns, polygons, and checkerboard arrangements, independently of subjective processing, if possible. The problem of structural quality seems to be under control of the researcher who has obtained measures of entropy and redundancy as a result of his operations.

In opposition to this artful twist of various S–R theorists are those who maintain that subjective reality is the starting point for psychological investigation. What counts behaviorally, they argue, is not the stimulus, but the percept, i.e., the product of perceptual transformation of the visual stimulus. The techniques of information theory are rejected because they are not regarded as an adequate reflection of subjective reality. Measuring redundancy is considered as doomed to failure insofar as it cannot account for the variety of phenomenal properties such as lively, dynamic, strained, etc. Moreover, some authors point to the fact that, for example, a pattern made up of a multitude of small pieces arranged haphazardly in close proximity has a very low redundancy for the information theorist, who painstakingly registers all the small pieces one by one. For the naive perceiver, however, such a "stimulus" is highly redundant, or to use more appropriate terms, it is perceived as a homogeneous "texture" (Heckhausen, 1964). Similarily, a mixture of the frequencies of a whole band of frequencies is not perceived by the hearer as a very complex structure, but as monotonous "white noise" (Berlyne & Peckham, 1966).

The authors who advocate the phenomenological approach, however, must also be criticized. They have not developed any descriptive system for phenomenal properties. These psychologists use such terms as "structure," "dynamics," and "liveliness" but when one asks what is meant they answer "Look at the picture and you will see what it is about." I am greatly in favor of the phenomenological approach, but I am dissatisfied with such a procedure. One cannot grasp subjective reality by uncontrolled verbal behavior nor by resorting to demonstrative gestures. It seems to me that a careful psychosemantic analysis of the terms and phrases denoting subjective experience is a necessary step in any research on behavior in which subjective experience is crucial. The semantic components are conceived as features which, while having their place in language, are principally independent of it. Only through an analysis of the complex meanings of verbal expressions into simple, invariant extralinguistic components will it be possible to find and define the phenomenal parameters of the subjective world.

Semantic Analysis

Under my supervision, Volkmann (1966) carried out a dimensional analysis on a sample of 45 bipolar adjectives using a semantic differential. The material used consisted of 50 abstract graphics, pictures, and other patterns in black and white. As in other earlier investigations of this kind (Ertel, 1965) repeated factorization and elimination of objects and scales led to a near optimal differentiation of the factors involved. There remained 16 scales representing the five rotated factors shown in Table 5-1.[2]

Besides the three general qualities, activity (A), evaluation (E), and potency (P), already well known through other investigations, two further object-specific dimensions were found: balance (B) and clarity (C). Interestingly enough, the degree of perceived balance and clarity in a figural pattern does not necessarily determine its evaluation or pleasantness. There are well ordered, clearly structured patterns which are low in evaluation as well as less ordered and diffuse patterns which are positively evaluated.

In the literature dealing with curiosity, the terms "incongruity" and "pleasantness" are widely used. These obviously correspond to the dimensions of balance (in the negative direction) and evaluation (in the positive direction). In addition to these, some authors use the terms "complexity" and "interestingness," and occasionally "prägnanz." The expressions "complex" ("simple"), "interesting" ("uninteresting") and "prägnant" ("not prägnant") were also included among our scales. They had to be eliminated, however, because they had appreciable loadings on more than one dimension (see Table 5-2). This point will be taken up in the discussion.

---

[2] The German scale descriptions have been translated into English. The original wordings for the scales were: 1. bewegt–ruhig; 2. belebend–beruhigend; 3. lebendig–unlebendig; 4. anziehend–abstoßend; 5. schön–häßlich; 6. freundlich–unfreundlich; 7. kraftvoll–zart; 8. mächtig–zierlich; 9. robust–nachgiebig; 10. ausgewogen–unausgewogen; 11. gestaltet–ungestaltet; 12. einheitlich–uneinheitlich; 13. klar–verschwommen; 14. deutlich–diffus; 15. scharf–unscharf; 16. Übergänge abgesetzt–Übergänge fließend. The left–right position of the polarities and the order of the scales on the test sheet were randomized.

TABLE 5-1

Factor Loadings of 16 Selected Scales after Varimax-Rotation

Scale	Factor					h^2
	Activity	Evaluation	Potency	Balance	Clearness	
(1) Moving–Static	.85	.05	.02	−.11	−.10	.75
(2) Arousing–Quieting	.82	.02	.15	−.07	−.05	.70
(3) Lively–Not lively	.71	.34	.01	−.07	.02	.63
(4) Attractive–Repellent	.15	.84	−.03	.30	.08	.83
(5) Beautiful–Ugly	.16	.84	−.05	.27	.01	.81
(6) Friendly–Unfriendly	.08	.72	−.23	.26	.13	.66
(7) Strong–Tender	.11	−.05	.85	.05	.14	.75
(8) Powerful–Delicate	.08	−.09	.85	−.02	.07	.74
(9) Robust–yielding	.00	−.08	.73	.01	.23	.60
(10) Balanced–Imbalanced	−.10	.33	.00	.72	.11	.66
(11) Organized–Unorganized	.10	.29	.09	.65	.32	.63
(12) Even–Uneven	−.11	.23	−.02	.67	.16	.54
(13) Clear–Hazy	.01	.15	.06	.21	.85	.80
(14) Distinct–Diffuse	−.05	.05	−.12	.22	.82	.74
(15) Sharp–Not sharp	−.13	.18	.15	.32	.68	.64
(16) Contours clearcut–Contours loose	−.12	−.10	.21	−.08	.61	.44
Percentage of total variance	12.7	14.8	13.3	11.5	15.5	$\Sigma Vg\% = 67.8$

TABLE 5-2

Factor Loadings of Three Selected Scales after Varimax-Rotation

Scale	Factor					h^2
	Activity	Evaluation	Potency	Balance	Clarity	
complex–simple	.53	.07	.19	−.27	−.12	.43
interesting–uninteresting	.57	.55	.17	.19	−.01	.69
pregnant–not pregnant	.21	.20	.37	.49	.13	.49

Exploratory Choice

The question of validation is the first to be raised: Are the semantic dimensions obtained related to nonverbal exploratory behavior?

The exploratory choice method was used for this investigation. The subjects were shown two pictures briefly in immediate succession. They were told to choose one of them for further inspection by pressing a button.

An experiment of this kind must take Berlyne's (1963) findings into account. His results indicated that the choice of a picture for repeated inspection depends on the duration of the initial presentation. After a presentation of only .5 sec, the subjects preferred to choose the more irregular of the two pictures for further inspection, whereas after a presentation of 4 sec the more regular picture was chosen. These results led Berlyne (Berlyne, 1963; Berlyne & Peckham, 1966) to the conclusion that two different types of exploratory behavior exist, namely a specific exploration whose purpose is completion of partial information (perceptual curiosity in the narrow sense), and a diversive exploratory behavior which aims at distraction, amusement, and aesthetic pleasure. In the literature on curiosity these two motivational sources of exploratory behavior are often not distinguished from one another.[3] The following experiment, however, will take full account of this interesting distinction. It is a challenge for our dimensional approach to see whether it is able to predict changes of perceptual choice over time as described by Berlyne.

Two groups of subjects were needed, one for the judgment task and another for exploratory choice (see Fig. 5-1). The subjects of the judgment experiment were presented with 20 pairs of slides, the pictures of each pair were shown successively. To one subgroup of the judgment subjects ($N = 24$) each picture was shown for .5 sec whereas for the other subgroup ($N = 24$) the presentation lasted 4 sec. The experimenter had paired the pictures in advance in such a way that qualitative contrasts between members of pairs for each dimension were likely to be obtained by the judgments of the subjects. Each subject had to judge each picture separately following the presentation of a pair using five bipolar rating scales, one scale for each dimension.[4] The sequence of

---

[3] A similar distinction has been made by Livson (1967) between "noticing curiosity" and "examining curiosity." "What can attract or distract, may not hold attention [p. 80]."

[4] At both end of the bipolar scales two adjectives were written, representing the opposite poles of the respective dimension. *Evaluation:* Schön, anziehend–häßlich,

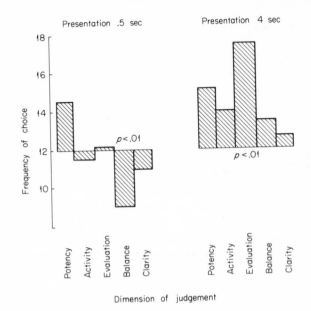

Fig. 5-1. The mean number of subjects choosing pictures with more potency, activity, evaluation, balance, and clarity, after looking at them for a short time (.5 sec) or a long time (4.0 sec). As there are 24 subjects, the number of 12 indicates no preference.

pictures and scales was varied by chance in order to avoid position effects. For the second experiment (exploratory choice), again two groups of 24 subjects each were used, one for each presentation time (.5 sec and 4 sec). The subjects were told that after the presentation of a pair of pictures they could choose one picture for further inspection, thereby following their first impulse.

The data were subjected to analysis as follows: For each pair of pictures an average difference score over all subjects (judgment group) was calculated. This showed whether or not picture A was more "pleasant," "balanced," etc. when compared with picture B and how large the difference was. Thereafter, those 10 pairs of pictures whose members

---

abstoßend (beautiful, attractive–ugly, repellent); *Potency:* mächtig, kraftvoll–zart, zierlich (powerful, strong–tender, delicate); *Activity:* bewegt, lebendig–ruhig, unlebendig (agitated, lively–quiet, still); *Balance:* ausgewogen, einheitlich–unausgewogen, uneinheitlich (balanced, congruous–imbalanced, incongruous); *Clarity:* klar, deutlich–verschwommen, diffus (clear, distinct–blurred, vague).

showed the greatest differences with respect to one dimension were selected. As there are five dimensions, five groups of 10 pairs of pictures resulted, and, as there were only 20 pairs of pictures in all, many pairs were included in several dimensional groups if they showed differences in more than one dimension. For each group of 10 picture pairs the average number of choices was determined. For example, it was determined how often the subjects chose the more pleasant picture for further inspection disregarding the less pleasant member of the pair. Of course, the judgmental results of one presentation condition were compared to the frequencies of choice of the same presentation condition.

The results confirmed the expectations. After short presentation (.5 sec) the more unbalanced of the two pictures was preferred for further inspection, whereas after longer presentation (4 sec) the picture having higher evaluation was chosen more frequently. Both of these differences were statistically very significant, and all of the other differences were insignificant. Important to note is the disappearance of the statistical relation between frequency of choice and judgmental difference when the ratings obtained after brief presentation are compared to the frequencies of exploratory choice after longer presentation, and vice versa. The qualitative judgments obviously change during inspection. Exploratory choice is dependent only on the impressions the pictures give to the subjects at the time of choice.

The results may be summarized as follows: After short presentation, the pictures preferred are those that, at first glance, appear to be more unbalanced, whereas after longer presentation, the pictures chosen are those that, at the time, are felt to be more pleasant.

The assumption that picture qualities may change during the time of inspection was first advanced by Heckhausen (1964) in his polemic against Berlyne (1963). It remains to be seen whether or not this change, as it is revealed in the ratings, shows any consistency and whether it is related to perceptual choice, as Heckhausen suspects.

The first interesting fact to be noted is that the greatest instability of picture qualities occurs with respect to evaluation. The correlation between the average evaluation ratings after brief and longer presentation is much lower than those for the other dimensions:

$$E: .40, \quad P: .95, \quad A: .74, \quad B: .86, \quad C: .90.$$

How can we explain this fact? If we calculate the differences in mean judgments for each picture and each dimension between the two presentation conditions, and if we correlate the differences so obtained for each dimension with each other, the following result is obtained: If a picture increases its "activity" during inspection time, it will also increase in evaluation, and vice versa ($r = .47$, $p < .01$). This also holds for balance, i.e., an increase in balance is accompanied by an increase in evaluation, a decrease in balance is accompanied by a decrease in evaluation ($r = .34$, $p < .05$). If we sum the differences for activity and balance for each picture pair, and correlate this total with the differences of evaluation ratings, the relationship becomes even more apparent ($r = .69$, $p < .01$). The changes in the other dimensions do not correlate. We now have an explanatory hint for the instability of evaluation. The changes in pleasantness during inspection of a picture seem to be a function of the direction and amount of change which the picture shows in balance and activity.

Could one expect perceptual choice to be affected by this? One could reason, with Heckhausen, that visual forms will attract the attention of a perceiver if they give an opportunity to perceptual grouping, organizing, and restructuring. If a picture, through its composition, allows this kind of active perceiving and shows more balance as a result of organizing processes, it will prompt longer viewing. The experimental results, in fact, give some support to this hypothesis. If one takes into account the relative frequencies of exploratory choice on the one hand, and the changes over time in the ratings for balance and activity for the respective pictures on the other hand, the following results are obtained. The more a picture gains in balance and activity in the time between .5 sec and 4 sec presentation in comparison to its partner picture, the greater the frequency of choosing this picture after 4 sec when compared with the frequency of choice after .5 sec ($p < .05$). These results help to resolve the controversy between Berlyne and Heckhausen. It is true that the initial curiosity is aroused by the perceived imbalance of a picture. The individual ignores for the moment even a more pleasant form if an unbalanced form is presented with it. However, if he is not successful in finding order or meaning in a picture after a certain time of inspection he will shift his attention to the more pleasant alternative. Only if the incongruent form permits of reorganization will the perceiver look at it for a longer time, and during that time the form will also become more pleasant.[5]

---

[5] One is reminded at this point of the dynamics of the humor response (Ertel, 1968) and the related process of the microgenesis of the orienting response (Froehlich & Laux, 1969).

A Replication Experiment

The conclusion that the motivational conditions of perceptual choice may change rapidly with increasing presentation time is not warranted unless the experiment is repeated with different pictures. Oberhoff (1967) carried out this investigation. He selected 14 new pairs of pictures such that picture A was far more unbalanced than picture B, put picture B was far more pleasant than picture A. Those differences were so large that even after a presentation of 4 sec the direction of these differences were the same as after a .5-sec presentation despite the above-mentioned changes in judgment which also occurred here. For example, if picture A was rated as more unbalanced and less pleasant than picture B after short presentation, the direction of these rating differences remained unchanged by longer presentation (see Fig. 5-2). The method of exploratory choice was the same as used by Volkmann (1966), but the longer presentation time was increased to 6 sec.

The results are shown in Fig. 5-3. There were 14 pairs of pictures and two presentation conditions. Differences in exploratory choice between pictures were observed in 26 out of 28 cases. The predicted preference resulted in 20 cases. In 12 of the 14 pairs of pictures the preference was different for the different presentation times. Out of these, 11 cases showed a change in the direction expected, three being very significant, one being significant. Only one change in preference was opposite to that expected, and this was not significant.

In this investigation, not enough attention was paid to an exact analysis of the possible interactions between qualitative parameters. Moreover, individual differences were totally neglected. There are consistent interindividual differences despite group trends in perceptual judgment and exploration (e.g., Munsinger & Kessen, 1964; Dorfman & McKenna, 1966; Vitz, 1966) and these should be considered in order to explain more of the variance occurring in exploratory behavior.

Final Discussion

The results obtained from the two experiments serve to substantiate the following assumptions:

1. The evaluation (pleasantness) of a perceived object does not appear to be linearly related to its degree of balance. This has been confirmed by a factor analysis of the judgmental data showing that these dimensions are independent, as well as by the results of the experiments

Fig. 5-2. Two examples of pairs of pictures used in the second experiment. The pictures on the left (1a, 2a) were judged as more imbalanced and as less positive in evaluation in comparison to the pictures on the right [1b, 2b (after short presentation as well as after long presentation)].

on exploratory choice, showing that the subjects chose either the more unbalanced or more pleasant picture for longer viewing, depending on presentation time.

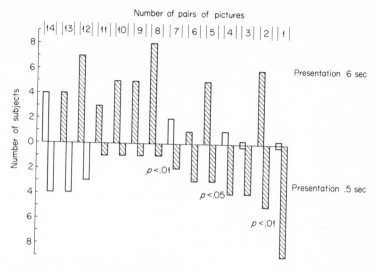

Fig. 5-3. Exploratory choice of 14 pairs of pictures: After having been presented a pair of pictures either 5 sec or 6.0 sec, two groups of 24 subjects each chose one of them for further inspection. The horizontal line represents the base line of random choices for any one picture, i.e. $N/2 = 12$ subjects. The bars represent the number of subjects more than 12 (hatched bars) or less than 12 (clear bars) choosing the picture consistent with prediction. The differences of choices between the presentation conditions are significant for pairs No. 1, 2, 5, and 8.

(2.) The motivation underlying perceptual choice is dependent on the duration of presentation. Shorter inspection favors the choice of a more unbalanced picture; longer inspection favors the choice of a pleasanter picture.

(3.) The phenomenal qualities of a picture change during inspection. For example, a picture that at first seems unbalanced, unpleasant and only slightly "active" may after further inspection become more balanced, pleasanter, and more "active."

(4.) The duration of looking at an initially unbalanced picture is dependent on the extent to which the picture gains in balance during perception. If the picture is such that its balance increases during perception the perceiver will spend longer with it than if this were not the case. An increase in "activity" also prolongs inspection time.

The last statements bring forward a point which has often been neglected in research on curiosity. Perception is a process. In the course of perception, the percept may change and, with it, the relation of the perceiver to it. The behavior of the perceiver in a given situation is dependent on the preceding perceptual experience, however short, and on the perceptual expectations resulting from this experience. An unbalanced object will induce the perceiver to construct a more balanced one. The parts which do not seem to fit to each other tend to be restructured toward greater fittingness. Those parts which do not seem related to each other tend to be brought into a closer relation. The perceiver feels obliged to solve the problem of organization that the object imposes upon him. So long as the perceiver feels he is progressing with this task he will continue visual exploration. But he will turn away from the object when, after some futile attempts, he has given up hope of finding organization in it. Every process of perceiving an unbalanced object is an attempt to solve the problem of balance, which ends either in success or in failure. Of course, perception is predominantly an autochtonous process, less open to intentional factors than the process of problem solving in thinking.

The fact that the properties of a perceived object may change during perception should be a warning to those who take visual qualities, e.g., complexity, for quasi-objective, invariant attributes. The search for a physical environment as the basis of behavior is likely to induce a researcher to regard figural properties of the visual world as parameters of the geometric world, without noticing that their source is perception. Descriptive terms like "complex," and "incongruous" are related to what is given to a perceiver, and as we have seen, those judgments are dependent upon the degree of organization that the perceiver has achieved at the point at which his judgment is made. This interpretation is confirmed by numerous results that Neisser (1967) quotes in order to substantiate his hypothesis that "perception is basically a constructive act rather than a receptive or simply analytic one [p. 94]."

A perceiver who has already studied a picture and has tried to organize it is in a different situation from one who perceives the picture for the first time and has yet to undergo this experience. If he is given a choice between two familiar pictures, he will avoid the one that does not improve with respect to balance. Instead, he will choose the picture that he knows can be organized by perceptual construction allowing a pleasant repetition of the successful perceptual activity.[6] A visual form of this sort is even preferred to those that offer a perfect structure immediately without constructive effort on the part of the perceiver.

---

[6] Success in perceptual organization is probably the basis for "aesthetic" pleasure. The question whether a concept "aesthetic pleasure" as distinct from "pleasantness" is a useful one needs discussion and further research.

The attractiveness of a visual form is not due to the degree of orderliness it provides "by itself," but to the degree of relative gain in orderliness and organization that the perceiver can achieve for it. Visual forms induce prolonged inspection "if they present some challenge or disturbance that can be resolved by 'making sense' of them or organizing them . . . [Berlyne & Peckham, 1966]." One component in

> aesthetic pleasure . . . is the job in reflecting, discriminating, making comparisons, understanding, examining; joy also in the discovery a more profound meaning and in seeing clearly . . . structures, phrasings, focusses, emphases, modes of structuring and re-structuring, . . . shifts of frames of reference, and . . . transformation of function of the different parts and subwholes . . . [Metzger, 1965].

Future research on curiosity, epistemic, and aesthetic behavior will have to take special account of the processual properties of perception.

Another pertinent question is why negative or neutral stimuli become more pleasant after frequent exposure. Zajonc (1968) found that nonsense words and Chinese characters become more pleasant with time than equivalent words and characters viewed for shorter periods. "If the function of orienting behavior is eventually to change the novel stimulus into a familiar one, it is also its consequence to render the stimulus object eventually more attractive (or perhaps merely less repulsive) [p. 21]." We have argued that individuals who do not succeed in finding meaning in a meaningless object do not choose to be exposed to it again. Therefore, a decrease of unpleasantness in this object is not likely to occur. If the individual, however, is not given a choice, but is repeatedly exposed to the object, he may eventually find some organization in it. If this does not occur, it is possible that the individual merely gives up hope of finding some organization. A form that no longer disappoints the perceiver will be less unpleasant for him than one that has just fallen short of his expectations. Finally, the pure assimilation of a visual object in memory schemata could bring about a certain affective gain, regardless of its internal balance.

A different question, over which consensus should be achieved as soon as possible, concerns the dimensionality of phenomenal qualities. The strategy used here tries to overcome the difficulty deriving from the dependence of the between—scale correlations of judgments on stimulus sampling. The proportion of the overall variance due to interindividual differences is negligible in comparison to the variance due to the variety of the pictures in the sample. The arbitrariness of sampling and the range from which the investigator chooses his sample are mainly responsible for the discrepancies found in factor analyses of verbal judgments. I have tried in my experiments to obey certain rules of sampling in order to minimize this kind of sampling bias. From among a large pool of many different pictures I always took pairs which appeared most different to me. When I found a lively, tender picture I then chose a lively powerful picture, after choosing a quiet tender picture I looked for a quiet powerful picture. To a clear, balanced picture a clear, unbalanced picture was opposed, to an interesting symmetrical picture an interesting asymmetrical picture etc. An investigation of tonal qualities would have to proceed in a similar manner. Both loud high tones, soft high tones and loud low tones and soft low tones must be included in the sample. If, for example, only loud high tones and soft low tones were included a factor analysis would hardly differentiate between volume and pitch. Despite remaining flaws, this method leads to a more pronounced differentiation of independent factors. The first factor analysis, however, usually still shows correlations between the factors. These can be reduced by eliminating pictures which contribute most to the correlation before the second factor analysis is done. In this manner the factorial structure of the scales (and the stimuli) becomes successively simpler and reaches the degree of distinction as shown in Table 5-1. Of course, the factors obtained by this method are still hypothetical. The most promising approach to further validation is to relate these factors to nonverbal behavior under experimental conditions (Ertel, 1969).

The use of one-dimensional scales instead of multidimensional scales is reasonable on the grounds that an instrument measuring only one parameter has to be preferred to an alternative that is an over-all measure of several parameters. The "interesting–uninteresting" scale was shown to be two-dimensional having loadings of "activity" and, to a smaller extent, "evaluation." [7] It is therefore reasonable to assume that there are

---

[7] In color judgments Oyama, Tanaka, and Chiba (1962) found that the "interesting–boring" scale had several substantial loadings when used with American subjects (evaluation, E, .74; Activity, A .54). The translated Japanese equivalents had the loadings .35 (E), .74(A) and .50 (potency, P). Tanaka, Oyama, and Osgood (1963) found that for color judgments on "interesting–boring" the loadings were .45(E), .82 (A) for Americans and .51 (E), .29 (A), .73 (P) for Japanese. When abstract concepts were judged on the same scale the following loadings were found .85 (E), − .34 (A), .30 (P) for Americans, .83 (E), − .29 (P) for Japanese. Berlyne (1972) also found that judgments of pictures on the "interesting–uninteresting" scale yielded more than one loading .51 (hedonic value = E), .80 (cortical arousal $\approx P, A$) .72 (complexity $\approx A,P$).

at least two conditions leading a person to say "This picture is interesting." The more "active" a picture appears and the more positive its evaluation, the more it will be judged as interesting. Moreover, as both factors are likely to contribute in an additive way to the judgment it is quite possible that a low contribution of one component be compensated by a higher contribution of the other component. In this way an object which is not very pleasant but very "active" might be judged as interesting as a very pleasant object with a lower degree of "activity." For example, there are interesting Thai boxing matches and interesting Thai dances; the former are repulsively exciting, the latter charmingly arousing. Both are interesting, but in different ways, i.e., the components underlying the judgment of interestingness when judged separately would differ considerably.

A similar problem arises with complexity. The criteria that have led us to discard interestingness as a unique dimension would also indicate that complexity is superfluous as a dimensional concept: Complexity is two-dimensional, incorporating mainly "activity" and also imbalance to some degree. However, the "complex–simple" scale has a very low communality. This could be interpreted as due either to low intersubjective consistency in meaning or to the existence of an additional meaning dimension which this factor analysis has not been able to reveal. I suspect the latter to be true. "Complex" might be related, perhaps primarily, to the amount of energy or effort which is felt to be required on the part of the individual in the process of cognitive–perceptual organization. This assumption is consistent with two observations. First, the term "complex" is often interchangeable with such terms as "difficult," "strenuous," "demanding," and the term "simple" often denotes the opposite, i.e., "easy." The fact that the hypothetical "energy" factor has not appeared in this analysis might be due to the lack of relevant scales in the sample. One scale cannot constitute a factor. The second observation is that in an unpublished factorial study on motivational verbs an "energy" (effort, Anspannung) factor has already been obtained, besides an "activity" (Erregung) factor orthogonal to it. The difference between "activity" and "energy," according to this analysis, appears to be related to the difference between passive stimulation (Erregung) and active concentration (Anspannung). Environmental stimulation does not necessarily involve internal concentration, although it may often be the consequence of it. The hypothesis is therefore warranted that the verbal judgment "complex," as opposed to "simple," denotes a perceptual or cognitive object that is felt to require a pronounced amount of energy expenditure in information processing. An "active" (arousing) object is more likely to be "complex" or effort demanding than a "passive" (less arousing) object. And an imbalanced object also is more complex, in this sense, than a comparable balanced one. But the essential meaning component of "complex" would neither be "activity" or degree of arousal nor imbalance, but amount of energy necessary to overcome the difficulties which the object presents to the information processing system.

Further support for this interpretation can be drawn from psychophysiological investigations as reviewed by Klix (1971), who concludes that "there is no doubt that a narrow correspondence exists between the degree of difficulty of complex information processing and the level of psychophysiological activation . . . [p. 502.]" Level of activation is here conceived of as the physiological correlate in the brain of phenomenal effort. This author also refers to the relation between effortful information gain and affect: ". . . the information gain is accompanied by (positive) affect which follows not only great discoveries but even minor problem solutions; perhaps it is also one of the factors underlying the motivation of the search for information and the pleasure of discovery [p. 503]."

"Complexity" in the sense of energy expenditure required for information processing might turn out to be a suitable concept for defining aesthetic pleasure. Granted that aesthetic pleasure is in fact a special kind of hedonic experience and behaviorally different from nonaesthetic hedonic experiences, the following assumption is worth considering: An object is aesthetically pleasant the greater its complexity (induced energy expenditure, effort) and the greater the degree of balance achieved as a consequence of energy expenditure. Aesthetic pleasure = Complexity × Balance. The multiplicative interaction between complexity and balance indicates that lack of complexity cannot be compensated by balance; the aesthetic evaluation of a low complex balanced object, a circle for example, would be near zero.

The proposal advanced here comes close to what writers seeking to capture the essence of formal beauty have proposed: Aesthetic pleasure is "uniformity in variety," "unity in diversity," and "order in complexity" (see Berlyne, 1971). It is tempting to approach the problem of complexity (diversity, variety) which is the main focus of theoretical divergences among aestheticians and psychologists by shifting one's attention from the aesthetic object to the amount of energy that the recipient feels to be needed to achieve uniformity, unity, and order in the object. The presence of many elements in an object, as well as a lack of order usually increases judged degree of complexity. Both factors combine to determine the demand for information processing. Future research must prove whether "complexity" in this sense is separable factorially from what we have hitherto achieved.

This discussion must have created the impression that the dimensional results we have obtained are not yet final. Of course, it is true that the problem of stimulus and scale selections requires a more elegant solution. Nevertheless, some confidence in the factorial solution which we have obtained seems justified even at this stage. It was possible to extract the E, P, and A factorial trias which after the extensive cross-cultural work of Osgood and his collaborators can be acknowledged to be universal. The factors "balance" and "clarity," which were revealed in this investigation are clearly distinct from E, P, and A. They are obviously less general, i.e., more specific for a range of visual displays. It is reasonable to postulate that the addition of new and more specific factors to those which have been shown to be invariant under many conditions should be made dependent on results showing that they are really unique.

A further problem which should be investigated soon is the interaction between dimensions. Factorial independence of dimensions does not exclude the possibility that the processes involved may interact. It has already been assumed that the pleasantness or evaluation of a picture is "dependent" on the degree of balance or the gradient of balance which develops in the process of perception. The "activity" of a picture could equally interact with its degree of balance. An unbalanced picture should be more "active" than a similar balanced picture, but an irretrievably unbalanced picture less "active" than a picture which has acquired some degree of balance at a later stage of perception. The problem of "interphenomenal relations" in the process of perception, the question of dependency of dimensions, and the question of their interactions (summative or multiplicative) requires careful investigation with well chosen picture material and one-dimensional rating scales together with the use of methods of multivariate analysis.

References

Berlyne, D. E. Complexity and incongruity variables as determinants of exploratory choice and evaluative ratings. *Canadian Journal of Psychology*, 1963, **17**, 274–290.

Berlyne, D. E. *Aesthetics and psychobiology.* New York: Appleton, 1971.

Berlyne, D. E. & Packham, S. The semantic differential and other measures of reaction to visual complexity. *Canadian Journal of Psychology*, 1966, **20**, 125–135.

Dorfman, D. D. & McKenna, H. Pattern preference as a function of pattern uncertainty. *Canadian Journal of Psychology*, 1966, **20**, 143–153.

Ertel, S. Standardisierung eines Eindrucksdifferentials. *Zeitschrift für Experimentelle und Angewandte Psychologie*, 1965, **12**, 22–58.

Ertel, S. Eine psychologische Theorie des Komischen. Münster: Philosophische Fakultät der Universität Münster, 1968. (Habilitationsvortrag, unveröffentlichtes Manuskript).

Ertel, S. Psychophonetik. *Untersuchungen über Lautsymbolik und Motivation*. Göttingen: Hogrefe, 1969.

Fröhlich, W. D. & Laux, L. Serielles Wahrnehmen, Aktualgenese, Informationsintegration und Orientierungsreaktion. *Zeitschrift für Experimentelle und Angewandte Psychologie*, 1969, **16**, 250–277.

Graefe, O. Versuche über visuelle Formwahrnehmung im Säuglingsalter. *Psychologische Forschung*, 1963, **27**, 177–224.

Heckhausen, H. Complexity in perception; phenomenal criteria and information theoretic calculus—a note on D. E. Berlyne's "complexity effects." *Canadian Journal of Psychology*, 1964, **18**, 168–173.

Klix, F. *Information und Verhalten*. Berlin: Deutscher Verlag der Wissenschaften, 1971.

Livson, N. Towards a differentiated construct of curiosity. *Journal of Genetic Psychology*, 1967, **111**, 73–84.

Metzger, W. The foundations of artistic experience. *Acta Psychologica*, 1965, **24**, 409–422.

Munsinger, H. & Kessen, W. 1964. Uncertainty, structure, and preference. *Psychological Monographs* **78** (9, Whole No. 586).

Neisser, W. *Cognitive Psychology*. New York: Appleton, 1967.

Oberhoff, B. Die perzeptive Zuwendung in Abhängigkeit von Bildqualität und Wahrnehmungsdauer. Münster: Psychologisches Institut der Univ. Münster, 1967. (Diplomvorprüfungsarbeit, Schreibmaschinenkopie).

Oyama, T., Tanaka, Y. & Chiba, Y. Affective dimensions of colors: a cross-cultural study. *Japanese Psychological Research*, 1962, **4**, 78–91.

Tanaka, Y., Oyama, T. & Osgood, C. E. A cross-culture and cross-concept study of the generality of semantic spaces. *Journal of Verbal Learning and Verbal Behavior*, 1963, **2**, 392–405.

Vitz, P. C. Preference for different amounts of visual complexity. *Behavioral Science*, 1966, **11**, 105–114.

Volkmann, H. R. Motivationale Änderungen der perzeptiven Zuwendung bei zunehmender Wahrnehmungsdauer. Münster: Psychologisches Institut der Universität Münster, 1966. (Diplomvorprüfungsarbeit, Schreibmaschinenkopie).

Zajonc, R. B. Attitudinal effects of mere exposure. *Journal of Personality and Social Psychology, Monograph Supplement*, 1968, **9**, 1–27.

CHAPTER 6

Personality and the Law of Effect

H. J. EYSENCK

University of London

In some form or other, the law of effect has been one of the most widely recognized generalizations in the whole of psychology. "The belief that rewards and punishments are powerful tools for the selection and fixation of desirable acts and the elimination of undesirable ones" (Postman, 1947) is almost universal, and although the law itself is usually associated with the name of Thorndike (1911) who first used this phrase, he had precursors, e.g., Bain (1868) and Spencer (1870), who brought together the contributions of Associationism, Hedonism, and Evolutionary Doctrine in a coherent form closely resembling Thorndike's own formulation. This formulation was as follows:

> Of several responses made to the same situation, those which are accompanied or closely followed by satisfaction to the animal will, other things being equal, be more firmly connected with the situation, so that when it returns, they will be more likely to recur; those which are accompanied or closely followed by discomfort to the animal will, other things being equal, have their connection with the situation weakened so that, when it recurs, they will be less likely to occur. The greater the satisfaction or discomfort the greater the strengthening or weakening of the bond [Thorndike, 1911, p. 244].

In this statement, Thorndike appears to have abandoned the Spencer–Bain tradition of frankly invoking pleasure and pain as agents responsible for the fixation and elimination of responses; as Postman (1947) put

133

it, "Thorndike's law has been a law of *effect,* not *affect.* [p. 496]" By
defining satisfiers and annoyers independently of subjective experience
and report, he seems to have abandoned hedonism; in his own words,
"By a satisfying state of affairs is meant one which the animal does nothing to avoid, often doing such things as to attain and preserve it. By
a discomforting state of affairs is meant one which the animal avoids
and abandons [Thorndike, 1911, p. 245]." But this of course raises the
danger of circularity, because of the absence of an *independent* determination of the nature of satisfiers and annoyers. "The satisfying or
annoying nature of a state of affairs can usually be determined fully only
in the course of a learning experiment and cannot then be invoked as a
causal condition of learning without circularity [Postman, 1947, p. 497]."

Actually it is doubtful whether these two main points of Postman's
evaluation, often reproduced by later writers, are in fact correct. Thorndike's law is one of affect, as well as effect; the very notion of satisfiers
and annoyers invokes hedonistic, affective connotations, and although
Thorndike avoids verbal and introspective references (which was in any
case inevitable, as he was dealing with animals) he clearly defines the
affective portion of his statement in behavioral terms, i.e., in terms of the
adient or abient behavior of the animal. Given this independent definition
of the *affective* portion of his law, there is clearly no circularity; the
adient and abient behavior of the animal is clearly differentiated from
the learning and/or performance increments which are being measured
as the dependent variable. The position may be pictured as below:

Reinforcement

(1) Connectionism:	(2) Affective consequences:
(a) Learning	(a) Verbal report
(b) Performance	(b) Adient/abient behavior.

The law of effect asserts that manipulation of the independent variable
(reinforcement) has two consequences. One set of these consequences
is listed above under 2a and 2b; these are the verbal and behavioral
results of administering the reinforcement. The other set of consequences
constitutes the dependent variable, i.e., 1a and 1b. The law also asserts,
and this is where it escapes from circularity, that these two sets of consequences are empirically found to covary; the notion of circularity
probably arises from our preconceived ideas that they always do covary.
It is possible to demonstrate that such covariation is not always found;
such a demonstration simultaneously proves that the law is not circular,
and also that it is not true—at least, that its truth can only be asserted
within certain limits which require to be ascertained empirically. As an

example of such a failure of the law of effect, a study by Kennedy (1970) will serve this purpose.

Using elderly psychotic females as her subjects, she selected as the response to be conditioned that of pressing a lever; a variable interval schedule with a mean interval of two minutes and a range of 10 sec to 4 min was chosen, and sweets, pennies, and small picture cards were used as reinforcers, with occasional "no reinforcement" extinction trials interpolated. Each subject attended eight 20-min operant conditioning sessions. Positive results were obtained, in that these severely ill patients learned to press the lever, although at rates lower than achieved by normal controls; there was also a high resistance to extinction. So far, the law of effect seems to be well supported. However, it was found, in a detailed comparison, that "responses to pennies, picture cards, and no reinforcement were almost identical, and significantly higher than responses to sweets [p. 117]." As Kennedy points out, "this relationship was not expected, inasmuch as sweets appeared to be the reinforcers most highly valued by the majority of subjects [p. 118]." Among control subjects, too, there were differences in the effectiveness of reinforcers, with pennies and no reinforcement more influential than sweets and picture cards; "these differences were not consistent with the subjects' preferences as given in the questionnaire [p. 123]." In addition, "some subjects in the experimental group who appeared to like the reinforcers very much, and who accepted them eagerly, were very low responders, and others who rejected the reinforcers or otherwise indicated displeasure continued to respond at high rates [p. 130]." In fact, 18 out of 130 psychiatric subjects rejected some or all of the reinforcers, but there was no consistent relationship between response rate and rejection. Subjects who rejected reinforcers appeared in all response rate groups, from high to low.

Kennedy discusses the contradictory nature of her results within the context of the law of effect; "the refusal or eager acceptance of a reinforcer is one of the behaviours which establishes its reinforcing value. In the present study, even when the reinforcing value of the stimulus was indicated by the refusal or eager acceptance of it, the operant response was not consistent with its reinforcement value [137]." Kennedy argues for an explanation in terms of compliance or "social reinforcement"; this is not an implausible suggestion, but it still leaves us with unresolved problems, such as why sweets are preferred to other reinforcers so-called, but lead to less lever pressing. In other words, the problem lies in the inconsistency of the results; if we use two criteria of "effect" or "reinforcement value," i.e., verbal and behavioral consummatory behavior, on the one hand, and lever pressing on the other, we find a negative correlation between them, rather than a positive one as confidently predicted and expected. This is a fairly unique study because it investigated in detail the actual reinforcement value of different "reinforcers" along more than one line; usually it is taken for granted that the "logical" implications of the law of effect are borne out in actual practice. It is only when we have more than one criterion of "reinforcement" that we can test the law apart from its circularity; it would be most desirable if further studies of this type were to be carried out in order to establish the conclusions reached once and for all. If Kennedy had not investigated the "reinforcement value" of the reinforcers in her study along independent lines, then the fact that "learning" occurred after the introduction of reinforcers would almost certainly have been interpreted in classical Skinnerian fashion as verification of the hypothesis that it occurred because of the introduction of these reinforcers. Science cannot be built upon such *post hoc ergo propter hoc* arguments.

The Law of Primary Reinforcement was put forward by Hull (1943) in order to overcome this difficulty, and also in order to make the law of effect applicable to conditioning experiments; it reads as follows:

> Whenever an effector activity occurs in temporal contiguity with the afferent impulse, or the perseverative trace of such an impulse, resulting from the impact of a stimulus energy upon a receptor, and this conjunction is closely associated in time with the diminution in the receptor discharge characteristic of a need, there will result an increment to the tendency for that stimulus on subsequent occasions to evoke that reaction [p. 80].

For Hull, then, *need reduction* (later substituted by *drive reduction*) was the critical factor in the reinforcement process, and by need is meant in this context a condition in which any of the commodities necessary for survival are lacking or deviate seriously from the optimum. To account for the many occasions where learning occurs in the absence of such lack, Hull introduced the principle of *secondary reinforcement:* "The power of reinforcement may be transmitted to any stimulus situation by the consistent and repeated association of such stimulus situation with the primary reinforcement which is characteristically of need reduction [Hull, 1943, p. 97]." The hedonistic implications of Hull's formulation are even more apparent in the writings of some other learning theorists (Mowrer, 1946; Muenzinger, 1938), it should be noted, however, that Hull has eliminated pleasure from the position of a motive, and has instead chosen to concentrate on tension reduction as the motive, with pleasure merely the result of tension reduction. This concept of secondary reinforcement is linked with that of *secondary drive* in extending the law of effect to learning which is not motivated by physiological need reduction; "secondary drives are acquired on the basis of primary drives, represent elaboration of them, and serve as a facade behind which the functions of the underlying drives are hidden [Miller & Dollard, 1941]." Of particular importance in this connection has been Mowrer's (1939, 1940; Mowrer & Lamoreaux, 1942, 1946) classical stimulus–response analysis of anxiety and fear; anxiety to Mowrer was the (conditioned) anticipation of noxious stimulation. This anticipation is a source of tension and discomfort, and thus acquired drive properties; those acts of the organism which are most active in reducing this tension lead to learning by reinforcing the behavior in question.

It is notable that all versions of the law of effect which have appeared in the literature have been *universal;* they make no provision for individual differences of a systematic kind. Laws in the hard sciences usually do make such provision. Consider Hooke's law of elasticity: Stress = $k \times$ Strain, where k is a constant (the modulus of elasticity) which depends upon the nature of the material and the type of stress used to produce the strain. This constant k, i.e., the ratio Stress/Strain, is called Young's modulus, and is an indispensable part of the law; without it neither verification nor falsification is possible. I shall be suggesting in this chapter that the law of effect as usually stated is equally incapable of verification or falsification unless we introduce a constant k which depends on the nature of the organism (personality) included in the experiment. This is but one application of a general principle I have elaborated in *The Biological Basis of Personality* (Eysenck, 1967), namely that psychological laws apply to persons, and can never be considered in isolation; in a conditioning experiment, for instance, we cannot study the reflex arc in isolation, but must be concerned with individual differences in motivation, arousal, ease of formation of connections, and many other relevant psychological parameters.

To put this point in a slightly different way, personality is an inescapable parameter in all psychological experiments, and attempts to formulate laws which do not include this variable are as useless as would be Hooke's law without the inclusion of the k term. Difficulties do of course arise in the precise method of inclusion; there are many complexities attending this operation, and no final answer can as yet be given. However, suggestions will be made, and exemplified by reference to two areas of research, namely, sexual responsiveness and the maintenance of the smoking habit.

Let me note here, however, that this same objection has been raised

by Allport (1943, 1946) in the course of a controversy about the law
of effect. "For Allport it is the person who learns, is rewarded, and
utilizes his success in his future adjustment. Allport thus pitted an
ego-oriented psychology of learning against the neo-hedonism of the
law of effect [Postman, 1947, p. 501]." In his own words, ". . . learning
proceeds because it is relevant to an interest system; it adds to knowledge, it differentiates items within the system, it broadens the range of
equivalent stimuli. . . . Pleasure attending a single response, or even
concatenations of responses, is not decisive [Allport, 1946, p. 346]." [1]
Allport's protest is well taken, but he has in effect nothing positive to
contribute; his idiographic insistence on a nondefined "ego" simply takes
refuge in ignorance. The ego is a kind of homunculus reference to which
can give a verbal answer to scientific problems, but which is not in
itself a scientific concept which might be used to make testable predictions.

In a sense, the errors committed by Allport and by the adherents of
the law of effect in its classical form are at opposite ends of a continuum.
For Allport, all persons are unique; from this he essentially argues against
the possibility of a nomothetic psychology, and by implication against
the possibility of a science of psychology at all—if uniqueness is really
universal in psychology, then how are we ever to have generalizations
which by their nature deny uniqueness? Conversely, Thorndike and
Hull in their formulations disregard all individual differences and in
effect treat all organisms as uniovular twins, reacting in a precisely
identical fashion to identical stimulus presentations. (Hull, in 1945, did in
fact suggest taking individual differences into account, but neither he nor
his followers have followed this advice.) In practice they may at times
act contrary to this view, but in their considered theoretical formulations
there is no trace of any realization that individual differences may systematically interact with the "laws" so promulgated. Clearly a compromise
is needed before we can properly proceed to study motivation scientifically, and I am suggesting that what is needed is some form of typology.
The typologist does not deny that *some* invariances do exist in the field
of psychology, contrary to Allport; and he does not deny the existence of
individual differences, contrary to Thorndike and Hull. How can such a

---

[1] According to Allport, the law of effect holds only for animals, small children,
mental defectives and in some peripheral phases of adult learning, i.e., with organisms where ego involvement is ruled out in large measure because the ego has
not yet been developed sufficiently to exert a directing influence.

typology be constructed, and how can it be applied to the field under discussion? It will be the burden of this chapter to provide some tentative answers to these important questions.

In mentioning the antecedents of the law of effect at the beginning of this chapter, associationism and hedonism are unlikely to have given rise to any questions; the law, particularly in the form given to it by Hull, clearly requires both some form of "connectionism," and also the connection to be formed with some form of hedonically positive or negative end product. The third variable, evolutionary doctrine, may have given rise to some doubt; why is evolution relevant in this context? The answer lies in Spencer's (1870) basic assumption

> that in the course of natural selection there has been established in the various species a correlation between the pleasant and the beneficial, and a similar correlation between the unpleasant and the injurious. That which is pleasant is maintained and repeated and proves beneficial to the biological organism. That which is painful is abandoned and the organism is protected from injury [Postman, 1947, p. 491].

Thus evolution is responsible for an innate hedonistic relation between certain kinds of stimulation and certain kinds of feelings and reactions; without this, survival would at best be accidental. On this showing, hedonic effects have strong biological roots, and are essential in securing the continuation of the species.

In looking at personality variables which might be useful in providing us with a scientifically valuable typology, we should perhaps first of all look at concepts which have a proper biological basis. I have argued that the two typological concepts of extraversion–introversion (E) and neuroticism–stability (N), conceived of as two orthogonal dimensions of personality, fulfill this function; they account for a considerable amount of everyday variation in behavior (Eysenck, 1970a), and they are firmly anchored in the physiology of the individual (Eysenck, 1967). In addition, they have been shown to be omnipresent in analyses of many different types of data (tests, ratings, self-ratings, laboratory measurements, physiological measures) and to have been postulated as explanatory and descriptive concepts by many workers in this field ever since the dawn of the Christian era and perhaps earlier (Eysenck & Eysenck, 1969). I will not here give any detailed description of these factors, but merely stress that in this theory extraverts are characterized by low cortical arousal, introverts by high cortical arousal—with ambiverts occupying intermediate positions with respect to arousal. It is further suggested, although this point will not be crucial to our discussion, that degree of arousal is mediated by individual differences in activation thresholds in the reticular activating system. Neuroticism, on the other hand, is related intimately to the autonomic system and the visceral brain, high N scorers being characterized by easy activation of this system (particularly the sympathetic branch), and by a slow deactivation after the cessation of stress.

It should further be noted that these dimensions of personality are conceived of as phenotypes based on strongly heritable physiological and anatomical structures; it is the genotype, interacting with environmental influences, which finally produces the observed outward behavior. I have reviewed the evidence for a strong genetic component in personality elsewhere (Eysenck, 1973a) and will not here repeat this discussion; suffice it to note that modern methods of genetic analysis enable us to answer many of the criticisms which have rightly been made of the so-called classical methods of twin analysis. We are no longer restricted, as were the earlier workers, to the analysis of within–family variance, and we do not have to put up with neglect of interaction effects; we can now study both between–family variance and interaction between environmental and genetic factors; the outcome of such analysis has been to suggest that between–family variance and interaction effects are both relatively unimportant in relation to E and N, and that heritability is in excess of 50%, and may be as high as 80%, in members of typical Western societies, at the present time. Thus the biological and hereditary nature of the law of effect finds a complement in the biological and hereditary nature of these dimensions of personality. American and Russian writers, in particular, have often denied the importance and relevance of genetics in this context, and have advocated a whole-hogging environmentalism which would leave no room for heredity; the facts are too clear to allow of any such one–sided approach (Jinks & Fulker, 1970).

As an example of the kind of interaction I am concerned with, let me look at a problem which has played an important part in the discussion of the law of effect, and which has in philosophical circles spelled the death knell of hedonism as a philosophical doctrine. As Postman (1947) puts the problem

> why do organisms so frequently persist in behavior which is clearly punishing, or, at least, more punishing than rewarding? It is, of course, possible to argue that whatever behavior subjects persist in must somehow be rewarding or it would be abandoned. Such reasoning would, however, be clearly circular and would beg the very question at issue in discussions of the law of effect [p. 546].

Mowrer and Ullman (1945) have sought an answer to this problem of "non-integrative learning" in the pattern of rewards and punishments. Our actions usually have consequences some of which are punishing, others rewarding; according to the doctrine of the "gradient of reinforcement" (which has strong experimental support), those consequences which immediately follow the act will be more influential in learning than effects which are temporally remote. Integrative learning occurs when remote consequences are brought to bear on the total hedonic state of the individual through symbolic behavior; in nonintegrative learning the organism fails to make this symbolic bridge to the future and remains at the mercy of the immediate gradient of reinforcement. "It is the failure to react to remote punishing consequences which is the basis for the persistence of behavior in the face of punishment [Postman, p. 547]." This explanation is well adapted to rat behavior, as in the Mowrer and Ullman (1945) study, but as Postman points out, "what about nonintegrative learning in humans capable of reactions to symbols [p. 547]?" Mowrer and Ullman (1945) are only able to produce an answer which involves us in the usual circularity so often attending discussions of the law of effect, and finally have recourse to Allport's *deus ex machina*, the "strength of the total ego," which, they say, "seems capable in ways which have not yet been clearly analyzed, of being mobilized in support of any single part (habit) for which the going is particularly hard [p. 85]." This is little more than a confession of ignorance.

Actually the Mowrer and Ullman study raises another problem not discussed at all by the authors. In this study the authors first trained rats to come to the trough when a buzzer sounded, in order to eat food placed therein. At this point of training a "rule" was introduced, to the effect that the rats were henceforth not to touch the food for a period of 3 sec after it appeared in the trough.

> One may think of this as a kind of rat "ettiquette," according to which it was not "polite" to eat until the prescribed length of time had elapsed. We could not, of course, "tell" our subjects about this rule, but we established conditions which were calculated to teach it to them. [Mowrer & Ullman, 1945].

This was done by giving the rats a shock if they took the food within the forbidden 3-sec interval; "in other words, the rats were 'punished' for eating within the tabu period but were free to eat, without punishment, if they waited a minimum of 3 sec after the food appeared [Mowrer & Ullman, 1945]."

Animals can react in three ways to this experimental situation: 1. They can take the food within the danger period and get shocked; Mowrer calls this the "delinquent" pattern. 2. They can avoid the shock by not eating at all; Mowrer calls this the "neurotic" pattern. 3. They can wait the 3 sec and then eat, thus avoiding the shock, but nevertheless obtaining the food; Mowrer calls this the "normal" or "integrative" reaction. The other two reaction patterns are called "nonintegrative." Mowrer studied the behavior of his animals as a function of the length of time elapsing between violations of the tabu and shock administered as a punishment; in addition to the 3-sec interval he used a 6- and a 12-sec interval. Mowrer demonstrates that with increasing interval delinquent behavior increases and neurotic behavior declines, which is in accord with his general hypothesis, but he does not answer the obvious questions why within each experimental paradigm different animals behave differently. This seems a crucial point; clearly no prediction about any particular animal's behavior is possible even if Mowrer's law should be true and valid. No physicist would be content with a law which did not enable him to make any quantitative prediction about the behavior of specific and specified classes of objects; it is difficult to see why psychology should adopt a less stringent criterion.

The writer replicated the Mowrer and Ullman experiment, using only the 3-sec interval of time elapsing between violation of the tabu and shock administration (Eysenck, 1963). Instead of varying this variable, he varied the strength of the shock (strong versus weak) and the constitutional emotionality of the animals tested (emotionally reactive versus emotionally nonreactive). This second variable was controlled by using the Maudsley reactive and nonreactive strains bred in our animal laboratories and numbered 163f and 163g, respectively, in the Catalogue of Uniform Strains. It was found that regardless of shock strength, nonreactive animals showed a larger number of normal, "integrative" reactions than did reactive animals; the differences were highly significant. Reactive animals produced more "delinquent" as well as more "neurotic" reactions. The writer, equating emotional reactivity in rats with neuroticism in humans, has drawn attention to the fact that in human subjects both delinquents and neurotics have much higher N scores than do normal subjects (Eysenck, 1964). The general theory advanced there was that "extraverted" humans and rats, because of their low arousal, condition poor, and hence do not acquire the conditioned responses which are required in order to avoid "delinquent" behavior. "Introverted" humans and rats, because of their high arousal, condition well, and hence acquire very strongly the conditioned responses which mediate normal behavior, and which might be characterized as "anxiety" or "fear" responses. Emotion may be regarded, following Spence, as a drive; this drive multiplies with the habits acquired by the animal during the experiment and determines his behavior. The "delinquent" has his food-seeking-and-eating habit multiplied by the strong drive of the emotionally reactive strain, and consequently acts in a delinquent fashion. Conversely, the "neurotic" has his conditioned fear responses multiplied by the strong drive of the emotionally reactive strain, and consequently acts in a neurotic fashion. Thus the strong emotional drive of animals of this strain drives them away, in opposite directions, from the integrative position; this position is much more easily reached by the nonreactive animals, where the drive which multiplies with the habit is much weaker. This hypothesis enables us to answer the question posed by Postman, both for rats and for humans. There is no need to invoke symbolic processes, or to wonder why despite these symbolic processes human beings often behave in nonintegrative ways.[2] Innate differences in arousal, related to extraversion–introversion, mediate different degrees of "conditionability"; it is this capacity to form conditioned responses which makes possible the removal of the individual from the immediate

---

[2] Cognitive theorists who appeal to "cognitive processes" are in error if they consider that such an appeal serves in any way as an explanation; we can only explain the less well known by an appeal to the better known, not by an appeal to something equally little known or understood. The phrase "cognitive processes" has no operational meaning, and does not refer to knowledge gained in large-scale and detailed laboratory experiments; it really refers to introspective notions and ideas which have not hitherto been fitted into any lawful framework. As such, they are not capable of bearing the burden imposed upon them by those who wish to explain "time spanning"; far from being able to offer any explanation, these "cognitive processes" are in need of explanation themselves. To take but the simplest case, why is it that psychopaths are apparently incapable of "time spanning," when there is no reason to doubt the existence of "cognitive processes" which are just as strong and well developed as those of more normal people? Psychopaths *know* very well what the contingencies are which are involved in their actions; they just disregard them. Cognitive theorists have no explanation to offer of this paradox. In saying this I do not wish to imply that cognitive theories are of necessity wrong and superfluous; I am only suggesting that as of now they have very little positive contribution to make. This position will undoubtedly change when a larger body of experimental knowledge has been accumulated; after all, even Pavlov acknowledged the importance of the "second signalling system," and its interaction with the primary system is a well recognized empirical problem.

gradient of reinforcement.[3] The stronger this ability, the greater his ability of "time spanning." It is particularly interesting that psychopaths, who by definition are least able to carry out this feat of "time spanning," and who are at the mercy of the immediate gradient of reinforcement, tend to have extraverted personalities (Eysenck, 1957) and to be characterized by low cortical arousal (Hare, 1970). The "remote punishing consequences," failure to react to which Postman alludes to as the basis for persistence of behavior in the face of punishment, are made present by a process of conditioning; the degree of conditioning determines the effectiveness of this "bridge to the future." By this hypothesis we not only circumvent an extremely embarrassing criticism of the law of effect, but we also explain the observed individual differences in experiments such as that of Mowrer and Ullman.

This example of the origin of "non-integrative behavior" illustrates the importance of personality in predicting human (or rat) behavior; a second example may be useful in illustrating how the very notion of a "psychological law" can be distorted by refusal to pay attention to individual differences. In *The Biological Basis of Personality* one such example was quoted, relating to the long continued theoretical struggles between Tolman and his followers on one side, and the Hull–Spence faction on the other; it seems likely that many of the issues in question arose simply because Tolman used an emotionally reactive strain of rats, while Spence used a nonreactive strain—widely different behavior of the animals of these strains seemed to justify the widely different theoretical accounts given by these authors. It is interesting that never, in all the critical exchanges between the two sides, is there as

---

[3] The literature concerning the relation between conditioning and introversion–extraversion has been reviewed by Eysenck (1965, 1967). Two frequently repeated criticisms of this position are (1) that the concept of "conditionability" implies that different tests of conditioning should intercorrelate positively; this degree of correlation is not usually found; (2) that experiments in the past have only used aversive conditioning, and that "positive conditioning" might not follow the same rules as "negative conditioning." Both objections are reasonable, but more recent experimental evidence has demonstrated that positive results in relation to both objections can be achieved by suitable choice of parameters (Barr & McConaghy, 1972). It does seem that the continued use of the concept of "conditionability" is justified, but it must certainly be recognized that conditioning is affected by many experimental parameters, and that choice of parameter values can in turn be decided on the basis of the writer's general theory (Eysenck & Levey, 1967). Many of the experiments responsible for critical evaluations of the writer's theories have been conducted without regard for such considerations, and are consequently less valuable for the development of the theory than they would otherwise have been.

much as a mention of these fundamental differences in the strains of the animals on which the theoretical generalizations were based. In this chapter I shall use a different example, related to what Mowrer has called the "neurotic paradox," i.e., the question of why neurotic behavior persists despite the fact that it is nonrewarding, i.e., seems to contradict the law of effect.

To take a very simplified case, consider a woman with a cat phobia (Freeman & Kendrick, 1960). Here a girl of 4 sees her favorite cat drowned by her father, and develops a strong fear of cats; this leads to a phobia so strong as to make her adult life a misery, and finally keeps her entombed in her room, afraid of going out because she might encounter a cat. This behavior is clearly not rewarding, in the sense of the law of effect; her life is extremely unhappy, and in addition she realizes full well that her fear is quite groundless and absurd (failure of "symbolic processes" to affect behavior). We may regard this neurotic illness as a simple case of conditioned fear responses (Eysenck & Rachman, 1965), and this may serve as a partial explanation of the phobia.

Note, however, that there are several problems still to be answered. In the first place, the phobia did not set in immediatey after the event which might be considered the crucial association between CS and UCS; onset was delayed by many years. In the second place, once the conditioned fear developed, we would have expected it to extinguish according to the classical laws of extinction theory; on every occasion that the girl saw a cat (CS) without any untoward UCS being associated with its appearance, an increment of extinction should occur, until finally the phobic fear would be completely extinguished. This does indeed seem to happen in many cases; the frequency of so-called "spontaneous remission" is probably due in large measure to simple extinction (Rachman, 1972). Why not in this case? Operant conditioning has been suggested as a possible cause (Eysenck & Rachman, 1965); the conditioned fear response is lessened if and when the woman, on seeing a cat, turns and runs. This reinforces the avoidance response, and thus "reality testing" is made impossible, and with it extinction. But this explanation is difficult to reconcile with the original slow development of the phobia; it can only be adduced as a reasonable cause once the phobia is fully developed. It will be seen that even an apparently simple case of neurotic behavior presents us with formidable difficulties as long as we fail to pay attention to individual differences; the case as described seems to violate both the law of effect and the law of extinction.

Let us consider the law of extinction, as stated by Kimble (1961): "If the CS is repeatedly presented unaccompanied by the usual reinforcement, the conditioned response undergoes a progressive decrement called extinction, and finally fails to occur [p. 281]." This is usually regarded as a universal law, as stated as such; yet, as I have pointed out, there are many exceptions in the literature (Eysenck, 1968), and these appear to afford some ground for restating this law. Such a restatement might read like this:

> If the CS is repeatedly presented unaccompanied by the usual reinforce-ment, the conditioned response undergoes a progressive change which may either lead to *extinction* (when the change is in the direction of diminution of the CR) or *incubation* (when the change is in the direction of increase of the CR). Extinction occurs when the UCS is weak, when the CS dura-tion is long, and when subjects are low on emotional reactivity. Incubation occurs when the UCS is strong, when CS duration is short, and when sub-jects are high on emotional reactivity.

Much of the evidence for this revised law has been reviewed else-where (Eysenck, 1968); additional work has since been published to give substance to some of the parts (e.g., Rohrbaugh & Riccio, 1970). It is not suggested that all the parts of this law are equally certain; indeed, the only part on which there can be no doubt at all is the statement that the law of extinction does not apply in all circumstances, but that incubation or enhancement of the CR will sometimes occur when the CS is presented without the usual reinforcement. The part of the revised law referring to the length of CS presentation is also well supported, and it has already been applied with considerable success in behavior therapy. "Flooding" therapy (also sometimes called "implosion" therapy) had been tried with no success (Rachman, 1966), sometimes even mak-ing the patients worse; in this method of treatment the CS is evoked for a short period of time, producing great emotion, in the hope that ex-tinction would occur. When "flooding" was tried with samples of obses-sive–compulsive patients by Rachman, Hodgson, and Marks (1971), attention was paid to the revised law of extinction, and lengthy periods of exposure to the CS attempted; the outcome was extremely successful, and extinction was achieved in a relatively short period of time with severely ill patients most of whom had experienced unsuccessful therapies of many different types.

The two other parts of the revised law are mutually complementary; they refer respectively to the strength of the UCS (i.e., the fear-producing properties of the stimulus) and the emotionality of the subject. Clearly the very definition of "emotionality" means that the subject (person or rat) reacts with a stronger degree of fear to a standard stimulus, so that this part of the revised law could also be made to refer to the strength of the UCR, the assumption being that this response strength would be determined both by the strength of the UCS and by the personality of the subject or patient. It is not accidental that the facts which led to a search for a law of incubation, to take its place beside the law of extinction, were largely derived from the behavior of neurotic patients, i.e., from people characterized by strong emotionality (high N). It is unlikely that strong UCRs are found in nonemotional subjects, because (in times of peace at least) stimuli sufficiently strong to promote incubation must be relatively rare as far as they are concerned; it is the innately reactive person who is likely to show these curious effects, even with UCSs which are only moderately strong—as in the case of our cat phobic woman, whose "paradox" may thus find an explanation in the law of incubation. I would suggest that without a law of this kind many features of neurotic behavior would be incapable of any scientific explanation.

The complementary nature of imposed stress and personality in producing a given response, mentioned in the preceding paragraph, is in my view a fact of major importance in psychology; it corresponds well with the position in physics, where a similar complementarity obtains. We have already mentioned Hooke's law of elasticity; let us consider Fig. 6-1, which illustrates this law (Savage & Eysenck, 1964). A and B are two metals differing in elasticity; they are stressed by increasing loads, and

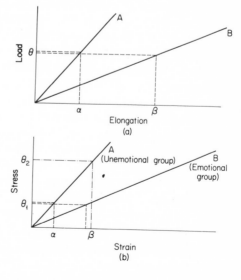

Fig. 6-1. Illustration of Hooke's Law (1a) as applied to the measurement of emotionality (1b).

the elongation corresponding to each load is plotted on the abscissa. It will be seen that identical loads θ give rise to quite divergent elongations, α and β (Fig. 6-1a). Figure 6-1b illustrates a similar analysis of rat (or human) behavior in an experimental situation productive of emotion. Again the stress (independent variable) is plotted on the ordinate, and the strain (dependent variable) on the abscissa; A and B represent the unemotional and emotional groups of animals respectively. Identical stress θ_1 gives rise to quite different strains α and β. It would require stress θ_2 to make the strain in A animals equal to that produced by θ_1 in B animals. Differences between θ_1 and θ_2 are the kinds of differences traditionally studied by experimental psychologists; differences between A and B are the kinds of differences traditionally studied by personality psychologists, believers in the importance of constitutional factors, and clinical psychologists. Physicists have never attempted to make a choice between these two sets of variables, or to study them in isolation; it seems equally futile for psychologists to do so.

Summarizing the argument so far, we may say that the law of effect cannot be understood or applied to individual cases unless we take into account individual differences, i.e., personality variables like emotionality–neuroticism, or introversion–extraversion. Identical experimental procedures (e.g., "flooding") may have exactly opposite effects on two subjects, simply because one is high, the other low on N. Identical environmental conditions may make one patient a neurotic, another a criminal, simply because one is extraverted, the other introverted. No general laws (e.g., that of extinction) are meaningful in psychology without explicit reference to personality variables. Experiments lacking such reference are unlikely to be replicable, unless restricted to highly selected groups of subjects (sophomores, or a given strain of rats).

In the examples so far given, we have been concerned mostly with general laws; in what follows we shall be dealing rather with specific experimental problems, selected to illustrate the way in which attention to personality variables can illuminate the application of the law of effect. In doing so we will also turn our attention from N to E, and in order to do this satisfactorily it will first be necessary to introduce a general law linking arousal and hedonic tone. This law resembles what Berlyne (1960, 1971) has called "Wundt's curve," after Wundt's (1874) generalization concerning pleasantness and unpleasantness (hedonic tone), conceived as attributes of the conscious experiences evoked by stimuli of different intensity. On this curve, stimulus intensity is plotted along the abscissa, hedonic tone along the ordinate; the curve rises from an indifference point at zero stimulation until it reaches a maximum, at some intermediate degree of stimulation. After this point has been reached, greater stimulation leads to a falling of the curve, until it crosses the indifference line and further increases in stimulation intensity become actually painful (negative hedonic tone). My own version of this curve (Eysenck, 1963, 1967) differs in two ways from the Wundt–Berlyne curve (Fig. 6-2). In the first place low levels of stimulation are associated with negative hedonic tone, not with indifference; work on sensory deprivation has shown that low levels of sensory stimulation can be as painful and aversive as very high levels. In the second place, personality differences are explicitly introduced into the picture, in a manner to be discussed presently. Apart from these differences, I agree with Berlyne when he identifies the abscissa with "arousal potential," i.e., attributes greater arousal potential to strong than to weak stimuli; [4] indeed, this identification forms the basis of my own attempt to introduce personality (in this case introversion–extraversion) into the curve.

Fundamental to the curve is the notion of an optimal level of stimulation (O.L. in Fig. 6-2); levels of stimulation below or above this will be less productive of positive hedonic tone. The O.L. of introverts is shown

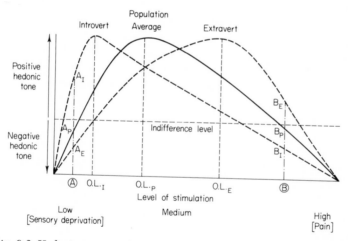

Fig. 6-2. Hedonic tone as a function of level of stimulation and personality.

---

[4] As Berlyne (1971) points out, "for us, the horizontal axis represents not merely stimulus intensity but arousal potential, which includes intensity but also other stimulus properties that tend to raise arousal, including biological significance and the collative properties like novelty and complexity. The vertical axis will represent hedonic value, which we just judge from effects on behavior, including reward value and punishment value, as well as from verbal reports [p. 90].

as displaced to the left, that of extraverts to the right, of the average or ambivert group; the reason for this of course that in our theory introverts have a higher level of arousal under identical conditions of stimulation than do ambiverts, and ambiverts than extraverts; thus identical levels of stimulation will produce an OL in ambiverts, will produce a lowered hedonic tone in introverts for whom the stimulation is supraoptimal, and an equally lowered hedonic tone in extraverts for whom the stimulation is infraoptimal. Thus an increase in stimulation from $O.L._I$ to $O.L._E$ will decrease the hedonic tone of the experience for introverts, will increase it for extraverts, and will first increase and then decrease it for ambiverts. At points A and B the average person will have his two indifference points, but at A introverts will experience positive hedonic tone, extraverts negative hedonic tone, whereas the reverse is true at B. Thus it will be clear that the theory cannot be tested in any rational manner without paying attention to individual differences and personality, particularly the dimension of extraversion–introversion. Changes in the independent variable may have contrary effects on introverts and extraverts, and the direction of these differences can be predicted from our diagram.

Several obvious and testable deductions can be made from Fig. 6-2, and the theory underlying it. Introverts should be better able to withstand sensory deprivation, while extraverts should be better able to withstand physical pain; both deductions have been tested several times, with results which on the whole support the prediction (Eysenck, 1967). Given a suitable experimental setup producing some low form of stimulation, extraverts should be found to indulge in lever pressing in order to achieve greater stimulation, whereas introverts should not so indulge; conversely, when the experimental set up produces some high level of stimulation, the opposite prediction would be made (Weisen, 1965). Generally, "sensation-seeking behavior" would be looked for in extraverts, seeking to approach their O.L., and avoided by introverts, seeking to approach theirs (Philipp & Wilde, 1970). Sensory thresholds should be lower for introverts than for extraverts (Eysenck, 1967). Taken together with the evidence for the general validity of the main curve in Fig. 6-2 (see Schneirla, 1959, on animal work, and Grastyan, Karmos, Vereczkey, & Kellenys, 1966, on electrophysiological work) these studies support the generalizations outlined in Fig. 6-2 fairly strongly, and we shall use it in the further development of our theory.

One extension of our general theory should at least be mentioned here, despite the rather speculative nature of the hypotheses involved. The theory in question may serve to explain the facts depicted in our Fig.

6-2, and consequently serve as a basis for the predictions we have made rather freely from the generalized relationship basic to that figure. Delgado, Roberts, and Miller (1954) and Olds and Milner (1954) have opened up a series of investigations demonstrating the existence of several pain and pleasure centers; Olds and Olds (1965) describe three such centers. First, we have the primary reward and aversion systems, which are believed to counteract each other; certainly the aversion system appears to inhibit the primary reward system upon activation, and diminishes the effects on behavior attributed to that system. No evidence has been found of reciprocal action of the primary reward system on the aversion system (Brady & Conrad, 1960; Olds & Olds, 1965). Now, as Berlyne (1971) points out

> the primary reward and aversion systems are . . . closely connected, and at least partially identifiable, with the brain structures controlling the manifestations of heightened arousal. Powerful and virtually insatiable rewarding effects can be obtained by stimulating the lateral hypothalamus and the medial forebrain bundle, and important tracts of nerves that pass along the sides of the hypothalamus. This is what Olds calls the "positive reinforcement focus [p. 84]."

However, it has been shown that even the elimination of large amounts of tissue from this area leaves strong primary rewarding effects intact (Valenstein & Campbell, 1966), suggesting that the essential focus of the system lies in the reticular formation, which is of course the area primarily concerned with arousal. The aversion system (Olds's "periventricular system") consists of fibres passing through the medial hypothalamus into the midbrain tegmentum, which is largely occupied by parts of the reticular formation. "A substantial body of experiments show that stimulation within either the primary reward system or the aversion system produces familiar signs of increased arousal, including changes in heart rate, high frequency EEG waves, and increased bodily movement [Berlyne, 1971, p. 85]."

The secondary reward system, on the other hand, appears to be more closely related to the trophotropic or dearousal system.

> Olds's experiments point to the existence of what he calls a "positive-reinforcement-field," which has a much larger extent than the positive reinforcement "focus" or primary reward system and is generally to be found rather higher up, toward the top of the brain-stem and in the limbic system, which occupies the lowest and most primitive parts of the cerebrum [p. 86].

Activation of this system results in dearousal; its stimulation leads to slow heart beats, the appearance of low-frequency EEG waves, and re-duced motor activity. It is suggested that the secondary reward system produces rewarding effects indirectly, i.e., by inhibiting the aversion system, which in turn ceases to inhibit the primary rewarding system. "Activation of the secondary rewarding system thus produces reward by releasing the primary rewarding system from inhibition [Berlyne, 1971, p. 86]."

Berlyne thus distinguishes between two mechanisms of reward, in-volving these three systems. One mechanism produces reward when arousal is lowered after rising to an uncomfortably high level; this he supposes to depend on the secondary reward system. "When food is presented to a hungry animal or when fear is alleviated through the appearance of a reassuring stimulus, the secondary reward system be-comes active. This, we have seen reduces the activity of the aversion system, which means a lowering of arousal and an alleviation of un-pleasantness [Berlyne, 1971, p. 86]." The other mechanism works through arousal increase rather than arousal reduction and comes into play when arousal is raised to a moderate extent.

Taking speculation just one step further, one might suggest that activa-tion of the secondary reward system, which produces reward by releas-ing the primary rewarding system from inhibition, is the more usual way for introverts to achieve pleasure. Berlyne's second mechanism, working through arousal increase rather than arousal reduction, is perhaps more likely to be used by extraverts in order to achieve pleasure. Of course these two mechanisms are not exclusive to one or the other type of person; both introverts and extraverts are likely upon occasion to make use of both. But taking an average over many different occasions, there is likely to be a difference in the direction suggested, because the start-ing level of arousal in the two groups is so different. Let us try and apply this model to one of the classical problems of pleasure-giving activity, namely sex. Consider a scale corresponding to the abscissa in Fig. 6-2, made up of items increasing in the degree of sexual stimulation. The scale, which is presented in Table 6-1, was derived from questionnaire responses of 400 male and 400 female students; percentage "Yes" answers were converted into scale distances by transformation in terms of the normal curve of distribution, and suitable multiplication and addition of a constant, in order to obtain a scale from 0 to 15. Zero on this scale means just no sexual arousal at all, while 15 means maximum possible sexual arousal.

In terms of our Fig. 6-2, we would predict that introverts, as compared with extraverts, would have a position somewhat to the left of center,

TABLE 6-1

Scale of sexual activity	Points
1. Social talking.	0
2. One minute continuous lip kissing.	3
3. Manual manipulation of female breast, over clothes.	4.5
4. Manual manipulation of female breast, under clothes.	5.3
5. Kissing nipples of female breast.	6.3
6. Manual manipulation of female genitals.	6.5
7. Manual manipulation of male genitals.	7.2
8. Mutual manual manipulation of genitals.	7.3
9. Sexual intercourse, face to face.	8.3
10. Manual manipulation of male genitals to ejaculation.	8.6
11. Oral manipulation of female genitals.	10.3
12. Oral manipulation of male genitals.	10.8
13. Sexual intercourse, man behind woman.	12.2
14. Mutual ora-genital manipulation.	12.5
15. Oral manipulation of male genitals to ejaculation.	12.8
16. Mutual oral manipulation of genitals to mutual orgasm.	15.0

whereas extraverts would have a position somewhat to the right of center; ambiverts would then be intermediate. Relevant information has been published by Giese and Schmidt (1968) and by Eysenck (1970b, 1971). These studies have shown that:

1. Extraverts will have intercourse earlier than introverts.
2. Extraverts will have intercourse more frequently than introverts.
3. Extraverts will have intercourse with more different partners.
4. Extraverts will have intercourse in more diverse positions than introverts.
5. Extraverts will indulge in more varied sexual behavior outside intercourse.
6. Extraverts will indulge in longer precoital love play than introverts.

Table 6-2 shows some of the results from the Giese and Schmidt study; those from Eysenck are similar.

In a general way, these results are in good accord with prediction; where there are some anomalies, these are susceptible to an obvious explanation. Thus with respect to such items as "long precoital love play" and "more than three different coital positions," men show the expected greater frequency of endorsements for extraverts as compared with introverts, but women do not. The reason almost certainly is that in these matters men take the initiative, women follow; hence the pattern of love

TABLE 6-2 [a]

	Males			Females		
	E_1	E_2	E_3	E_1	E_2	E_3
(1) Masturbation at present	86	80	72	47	43	39
(2) Petting: at 17	16	28	40	15	19	24
Petting: at 19	31	48	56	30	44	47
Petting: at present age	57	72	78	62	71	76
(3) Coitus: at 17	5	13	21	4	4	8
Coitus: at 19	15	31	45	12	20	29
Coitus: at present age	47	70	77	42	57	71
(4) Median frequency of coitus per month (sexually active students only)	3.0	3.7	5.5	3.1	4.5	7.5
(5) Number of coitus partners in last 12 months; unmarried students only 1	75	64	46	72	77	60
2-3	18	25	30	25	17	23
4+	7	12	25	4	6	17
(6) Long precoital sex play	21	25	28	21	16	18
(7) Cunnilingus	52	62	64	58	69	69
(8) Fellatio	53	60	69	53	59	61
(9) More than three different coital positions	10	16	26	12	18	13
(10) Experience of orgasm nearly always	—	—	—	17	32	29

[a] Sexual activities of introverts (E_1), ambiverts (E_2), and extraverts (E_3). [From Giese & Schmidt (1968).]

making tends to represent the inclinations of the male, rather than of the female. If this were true, then we would expect men who had indulged in *fellatio* and *cunnilingus* to say that they had enjoyed these activities, whereas in the case of women this would be more questionable; in actual fact, men do report enjoyment in over 90% of the cases, whereas women only do so in less than 50%.

The analysis so far presented is of course only partial; in thinking about any form of behavior we must consider both approach and avoidance gradients, and our concern so far has been mainly with approach gradients, i.e., degrees of "sensation-seeking." Also involved are undoubtedly avoidance gradients due to social pressure, the mores of our society, and parental approval and disapproval; these would be linked with such concepts as asocial or antisocial behavior (Eysenck, 1972b). When we analyze these concepts, as for instance in *Crime and Personality* (Eysenck, 1964), we find that here extraverts are less likely to acquire the internalized social "conscience" which would keep them within the lower bounds of the activities listed in Table 6-1 because of their lower "conditionability," itself due to low arousability. This is not the place to go into details about this process of "conscience formation"; the point is merely mentioned in passing in order to indicate that our analysis, correct though it may be as far as it goes, only concerns itself with a part of the whole story. Other considerations which must enter into the account are of course physiological factors, like sex hormone secretion; constitutional factors, like beauty and virility; accidental factors, like opportunities for sexual activities; and many others. But of course the point of this example was not to give an all-embracing account of sexual activity, but merely to indicate a way along which predictions could be made concerning the relation between personality factors and sexual behavior, through the mediation of arousal and hedonic tone.

We must now turn to the cigarette smoking habit, a habit seemingly as firmly ingrained, and as difficult to break, as that attaching to the topic just discussed. I have discussed this problem in considerable detail elsewhere (Eysenck, 1973b); I will here only summarize the more important conclusions. My general theory postulates (a) that smoking cigarettes introduces nicotine into the organism; (b) that the effects of the nicotine are the crucial factor in maintaining the smoking habit in confirmed smokers; and (c) that these effects are variable, leading to an *increase* in arousal when the amount of nicotine involved is small, and a *decrease* in arousal when the nicotine involved is large. The evidence for these propositions is of varying strength; I consider (a) to be undoubtedly true, (b) to be strongly supported by the evidence and (c) to be only weakly supported by the evidence. In terms of our Fig. 6-2, we would deduce from these propositions that people to the left of the point of optimal arousal would attempt to *raise* their level of arousal either by change of environment, activity, etc., or by pharmacological means, e.g. by drinking coffee, or by the intake of nicotine through smoking—provided the amount of intake was limited so that it produced an increase and not a decrease of arousal. The choice between these two different types of reaction is presumably governed by such factors as environmental constraints, availability of cigarettes or arousal-producing activities, pre-existing habits, knowledge of the arousal-producing effects of nicotine, etc. This hypothesis would integrate the fact that extraverts smoke more cigarettes than introverts into our model, because according to Fig. 6-2 the optimum level of arousal for extraverts is displaced to the right; in other words, *ceteris paribus* they will be more likely to be in a state of underarousal than will introverts. It would follow that they would have recourse to pharmacological methods of raising their level of arousal more frequently than would intoverts, i.e., would smoke more cigarettes. We have already noted that extraverts are also characterized by behavioral methods of increasing arousal level, i.e., through increase in sensory stimulation, environmental change, sexual adventures, etc.; smoking thus takes its natural place as one of many ways to achieve this end. Conversely, people to the right of the point of optimal arousal would attempt to *lower* their level of arousal either by a change of environment, activity, etc., or by pharmacological means, e.g., by taking tranquilizers, or by the intake of nicotine through smoking—provided the amount of intake was large enough to produce a decrease and not an increase in arousal.

One testable deduction from this hypothesis would be that under controlled laboratory conditions (i.e., when recourse to arousal-producing activity is made difficult or impossible) there should exist for each individual a preferred intake of nicotine, such that it brings him up to, or at least near, his optimum level of arousal; less intake of nicotine would make him fall short (underarousal), more intake of nicotine would make him exceed this point (overarousal). Quite generally, then, it is postulated that the tobacco habit is maintained because it is an artificial aid in producing a preferred level of arousal; it is the change from a less preferred to a more perferred level which constitutes the positive reinforcement which the smoker derives from this habit. There is some evidence from animal work (monkeys) that nicotine by itself can become a reinforcement (Deneau & Inoki, 1967; Jarvik, 1967); as Jarvik says, "we conclude that it is possible to elicit and maintain smoking behavior in monkeys with no other incentive and on a free choice basis, but it is relatively weak compared to other ingestive behavior, such as drinking, which satisfies an obvious physiological need [p. 294]." Such results are reassuring, but they cannot of course take the place of human experiment where much finer grading of responses can be expected.

Perhaps the early work of Johnston (1942) is relevant here; he showed that the craving of habituated smokers could be successfully appeased by nicotine injections instead of smoking. Similarly, Proosdy (1960) reports that during World War 2, chewing tobacco and snuff became popular among workers in munition factories where smoking was prohibited. Studies such as these indicate fairly clearly that it is the nicotine in the cigarette which plays the crucial role in the reinforcement process; apparently it is the ability of the nicotine to change the arousal level in the desired direction, and to the desired extent, which is responsible for the maintenance of the smoking habit.

A crucial experiment along these lines was performed by Frith (1971a), who got his subjects to smoke three different types of cigarettes, differing in nicotine content. He measured the number of cigarettes smoked during three 8-hour periods, the desire for a cigarette immediately before and after smoking, the time taken to smoke a single cigarette, and rate of puffing and the volume per puff.

Frith (1971a) concluded that

> this experiment has provided some data in support of the hypothesis that smokers can alter their behaviour to suit the nicotine content of their cigarettes. In particular the smokers in this experiment took longer to smoke a cigarette with more nicotine in it. Presumably this change in behaviour enabled the smoker to obtain the physiological and psychological effects he desired of the nicotine whatever the nicotine content of his cigarettes [p. 191].

Frith also argued that this might constitute a useful experimental technique because

> if the nicotine content of the cigarettes remained constant and yet the smoker changes his behaviour, then it could be assumed that the amount of nicotine he desired had changed, for example as a result of a stressful situation. It might thus be possible to measure rapid fluctuation in a person's desire for nicotine by measuring how long he took to smoke a standard cigarette [p. 191].

Confirmation comes from the work of Ashton and Watson (1970) who used different filters to produce high nicotine and low nicotine cigarettes. They tested their subjects under three conditions, resting, easy simulated driving task, and stressful driving task. They found that

> during both the driving tasks and during the resting period after the tasks the subject smoking the low-nicotine cigarettes took more frequent puffs than those smoking the high nicotine cigarettes. . . . As would be expected from the increased puff frequency, the average time taken to finish a cigarette was less in the groups smoking the low-nicotine cigarettes. Records of respiration made during the smoking showed no differences in overall rate or in the depth of respiration at or after each puff between the two groups of smokers. Hence these results suggest that the subjects smoking the low-nicotine cigarettes were attempting to compensate for the high filter retention of nicotine by a faster puffing rate [p. 681].

These results support the general position taken in relation to the effects of smoking; how about the doubtful postulate about the contradictory effects of nicotine in small and large doses?

We may begin by noting the well-known fact that nicotine injection is accompanied by cortical arousal and also by an increased production of acetylcholine, a transmitter substance for the propagation of nerve impulses in the cerebral cortex; Armitage, Hall, and Morrison (1968) have shown that, with small doses of nicotine, arousal and increased production of acetylcholine were observed. With slightly larger doses, there occurred a similar pattern in some experiments, while in others the result was a lowering of arousal and a decrease in the production of acetylcholine.

> It appears, therefore, that nicotine can have two effects, it can either cause an increase or a decrease in the acetylcholine release from the parietal cortex and can cause changes in the EEG consistent either with increased or decreased cortical activity. It seems likely that the effect varies from cat to cat, and even with the small changes in the dose of nicotine and the rate of injection [Armitage et al., 1968, p. 334].

And finally Armitage et al. conclude that "we suggest that the effect of nicotine in man probably depends critically on the dose and rate of self-administration and also on whether he is excited or depressed [p. 334]."

Possibly a general solution to the problem raised can be found in the application of principles familiar from the work on the sedation threshold, and Pavlov's principles of the "law of strength" and of "paradoxical reactions." Work on the sedation threshold has shown us that less of a depressant drug is needed to bring an extraverted subject to the sedation threshold; presumably this rule can be reversed to state that less of a stimulant drug is needed to bring an introverted subject to the arousal threshold. Such a law would tell us that under quiet laboratory conditions the amount of nicotine required to reach this threshold differs from person to person according to his introversion–extraversion score. How can we define such a threshold? Pavlov suggested that an increase in what we would now call cortical arousal was accompanied by an increase in "output"; this is the law of strength. He also suggested, however, that this law only applied up to a certain point; beyond this point "protective inhibition" set in and produced paradoxical effects, such that with increasing arousal "output" was in fact decreased. It is difficult to deal with Pavlov's physiology in modern terms, and we may with advantage drop reference to it and restate our suggestion in somewhat different terms. We would suggest that the effects of nicotine depend on the degree of arousal in the cortex; when arousal is high, the effects are depressing, whereas when arousal is low, the effects are stimulating. The degree of arousal in primarily a function of two factors: (a) the personality of the subject (primarily his position on the introversion–extraversion continuum), and (b) the conditions obtaining at the time, i.e., external determinants of arousal such as degree of sensory stimulation, etc. Certain minor factors may have to be added to this list (time of day, for instance) and these minor factors [as well as the major ones mentioned under (b)] may interact with personality; extraverts have relatively low arousal in the morning, relatively high arousal in the evening (Blake, 1967a, b). However, the final common pathway of these various factors must be the state of arousal, as indexed by the EEG or some other suitable measure, and the theory suggests that depending on this state the effects of nicotine will be positive or negative, arousing or depressing. This would mean that nicotine would be uniquely reinforcing, tending under all conditions (in suitable doses) to produce a shift in arousal directed toward the optimum degree shown in our Fig. 6-2. Possibly this is the reason why this habit is so difficult to give up, and to strongly reinforcing for so many people. (A similar slight ambiguity has sometimes been observed in relation to alcohol also, where small and large doses may appear to have antagonistic properties.)

Note the phrase: "in suitable doses," inserted in the sentence above suggesting that the shift produced by nicotine in the arousal level could always be reinforcing. As Armitage et al. (1968) have suggested, the smoker has "finger-tip control" over the actual uptake of nicotine; he can vary the interpuff interval, the strength and length of puff, the total number of puffs taken; he can inhale or not, as he pleases, and he can select cigarettes having a nicotine content most suitable for his habitual requirements. Thus we can combine our two sets of hypotheses and state that the selection and manner of smoking a cigarette interact with the personality type of the smoker, and the situation, to produce the final end effect—the change in arousal level which will be most reinforcing. None of these elements can fruitfully be studied by itself, as all interact in complex ways to produce the final result. (Possibly another point should be emphasized here; the effects of nicotine are likely to be profoundly different depending on the previous exposure of the smoker to the drug. This factor in turn can be split up into two quite different factors; short-term exposure, i.e., length of time since smoking the last cigarette, and long-term exposure, i.e., habitual intake of nicotine, over the last few years. For the sake of simplifying our exposition these factors have been kept implicit rather than made explicit; for serious experimental work they must always be borne in mind, however.)

Armitage et al. (1968) remark that "tobacco smokers have frequently stated that they are either 'tranquillized' or 'stimulated' as a result of smoking a cigarette and although this evidence is purely subjective it cannot be dismissed [p. 331]." In terms of our theory, it would seem to follow that (a) introverts should more frequently use nicotine for tranquillizing purposes, extraverts for stimulating purposes, and (b) people smoking under conditions of "boredom" should use nicotine for stimulating purposes, people smoking under conditions of "stress" should use nicotine for tranquillizing purposes. An experiment relevant to those hypotheses have been performed in our laboratory by Frith (1971b). In his own words

> if nicotine acts as a stimulant, then a person is most likely to smoke when he has an undesirable low level of arousal. Such a low level of arousal would probably result from a combination of circumstances. The person would be particularly prone to low levels of arousal by his very nature and would also be in a situation inducive of a particularly low level of arousal (tiring, boring, etc.). Another person might smoke because he was particularly prone to high levels of arousal and found himself in a highly arousing situation. It seems very likely that these two would be different people Thus it should be possible to isolate two extremes of smoking behaviour. There should be one group of people who smoke mostly in situations inducing low levels of arousal in order to increase their arousal level, and there should be another group of people who smoke in situations which induce high levels of arousal in order to reduce their arousal level [p. 73].

As a test of his hypothesis, Frith constructed a questionnaire listing 22 situations which might make it likely that a person would be tempted to light a cigarette; 12 of these were high-arousal and 10 low-arousal situations. The subjects had to imagine themselves in each of these situations and indicate what their desire for a cigarette would be on a seven-point scale. Ninety-eight subjects, of both sexes, took part in the experiment; ages ranged from 18 to 50. All were cigarette smokers. The 25 variables (including sex, age, and number of cigarettes smoked per day) were intercorrelated and factor analyzed; two main factors were extracted. All questionnaire items have loadings with identical sign on the first factor; this suggests that a person who is tempted to light up in one situation is also likely to light up in another. The highest loading is for number of cigarettes smoked per day. The second factor opposes the low-arousal situations to the high-arousal situations, in conformity with expectation. It is interesting to note that sex has the highest loading on this factor: "the men tended to have the highest desire for a cigarette in situations inducing boredom and tiredness, while the women had their highest desire in stress inducing situations [Frith (1971b), p. 74]." It is relevant to note that men have always been found to have higher extraversion scores than women (Eysenck & Eysenck, 1969), as well as lower neuroticism scores; this suggests that a repetition of the experiment using personality questionnaires might indicate that extraverts smoke to increase arousal, introverts to reduce it.

LIST OF SMOKING SITUATIONS

1. You are having an important interview for a job.
2. You have to fill in a complicated tax form.
3. You have to look through several hundred coins to see if there are any rare and valuable ones.
4. You are having a quiet evening with friends.
5. You are witnessing a violent and horrifying film.
6. You have to drive at speed in heavy traffic.
7. You have to wait for your train home, which is very late.
8. You are having a restful evening alone reading a magazine.
9. You are sitting in a dentist's waiting room knowing that you are to have a particularly difficult filling.
10. You are trying to hold a conversation at a large and very noisy party.
11. You are very tired and need to keep awake.
12. You have to ask your boss for a raise at a time when he is known to be in a bad mood.
13. You are trying to account for the discrepancy between your spending for the month and your bank statement.
14. You are looking through a long list of names to see if you can find anyone you know.
15. You are chatting with friends during a tea-break.
16. You have just been informed of a death of a close friend.
17. You have to do some rapid mental arithmetic for an intelligence test.
18. You are travelling on a train for several hours.
19. You go for a solitary walk in quiet countryside.
20. You have just heard the announcement of a plane crash and you think a friend may have been involved.
21. You are having an important telephone conversation in a very noisy office.
22. You have just had a very big meal.

Frith's factor contrasting different occasions for smoking finds some support in a study by McKennell (1970), where a factor analysis of occasions to smoke brought to light several factors, of which two relevant ones were "relaxation smoking" and "nervous irritation smoking"; he too unfortunately failed to administer personality questionnaires. However, sex comparisons gave results similar to Frith's. The data are a little difficult to disentangle because they are confounded by differential smoking habits of men and women (sex is not included in the factor analysis, but percentage figures for males and females are given in his Table 7); nevertheless, it is clear that for his adults men exceed women for "relaxation" smoking, women exceed men for "nervous irritation" smoking, when allowance is made for the fact that men are heavier smokers than women.

There is also some support for Frith's finding from a study by Horn (1969). As a small part of his survey, Horn asked people how much they agreed with statements like "when I feel uncomfortable or upset about something, I light up a cigarette." There were five such statements with which women agreed significantly more often than men. All described situations of stress and high arousal (e.g., feeling worried, angry, upset, etc.). Unfortunately there were no questions describing low-arousal states. However, with one statement, "I smoke cigarettes to stimulate me," more men than women agreed, although not significantly so.

The model of smoking behavior and its maintenance here sketched out has some obvious relevance to attempts to reduce or eliminate the habit. The growing importance and success of behavior therapy (Eysenck & Beech, 1971) has brought about a flood of attempts to use techniques such as aversion therapy and desensitization for the purpose of smoking behavior modification. The outcome of all this work has not been commensurate with effort (Keutzer, Lichtenstern, & Mees, 1968; Berstein, 1969); this is not surprising when we consider the methods used in terms of our model. We have postulated (a) that different people smoke for different reasons, primarily to either increase or decrease cortical arousal, and they do so (b) in different situations, producing either too little or too much arousal. This suggests immediately that no general method of treatment would be likely to be effective for all subjects; indeed, a method which might help some individuals might have the opposite effect on others! A person using smoking as a tranquillizer might benefit from desensitization, but might in fact get worse under aversion therapy, where the electric shocks and other strong stimuli used might increase his already too-high degree of arousal. It seems clear that most of the attempts to modify smoking behavior have suffered from a lack of theoretical sophistication; in most cases an existing method has been adapted to the problem without any attempt to take into account important variables relevant to the situation. Any attempt to "cure" people of the smoking habit should incorporate an investigation of their personality structure, their response for smoking [along the lines of Frith's (1971b) study], their method of smoking (number of cigarettes, number and spacing of puffs, inhalation or not, etc.); on the basis of this knowledge it might then be possible to prescribe *for that particular person* a course of treatment which should of course be based on a detailed analysis of the problem presented, as well as thorough knowledge of the methods available, and their theoretical justification and background. Studies which are treatment centered, i.e., start out with the notion of testing a given type of treatment by administering it to every member of a randomly constituted experimental group, for comparison with an equally randomly constituted control group, are doomed to failure; they resemble a hypothetical attempt in the medical field to bring together a random sample of ill people and administer to them a particular type of treatment irrespective of the particular ills with which they happened to be afflicted. Such attempts are motivated by the belief that all smoking is caused and reinforced by a single, uniform factor common to all smokers; as we have seen, such a belief is hardly tenable any longer. Such undirected activity can have no other result than to bring into disrepute the methods of behavior therapy which, like all methods of behavior modification, require careful analysis and theoretical insight before they can be applied with success; they are not to be regarded as foolproof panaceas to be dispensed at random (Eysenck & Rachman, 1965).

This concludes the discussion of the two examples I have chosen to illustrate my contention that any consideration of "pleasure, reward, and preference" must perforce include personality as a crucial variable. By saying that this variable is crucial I mean that its inclusion in a proper experimental design is *mandatory;* we cannot put it in or leave it out as the fancy takes us. All other variables act in interaction with personality; leave out personality from the experimental design, and the whole pattern of interaction becomes confused and impossible to disentangle. The law of effect tells us that the effects of our actions dictate the future course of our behavior; it does not tell us that these effects are crucially dependent on the personality of the person concerned. Identical amounts of nicotine, administered under identical external circumstances, may have contradictory effects on an extravert and on an introvert; failure to control or measure the degree of extraversion–introversion of the subjects of the experiment must lead to failure to obtain replicable and meaningful results. Experimental psychology and personality study are not different and separate areas of study, which can afford to disregard each other; they are completely and utterly interdependent, and experiments, to be fruitful, must be set up in such a way as to take into account both aspects. The sad state of both sides illustrate the dangers of "going it alone"; no integrated science of psychology is likely to arise from such piecemeal endeavors.

References

Allport, G. V. The ego in contemporary psychology. *Psychological Review*, 1943, **50**, 451–478.

Allport, G. V. Effect: A secondary principle in learning. *Psychological Review*, 1946, **53**, 335–347.

Armitage, S. K., Hall, G. H. & Morrison, C. F. Pharmacological basis for the tobacco smoking habit. *Nature*, 1968, **217**, 331–334.

Ashton, H. & Watson, D. W. Puffing frequency and nicotine intake in cigarette smokers. *British Medical Journal*, 1970, 3, 679–681.

Bain, S. *The senses and the intellect* (3rd. ed.). New York: Longmans, Green, 1868.

Barr, R. F. & McConaghy, N. A general factor of conditionability: A study of galvanic skin responses and penile responses. *Behaviour Research & Therapy*, 1972, (in press).

Berlyne, D. E. *Conflict, arousal, and curiosity.* New York: McGraw-Hill, 1960.

Berlyne, D. E. *Aesthetics and psychobiology.* New York: Appleton, 1971.

Bernstein, B. A. Modification of smoking behaviour: an evaluational review. *Psychological Bulletin*, 1969, **71**, 418–440.

Blake, M. J. F. Relation between circadian rhythm of body temperature and introversion-extraversion. *Nature*, 1967, **215**, 896–897. (a)

Blake, M. J. F. Time of day effects on performance in a range of tasks. *Psychonomic Science*, 1967, **9**, 349–350. (b)

Brady, J. V. & Conrad, R. G. Some effects of limbic system self-stimulation upon unconditioned emotional behaviour. *Journal of Comparative & Physiological Psychology*, 1960, **53**, 128–137.

Delgado, M. M. R., Roberts, W. W. & Miller, N. E. Learning by electrical stimulation of the brain. *American Journal of Psychiatry*, 1954, **179**, 587–593.

Deneau, C. A. & Inoki, R. Nicotine self-administration in monkeys. In H. B. Murphree (Ed.). *The effects of nicotine and smoking in the central nervous system. Annals of the New York Academy of Sciences*, 1967, **142**, 277–279.

Eysenck, H. J. *The dynamics of anxiety and hysteria.* London: Routledge & Kegan Paul, 1957.

Eysenck, H. J. Emotion as a determinant of integrative learning: An experimental study. *Behaviour Research & Therapy*, 1963, **1**, 197–211, (a)

Eysenck, H. J. *Experiments with drugs.* Oxford: Pergamon, 1963. (b)

Eysenck, H. J. *Crime and personality.* New York: Hampton Mifflin, 1964.

Eysenck, H. J. Extraversion and the acquisition of eyeblink and GSR conditioned responses. *Psychological Bulletin*, 1965, **63**, 258–270.

Eysenck, H. J. *The biological basis of personality.* Springfield, Illinois: Thomas, 1967.

Eysenck, H. J. A theory of the incubation of anxiety/fear responses. *Behaviour Research & Therapy*, 1968, **6**, 309–321.

Eysenck, H. J. *The structure of human personality* (3rd. ed.). London: Methuen, 1970. (a)

Eysenck, H. J. Personality and attitudes to sex: a factorial study. *Personality*, 1970, **1**, 355–376. (b)

Eysenck, H. J. Personality and sexual adjustment. *British Journal of Psychiatry*, 1971, **118**, 593–608.

Eysenck, H. J. *Psychology is about people*, London: Allen, 1972.

Eysenck, H. J. Genetic factors in personality development. In A. R. Kaplan (Ed.). *Human Behavior Genetics*. (In press, 1973). (a)

Eysenck, H. J. Personality and the maintenance of the smoking habit. In: W. L. Dunn (Ed.) *Smoking behavior, motives, and incentives*. New York: Wiley, 1973. (b)

Eysenck, H. J. & Beech, R. Counter conditioning and related methods. In A. E. Bergin and S. L. Garfield (Eds.) *Handbook of Psychotherapy and Behaviour change*. New York: Wiley, 1971, 543–611.

Eysenck, H. J. & Eysenck, S. B. G. *The structure and measurement of personality*. London: Routledge & Kegan Paul, 1969.

Eysenck, H. J. & Levey, A. Konditionierung, Introversion-Extraversion und die Stärke des Nervensystems. *Zeitschrift für Psychologie*, 1967, **174**, 96–106.

Eysenck, H. J. & Rachman, S. *The Causes and cures of neurosis*. London: Routledge & Kegan Paul, 1965.

Freeman, H. L. & Kendrick, D. C. A case of cat phobia. *British Medical Journal*, 1960, **11**, 497–502.

Frith, C. The effect of varying the nicotine content of cigarettes on human smoking behaviour. *Psychopharmacologia*, 1971, **19**, 188–192. (a)

Frith, C. D. Smoking behaviour and its relation to the smoker's immediate experience. *British Journal of Social & Clinical Psychology*, 1971, **10**, 73–78. (b)

Giese, H. & Schmidt, S. *Studenten Sexualität*. Hamburg: Rowohlt, 1968.

Grastyan, E., Karmos, G., Vereczkey, L. & Kellenys, I. The hippocampal electrical correlates of the homeostatic regulation of motivation. *Electroencephalography and Clinical Neurophysiology*, 1966, **21**, 34–53.

Hare, R. D. *Psychopathy: Theory and research*. New York: Wiley, 1970.

Horn, D. *Use of Tobacco*. U.S. Dept. of Health, Education and Welfare, 1969.

Hull, C. L. *Principles of behavior*. New York: Appleton, 1943.

Hull, C. L. The place of innate individual and species differences in a natural-science theory of behavior. *Psychological Review*, 1945, **52**, 55–60.

Jarvik, N. E. Tobacco smoking in monkeys. In H. B. Murphree (Ed.). *The effects of nicotine and smoking on the central nervous system*. Annals of the New York Academy of Sciences, 1967, **142**, 280–294.

Jinks, J., & Fulker, D. W. Comparison of the biometrical, genetical, M.A.V.A. and classical approaches to the analysis of human behavior. *Psychological Bulletin*, 1970, **73**, 311–350.

Johnston, L. M. Tobacco smoking and nicotine. *Lancet*, 1942, Oct.–Dec., 742.

Kennedy, M. J. Operant conditioning of elderly female psychiatric patients. University of London: Unpublished Ph.D. Thesis, 1970.

Keutzer, C. S., Lichtenstern, E., & Mees, H. C. Modification of smoking behaviours: A review. *Psychological Bulletin*, 1968, **70**, 520–533.

Kimble, G. A. *Hilgard and Marquis' conditioning and learning*. New York: Appleton, 1961.

McKennell, A. C. Smoking motivation factors. *British Journal of Social & Clinical Psychology*, 1970, **9**, 8–22.

Miller, N. E. & Dollard, J. *Social learning and imitation*. New Haven, Connecticut: Yale Univ. Press, 1941.

Mowrer, O. H. A stimulus-response analysis of anxiety and its role as a reinforcing agent. *Psychological Review*, 1939, **46**, 553–565.

Mowrer, O. H. Anxiety-reduction and learning. *Journal of Experimental Psychology,* 1940, **27,** 497–516.

Mowrer, O. H. The law of effect and ego psychology. *Psychological Review,* 1946, **53,** 321–334.

Mowrer, O. H. & Lamoreaux, R. R. Avoidance conditioning and signal duration—a study of secondary motivation and reward. *Psychological Monographs,* 1942, **54,** No. 5.

Mowrer, O. H. & Lamoreaux, R. R. Fear as an intervening variable in avoidance conditioning. *Journal of Comparative Psychology,* 1946, **39,** 29–50.

Mowrer, O. H. & Ullman, A. D. Time as a determinant in integrative learning. *Psychological Review,* 1945, **52,** 61–90.

Muenzinger, K. F. The law of effect: A round table discussion. *Psychological Review,* 1938, **45,** 215–218.

Olds, J. & Milner, P. Positive reinforcement produced by electrical stimulation of septal area and other regions of rat brain. *Journal of Comparative Physiology,* 1954, **47,** 419–427.

Olds, J. & Olds, M. Drives, rewards and the brain. In *New directives in psychology, II.* New York: Holt, 1965.

Philipp, G. L. & Wilde, G. J. S. Stimulation seeking behaviour and extraversion. *Acta Psychologica,* 1970, **32,** 269–280.

Postman, L. The history and present states of the law of effect. *Psychological Bulletin,* 1947, **44,** 489–563.

Proosdy, C. van. *Smoking.* Amsterdam: Elsevier, 1960.

Rachman, S. Studies in desensitization—II: Flooding. *Behaviour Research & Therapy,* 1966, **4,** 1–6.

Rachman, S. *The effects of psychotherapy.* Oxford: Pergamon, 1972.

Rachman, S., Hodgson, R. & Marks, I. M. The treatment of chronic obsessive-compulsive neurosis. *Behaviour Research & Therapy,* 1971, **9** 237–248.

Rohrbaugh, M. & Riccio, D. C. Paradoxical enhancement of learned fear. *Journal of Abnormal Psychology,* 1970, **75,** 210–216.

Savage, R. D. & Eysenck, H. J. The definition and measurement of emotionality. In: H. J. Eysenck (Ed.). *Experiments in motivation.* Oxford: Pergamon, 1964, 292–314.

Schneirla, T. C. An evolutionary and developmental theory of biphasic processes underlying approach and withdrawal. In M. R. James (Ed.). Nebraska symposium on motivation. Lincoln: Univ. of Nebraska Press, 1959.

Spencer, H. *Principles of psychology.* London: Williams and Norgate, 1870.

Thorndike, E. L. *Animal intelligence: Experimental studies.* New York: Macmillan, 1911.

Valenstein, E. S. & Campbell, J. F. Medial forebrain bundle-lateral hypothalmic area and reinforcing brain stimulation. *American Journal of Physiology,* 1966, **210,** 270–274.

Weisen, A. Differential reinforcing effects of onset and offset of stimulation on the operant behavior of normals, neurotics and psychopaths. Univ. of Florida: Unpublished Ph.D. Thesis, 1965.

Wundt, W. M. *Grundzüge der physiologischen Psychologie.* Leipzig: Engelmann, 1874.

CHAPTER 7

A Common Model for Affectivity and Perception: An Adaptation-Level Approach

HARRY HELSON

El Cerrito, California

Traditionally, the subject matter of psychology has been divided into sensations, images, and feelings by content psychologists and into judging, ideating, and loving–hating by *Akt* psychologists (cf. Boring, 1950). Thus the earliest systems attempted to provide for the affective, motivational side of mental life and behavior. While Titchener believed he had achieved a purely unitary basis for structural psychology by reducing images and feelings to sensations, his reduction in the number of mental elements to one did not solve or advance the study of affects and motivation. Similarly the Gestalt psychologists, while stressing the dynamic character of perception, as opposed to the elementarism of the Wundtian structural approach, had little to say about the role of affective states in the formation and functioning of behavior patterns.

A frontal attack on the problems of perception and affectivity was attempted by the so-called New Look psychologists (cf. Helson, 1953, for a review and critique of this movement). They insisted that needs, values, and motives play a part in structuring perceptual processes. Autochthonous forces within Gestalten are not sufficient, they asserted, to account for the role of inner factors in perception. In the New Look account inner dynamisms seemed to stand outside perception and appeared to influence it only to distort experience toward subjective ends.

Werner and Wapner (1952) pointed out the difficulty in the New Look assumptions most succinctly when they said:

> This difficulty is concerned with the question how two alien elements, such as emotion, motivation, etc., on the one side, and visual and tactual processes, etc., on the other side, can influence each other and even fuse [p. 324].

Simply stating that there is an interaction of sensory and motivation factors does not solve the problem; rather it poses the crucial problem, they say, of how such interaction can take place. The solution proposed by Werner and Wapner, sensory-tonic theory, was to posit a tonic component in all perceptual processes, e.g., visual, auditory, etc. Covert or overt muscular changes in tonicity accompany every sensory impression they assume, and thus furnish the basis for the motivational, affective aspects of perception. While this theory broadened perception to include tonic factors in all sense modalities, it did not help explain other context effects, the influence of backgrounds and anchors on perception and judgment, and the role of altered states of the organism in stimulus–response relationships.

While it is true that inner states like needs, values, and drives affect perception, as the New Look psychologists maintained, it is equally true that perceptual states arouse feelings and emotions, drives, and the muscular and glandular changes accompanying them. Nowhere is the operation of feedback loops so clear and patent as in the perception–emotion–action systems involved in even the simplest types of responses. To ask which is first, needs or perception, is like asking: "Which came first, the hen or the egg?" And insofar as sensory-tonic theory is a theory of mental contents basically like the older structuralism it is subject to the same defects. A unitary theory is needed that envisages all processes, whether needs, values, perception, or cognition, as expressions of the organism's adaptations to the world around it.

At first sight, it might seem there is no essential connection between sensory processes and psychophysical judgment, where our theory originated, and affectivity and motivational processes, but when considered as adaptive in nature a common frame of reference is thereby immediately provided for them. In addition, we must not forget that affective, motivational, and preferential types of behavior have been scaled and indeed have given rise to special psychophysical methods, e.g., method of paired comparisons, order of merit, method of production, choice methods, and category ratings, each with appropriate statistics for evaluating measures of central tendency, dispersion, and correlation. But scalability in itself is not enough if it does not allow for the bipolar nature of feelings and emotions, for the influence of background and contextual stimuli, and for effects of previous experience.[1] Finally, inner and outer sources of stimulation must also be brought within a unitary theory so that special assumptions are unnecessary to account for their interaction.

The theory we propose assumes that all behavior is adaptive in nature and is referable to internal norms that are products of all relevant environmental and internal stimuli. These norms have proven to be weighted averages of focal, background, and residual stimuli in a variety of experimental situations ranging from psychophysical judging situations to interpersonal interactions (Helson, 1964). Instead of taking absolute thresholds or so-called effective thresholds, or complete lack of physical stimulation as representing behavioral zero, we take the adaptation-level (AL) as the zero or neutral of function. Since values of AL are nonzero and positive, stimuli above AL have qualities and magnitudes opposite to those below AL, whereas stimuli near AL are either neutral or ineffective. From this formulation the bipolar nature of all types of behavior immediately follows, especially affective and emotional responses whose bipolarity has long been recognized. These well-known propositions at the basis of AL theory are repeated here because they apply to feeling and emotion no less than to sensory processes and psychophysical data. Concretely, whether a stimulus is sensed and reacted to as loud or soft, bright or dim, beautiful or ugly, simple or complex, novel or hackneyed, and so on, depends upon its relation to prevailing ALs.

Before dealing specifically with affect and preference, it is necessary to define a few simple terms and to give illustrations of them in sensory and psychophysical data. We have already referred to focal, background, and residual stimuli and their meanings are self-evident in particular cases although it is difficult to draw sharp lines between them on purely a priori considerations. Since a number of stimuli of a certain kind are usually presented in psychological experiments, e.g., a series of weights to be lifted, or sounds to be judged, or colors to be rated for pleasantness, we refer to these as *series* stimuli and they are focal only during the time they are exposed. When a stimulus stands out from the others in a series by being exposed for a longer time, or by being much more intense, or by being presented more often than the other series stimuli,

---

[1] Neglect of background, anchoring, and contextual stimuli has probably been due in large part to the need for getting subjects, particularly subhuman and very young children, to attend and respond to what the experimenter wishes them to respond to; hence, the main concern with focal stimuli to the neglect of the others.

we refer to them as *predominant* stimuli. Special instructions serving to direct attention to one of a series of stimuli may make it a predominant stimulus. If a stimulus outside the series stimuli is presented but the instructions do not require subjects to judge or even attend to it, we call this an *anchor* or *background* stimulus. The backgrounds used in visual sensitivity experiments and in pleasantness ratings of colors are perhaps the best-known anchor or background stimuli. Finally, if series stimuli are compared with some designated stimulus, we refer to it as a *standard*. It is at once apparent that the amount of influence exerted by a stimulus on AL or its contribution in the pooling that results in the formation of ALs, will increase from series to predominant to anchor to standard stimulus, since there is more stimulation and involvement on the part of the subject as we go from the first to the last of these defined stimuli. While an individual series stimulus may have less weight in determining AL than, say, the background stimulus, the series stimuli taken as a whole may exert more weight than the background stimulus. Thus, in lifted weights experiments, the log mean of series stimuli had to be weighted three times as heavily as the anchor stimulus in approximating values of AL but in visual studies, the reverse was true: The background had to be weighted three times as heavily as the mean of the series stimuli. And when standards are provided their influence may be so great as to practically coincide with AL. The coefficients denoting the contributions of the various classes of stimuli must be determined from the results of particular experiments.

Adaptation Level and Psychophysical Judgments

Let us now consider some anchor effects in a simple psychophysical judging situation (Helson & A. Kozaki, 1968). Five squares, 36, 45, 54, 63, and 72 mm per side, were exposed in random order for .55 sec to five groups of subjects, 10 in each group. In the case of the control group, denoted by open circles in Fig. 7-1, the series stimuli were presented without an anchor. A second group was shown a small square, 18 mm on a side, for .10 sec, before each of the series stimuli but were not asked to make any judgment concerning its size. A third group had the small anchor which was exposed for 1.0 sec. A fourth group was presented an anchor 90 mm on a side serving as the large anchor for .10 sec and the fifth group was given the large anchor exposed for 1.0 sec. Judgments were made in terms of nine categories ranging from very, very small through medium to very, very large with numbers from 1 to 9 assigned to the categories for purposes of computation. As seen from Fig. 7-1,

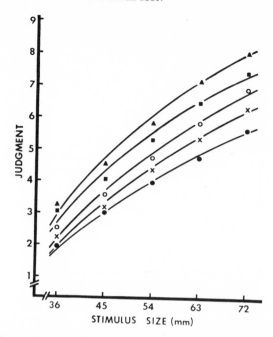

Fig. 7-1. Effects of size and duration of anchors on judgments of size of series stimuli. (From Helson and T. Kozaki, 1968, with permission from the *American Journal of Psychology.*) [(○): Control; (■): small anchor − .1 sec; (▲): small anchor − 1.0 sec; (×): large anchor − .1 sec; (●): large anchor − 1.0 sec.]

the judgments of the five groups are distinctly different. Large anchors depress and small anchors elevate judgments of all the stimuli. Moreover, the longer an anchor is exposed, the greater its effectiveness as either a large or a small anchor. Thus the judgments with small anchor exposed 1.0 sec are elevated more than with the same anchor exposed .10 sec; contrariwise, judgments with large anchor exposed for 1.0 sec are depressed more than with anchor exposed for .10 sec. It is evident that size and duration of exposure pool in the formation of AL underlying judgments of size.

In another experiment (Helson & T. Kozaki, unpublished), when the same series stimuli used above were presented in red and green colors in random order, effects of anchors acted selectively although no instructions were given the subjects to take the anchor into account: With large red anchor the red stimuli were depressed more than the green stimuli and vice versa when the large anchor was green (Fig. 7-2). Similarly, the small anchors had greater elevating effect on series stimuli of the

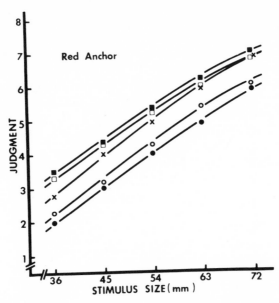

Fig. 7-2. Anchors have greater effects on judgments of size of series stimuli when both are of the same color, i.e., red on red, green on green. But anchors of different color still affect size judgments but to a lesser extent. (From Helson & Kozaki, unpublished study.) [Anchor: (●): large; (○): large; (■): small; (□): small; (×): control. Series stimuli: red, green, red, green respectively.]

same color than on stimuli of the other color. Taking such curves as are shown in Figs. 7-1 and 7-2 as indicative of the way the stimuli are organized, we must conclude that organization depends upon prevailing AL and thus becomes a derivative rather than a primitive concept contrary to the Gestalt point of view.

Shifts in judgments due to anchors such as those previously discussed have been explained as mere semantic changes or as due to changes on the response side only with no change in the sensory process itself. Such explanations are, in principle, the same as the old Helmholtzian explanation of simultaneous color contrast as errors in judgment but hardly any psychologists now living deny that the blue inducing effect of a yellow surround on an infield is a dimensional, sensory change. Why, then, should not a weight hefted after a heavier weight feel lighter, a tone heard after a louder tone sound softer, and so on through the whole gamut of perceptual processes? That these effects are not merely cases of classical contrast will be shown following a brief account of an *experimentum crucis* designed to lay the ghost of Helmholtzian-type explanations for context, and background effects. In this experiment (Helson & A. Kozaki, 1968), random patterns of 10, 12, 14, 16, and 18 dots were presented for .20 sec and subjects were required to report the number of dots perceived in *numbers*. The use of numbers in place of category ratings was to make sure subjects were reporting the actual number of dots seen under control and anchor conditions and not merely using a different response language. Four groups of five subjects observed under the following conditions: (1) series stimuli only were presented in random order; (2) a 4-dot anchor preceded each of the series stimuli; (3) a 13-dot anchor preceded each of the series stimuli; and (4) a 32-dot anchor preceded each series stimulus. The results, shown in Fig. 7-3, are similar to those obtained when category rating are used: small anchor raises, and large anchor reduces, the number of dots reported. The differences between the small and large anchor conditions are highly significant

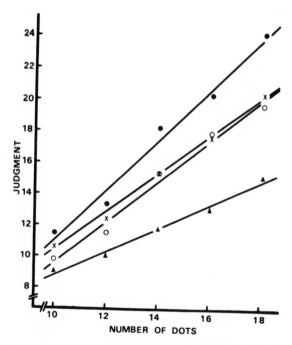

Fig. 7-3. Reports of number of dots perceived in random dot patterns are depressed with large (more numerous) dot anchors, raised with small (less numerous) dot anchors, and practically unaffected with anchor having the number of dots approximately at calculated AL for the series. (From Helson & A. Kozaki, 1968, with permission from *Perception and Psychophysics*.) [Number of dots of anchor: (●——●): 4; (×——×): 13; (▲——▲): 32; (○——○): control.]

$(F = 146.527; df = 4,64; p < .001)$ as is also the interaction between anchors and series stimuli $(F = 3.280; df = 12,24; p < .01)$. Use of the 13-dot anchor was to test anew the deduction from AL theory that stimuli at or near AL should neither raise nor depress judgments of series stimuli. This anchor was close to the value of AL calculated for a series of 12 to 18 dots, and as seen from Fig. 7-3, judgments with this anchor are not significantly different from the judgments of series stimuli without any anchor.

Having disposed of the argument that shifts due to anchors merely represent changes on the response and not on the sensory side, let us now consider an oft-made assumption that context and anchor effects are explainable in terms of classical contrast mechanisms with the implication that AL theory can handle contrast but not assimilation effects. Because contrast is an almost universal phenomenon in behavior, being found, for example, in sensory processes, in affective and motivational behavior, in reinforcement (in extinction as well as in conditioning), in attitude scaling, and in judgments of personality traits, etc., it is necessary to examine this concept in some detail. According to classical contrast theory, which is usually the prototype for its use in other areas, contrast is greater the nearer the contrasting elements. Carried over to the field of affectivity, it has been assumed that the pleasantness of a stimulus is enhanced or depressed by *immediately contiguous* or *preceding* stimuli. This view of contrast, no matter where it has been employed, does not account for the wider, more pervasive influence of stimuli more remote in space and/or time on stimuli in the focus of attention. Long ago Beebe-Center (1929, 1932) found that the pleasantness of individual colors was influenced not merely by the immediately preceding stimuli but by the whole series of colors preceding the focal stimulus. In reinforcement studies, including the extinction phase, a running average model has been more successful in predicting responses than models dealing with effects of single stimuli upon specific responses (Bevan, 1966; Bevan & Adamson, 1960, 1963). In short, contrast effects require that all parts of the visual field, the whole series of stimuli in affective and reinforcement situations, and even all the items in Thurstone-type scales when determining attitudes toward issues (Fehrer, 1952), or liking for foods (Jones, Peryam, & Thurstone, 1955), must be taken into account.

Since assimilation as well as contrast has been found in personality ratings and studies of attitudes, as well as in classical visual contrast situations, it should be pointed out that these phenomena are not separate, fundamentally opposed behavioral patterns but, as my co-workers and I have shown in a series of studies (Helson & Rohles, 1959; Helson

& Joy, 1962; Steger, 1969), there is a continuum of conditions giving rise at one end to classical contrast and to assimilation (reversal of classical contrast) at the other end with a neutral zone between in which there is neither contrast nor assimilation. And in scaling attitudes it has been shown (Helson, 1964) that if items are displaced away from each other (contrast) in one part of the scale, they must move closer together in other parts of the scale (assimilation) if the scale is finite and has fixed end points.

We can best demonstrate the difference between classical contrast theory and AL theory by an experiment dealing with shifts in judgment due to the influence of predominant stimuli. A series of gray squares, 36, 45, 54, 63, and 72 mm per side, were exposed randomly in the case of one group for .20 sec; a second group was shown the squares for .20 sec, with the exception of the topmost member of the series, 72 mm, which was exposed for 1.0 sec, thereby making it a predominant member of the series; the third group was shown the squares for .20 sec, except for the bottom series stimulus which was exposed for 1.0 sec, making it the predominant member of the series. As seen in Fig. 7-4, overexposure of the largest square caused a downward shift in judgments of *all* the stimuli, including the largest square itself, whereas overexposure of the smallest square caused an upward shift in the three smaller members of the series, including the smallest square. Since the shifts in judgment included the stimuli responsible for the shifts they cannot be attributed to contrast for if the largest square contrasted with the other members of the series it should have been judged larger, not smaller, when made the predominant stimulus; and the same holds true for the upward shift in the judgment of the smallest stimulus when it was made predominant. We explain the shifts as due to change in AL which affects judgments of all the stimuli. The more extended study dealing with pooling of size and duration and the quantitative treatment of the results has been referred to earlier (Helson & T. Kozaki, 1968). The fact that judgments of the two top members of the series with 36 mm as predominant stimulus were not elevated above the control judgments may be attributed to the use of independent groups with normal variation in group ALs. However, since our argument concerns the judgments of the predominant stimuli primarily its validity is not impugned (Helson & T. Kozaki, unpublished data).

Finally, regarding the question of contrast it should be pointed out that contrast lies on a continuum extending from classical brightness and chromatic contrast to assimilation of the von Bezold type wherein brighter areas *lighten* surrounds and darker areas darken surrounds with

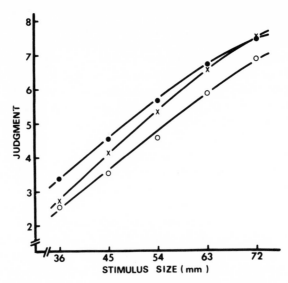

Fig. 7-4. Longer exposure of a series stimulus (72 mm in the case of the lower curve and 36 mm for the upper curve) makes it a predominant stimulus with resultant shifts in judgment as compared with each other and with the control curve. Since the predominant stimulus is depressed in the one case and raised in the other, the shifts in judgment cannot be attributed to contrast which must predict exactly the opposite shift to what was found. (Helson & T. Kozaki, unpublished study.) [(×): Control; (○): 72 mm; (●): 36 mm.]

an intermediate region in which there is neither contrast nor assimilation (Helson & Rohles, 1959; Helson & Joy, 1962; Helson, 1963; Steger, 1969). Bringing these apparently opposed processes within a common frame of reference in the sensory–psychophysical area can serve as a model in handling their counterparts in other fields of psychology.

Adaptation Level and Affective Judgments

Transfer of the AL model from its origin in sensory and psychophysical processes to the field of affectivity and preference can be made without new assumptions or stretching the theory beyond its legitimate limits, for affective states offer even more fertile grounds for its application then sensory and perceptual processes for a number of reasons. First, affects and preferences are more subject to adaptation and contrast-assimilation than are perceptual processes. Had the author of AL theory worked originally in feelings and emotions, instead of in perception and psychophysics, AL theory could well have originated there. Second, nowhere is the bipolarity of behavior more evident than in the field of affectivity and preference as shown by the opposition of pleasantness–unpleasantness, emotions that expand or contract the personality, acceptance–rejection forms of response, positive and negative reinforcement, and, in behavioristic terms, approach–avoidance behavior. Shifts in affective ratings due to anchors parallel those found in sensory and psychophysical judgments and are just as great as shown by the following experiments.

In an experiment conducted some years ago, 9 subjects first rated 40 advertisements of various kinds: large, small, colored, black and white, pictorial or mostly printed matter, etc., on a scale from extremely unpleasant (10) through indifferent (50) to extremely pleasant (90). From the 40 ads 8 were selected for each subject on the pleasant side (mean rating 58.6) and again rated with one of their most pleasant choices casually exposed in the field of view but without any instructions to use them as standards. The second ratings dropped to 37.7, definitely on the unpleasant side. Similarly, another 8 ads on the unpleasant side with mean of 36.5 were rated again with one of the most unpleasant ads for each subject plainly in the field of view whereupon the ratings rose to 50.9, slightly pleasant. These affective shifts seem to be as automatic and nonreflective (except for the necessity of assigning a category rating) as psychophysical judgments are when the absolute rating method is employed. Long ago Hunt and Volkmann (1937) found that merely "keeping the most pleasant color in mind" when making ratings of pleasantness judgments caused a drop in the judgments compared with the "no anchor" condition. These workers also found that colors nearest the mental anchor shifted more than farther removed stimuli, a finding exactly similar to psychophysical judging with real anchors. Indeed, mental anchors seem to be more effective in the field of affectivity than in the field of sensation–perception, a result that fits a priori considerations based on everyday experience where affects are more easily aroused by imagining and thinking than are sensory processes.

According to the theory proposed here, all conditions in the stimulating situation, not to mention residuals within the organism, affect AL with resultant effects on what is perceived and responded to. The next and final study to be discussed in this paper was designed to investigate the role of source of illumination and background on the pleasantness of object colors. These sources of variance were singled out for study because they have been largely neglected in the voluminous literature dealing with color preferences. Almost without exception color preferences have been studied in one source of illumination (often unspecified), and with the colors exposed on neutral backgrounds. The conditions for this study (Helson & Lansford, 1970), were are follows: subjects viewed 125 Munsell colors, 2.5 × 2.5 cm on 25 colored backgrounds in five sources of illumination. Both the object and background colors included a white, gray, and black. The object colors were exposed about 12 at a time on a given background (43.2 × 55.9 cm) in a given illumination with enough of the background around each object color to provide contrast. The sources ranged from warm white (2854 K) to cool daylight (6500 K) and included two tungsten and three fluorescent lamps as given in the key in Fig. 7-5. Ten subjects, five men and five women, rated the object colors in terms of a rating scale ranging from very, very

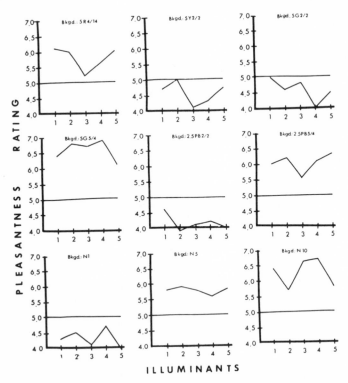

Fig. 7-5. Changes in ratings of pleasantness of Munsell 5R 2/2 due to changes in source of illumination and to color of background as shown at the top of each panel. The sources are keyed as follows: 1 = filtered tungsten (6500 K); 2 = incandescent filament (2854 K); 3 = fluorescent standard warm white (3000 K); 4 = fluorescent cool white, deluxe equivalent (4500 K); 5 = fluorescent daylight (6500 K).

unpleasant (1) through indifferent (5) to very, very pleasant (9). Colors and backgrounds were randomized for each subject within a given illuminant. In addition, ratings were made of the backgrounds with no object colors present in order to obtain judgments of relatively large areas of color without contrast effect.

Considering the effects of sources, we find that differences due to sources were small but statistically significant. The best source judged by the average of the 125 object colors across all backgrounds was 4500 K fluorescent cool white, whereas that for the large areas was 6500 K filtered incandescent daylight (Macbeth daylight). Differences due to sources appear very clearly in Figs. 7-5 and 7-6. In Fig. 7-5, Munsell 5 R 2/2 (a red of low chroma and low value or lightness), is plotted in five sources on nine different backgrounds. These plots show that color of background is much more important than spectral energy of the source but the latter cannot be neglected in studies of the aesthetics of colors. The plots in Fig. 7-6 of 5 R 4/14 on 25 different backgrounds in two

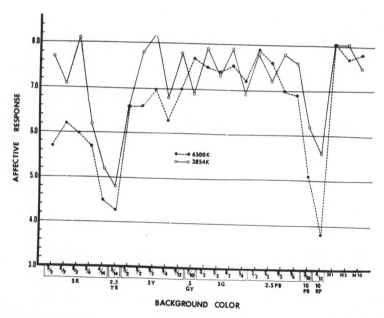

Fig. 7-6. Pleasantness ratings of Munsell 5R 4/14 on 25 colored backgrounds viewed in 6500 K incandescent filament filtered light and 2854 K incandescent lamp light. It is seen that 2854 K yields generally higher ratings than the 6500 K lamp and that the ratings on certain backgrounds drop sharply in the case of this object color.

sources show that one of the sources, 2854 K incandescent lamp light, is generally rated higher than the other, which is 6500 K incandescent filtered light (Macbeth daylight).

From the data in Figs. 7-5 and 7-6 it is evident that effects of sources on the pleasantness of colors cannot be divorced from the effects of the backgrounds forming a context for the perceived object colors. Thus in Fig. 7-6, 5 R 4/14 is rated pleasant in most cases but this color drops sharply when viewed on a background of the same color, 5 R 4/14 and on a similar color, 2.5 YR 5/14, and again on 10 RP 4/12. Background colors good in one source tend to be good in all but there may be important exceptions as seen from Table VII in the publication from which we are quoting (Helson & Lansford, 1970). The best background colors are either light or dark because they provide maximum lightness contrast. One of the most surprising results of this study was the fact that white (Munsell 10/) was the best background color in four of the five illuminants and it rated third in the fifth source judged by the average ratings of all 125 Munsell colors. The interaction of source and background color is perhaps most strikingly demonstrated by the fact that some backgrounds do not appear among the top third in some sources: For example, in 2854 incandescent lamp light no blue background is among the top eight; in 6500 K fluorescent light no green background is among the top eight; and in 6500 K incandescent filtered light no red background appears among the top eight. Since the backgrounds were evaluated in terms of the average ratings of all the object colors on each background this means that the ability of background color to enhance object colors depends not only on its own (daylight) color but also on the spectral energy distribution (or color) of the source. Conversely, a color may be pleasant or unpleasant, depending upon the color of source and background in which it is viewed (cf. Helson & Lansford, 1970, Table XIV, pp. 1526 ff.).

Just as illuminant and background colors cannot be separated in their effects on object colors, so the latter cannot be separated from the former. Whether or not it is true that all colors are inherently pleasant, as some have maintained, it is certain that the pleasantness of object colors depends upon background and predominant colors in the field of view, and even on the colors of other, smaller objects in the field. Insofar as generalizations can be made by averaging across sources and backgrounds, it appears that the pleasant hues are found mostly in the blue, purple–blue, green and blue–green color families. Whereas the unpleasant colors tend to be green–yellow, or yellow (cf. Guilford, 1934) and are very weakly saturated (/2 in the Munsell system). However, we shall see that there are important sex differences in color preferences. Cutting across source and background effects we must consider the roles of hue, value (lightness), and chroma (saturation) and the contrasts of these with their background counterparts. In general, more saturated colors are preferred to the less saturated ones as shown by the fact that the 25 highest average rankings (20% of the 125 object colors) have Munsell chromas of /6 or higher with only two exceptions; conversely, of the 25 lowest pleasantness rankings, all except five, have chromas of /2 which is the first step in chroma beyond the gray scale in the Munsell system. (Helson & Lansford, 1970, Table IX, p. 1523). The results for value (lightness, brightness) are not so clear-cut, since the top 25 object colors have low to intermediate values (2/-5/) whereas the bottom 25 have values ranging from 2/ to 8/.

The story with respect to the role of hue is also not a simple one. It is often asserted that differences in hue should be either zero, small, or large but not intermediate in order to make pleasant color combinations. The average hue differences between the best and poorest color combinations in our study give minimal support to this rule of thumb. Hue differences of either zero, 40, 45, and 50 in the Munsell 0–100 hue scale are slightly more often pleasant than unpleasant but the opposite is true for hue differences of 5 to 25 hue steps. Another oft-quoted rule, that complementary colors make the best color combinations also receives no support from our data (cf. Helson & Lansford, 1970, Table XX, p. 1535). We must conclude that hue differences of any size may be pleasant or unpleasant. The finding that colors of the same hue (zero difference) may be pleasant is very surprising but this happens only when there is lightness or chroma contrast, subjects to which we now turn.

Pleasant contrasts in chroma must be fairly large—from 6 to 14 Munsell chroma steps as seen from Table 7-1, where the frequency of these chroma differences is greater in the pleasant than in the unpleasant color combinations. While the smaller chroma contrast of four steps numbers 102 among the pleasant color combinations there are 135 of this magnitude among the unpleasant combinations. With zero chroma difference between object and background color the result may be pleasant or unpleasant as shown by the frequencies of 204 and 188, respectively. The results on chroma contrast are probably biased because there were 63 colors with low chroma, /2, as against 39 with high chroma, /6-/14. It is to be hoped that, in future studies, a larger proportion of high chromas will be used but this will be difficult because it is not possible to obtain as high saturations in some colors as in others, e.g., the maximum chroma for 5G at the 5/ value level is only /8, all other maxima

TABLE 7–1

Frequencies of Chroma Contrasts in the Five Best and Five Poorest Object–Background Color Combinations [a]

Difference in Munsell chroma steps	Best combinations	Poorest combinations
14	3	0
12	30	1
10	72	33
8	92	55
6	90	73
4	102	135
2	95	158
0	204	188
Total	688 [b]	643 [b]

[a] From Helson and Lansford (1970), with the permission of the Optical Society of America.

[b] The total number of best and poorest color combinations is not the same because of tied values necessitating inclusion of more than five ratings for some object colors.

being no more than /6 for this color and /6 for all 7.5 greens, 10.0 greens, and 2.5, 5.0, and 7.5 blue–greens.

We now come to the most important and most clear-cut finding in our study of color preferences, that of the effect of lightness contrast. Inspection of Table 7-2 shows that value differences of three or more are far greater among the pleasant color combinations than among the unpleasant combinations and that small or zero lightness contrasts (differences of zero or two in the Munsell value scale) almost guarantee an unpleasant effect. Our conclusions regarding chroma and lightness contrast are borne out by statistical analysis given in the original report (cf. Helson & Lansford, 1970, Tables XVIII and XIX, p. 1534).

Next to the clear-cut effect of lightness contrast are the sex differences between men and women in their color preferences which hold for object colors, background colors, and color of sources of illumination. Women rate object colors of warm hues (red to yellow) higher in all sources than do men while the latter rate the cool colors (green–yellow to blue to red–purple) higher (Table 7-3). Ratings of preference for the warm colors are also higher in the case of women on 23 to 25 of the backgrounds whereas the preference for the cool colors by men shows itself on from 17 to 23 of the 25 backgrounds as seen in Table 7-4.

TABLE 7-2

Frequencies of Lightness Contrasts of the Best and Poorest Five Object–Background Color Combinations [a]

Difference in Munsell value steps	Best combinations	Poorest combinations
8	15	0
7	58	1
6	194	4
5	95	5
4	85	3
3	195	20
2	28	42
1	9	172
0	9	396
Total	688 [b]	643 [b]

[a] From Helson and Lansford (1970), with the permission of the Optical Society of America.

[b] See footnote to Table 7-1.

A question never before raised in psychological studies of color preferences and color harmonies is answered for the first time so far as the data of this investigation are concerned: What neighboring or similar colors may be interchanged and still yield a pleasant combination with any given colored background? This question arises when it is not possible to obtain the exact color desired in a color combination. The answer is contained in a threefold classification of color pairs: (1) Some colors are judged almost identically on all backgrounds and so may be substituted one for the other. These colors are: 5R and 10R, 5YR and 10YR, 5Y and 10Y, 5G and 10G, 5B and 10B, and 5P and 10P. (2) Some hues are not interchangeable because one is better on all backgrounds than the other. The hues in this class are: 10YR and 5Y, 5GY and 10GY, and 5PB and 10PB. (3) Neither consistently the same nor better over all backgrounds are the hues in the third class which consists of 10R and 5YR, 10Y and 5GY, 10GY and 5G, 10G and 5BG, 5BG and 10BG, 10BG and 5B, 10B and 5PB, 10PB and 5P, 10P and 5RP, and 10RP and 5R. Inspection of Figs. 6-15 in the original study (Helson & Lansford, 1970) yields the graphical evidence for distinguishing between these three classes of colors. Space does not permit reproduction of these figures in this discussion. A single generalization, however, can be made from these

TABLE 7–3

Sex Differences in Effects of Sources of Illumination on Pleasantness Ratings of Color Families [a]

Color family	Illuminants preferred by women	Illuminants preferred by men
5R	1,4,5 [b]	2,3
10R	1,2,3,4,5	
5YR	1,2,3,4,5	
10YR	1,2,3,4,5	
5Y	1,2,3,4,5	
10Y	1,4,5	3
5GY	4,5	1,2,3
10GY	1	2,3,4,5
5B		1,2,3,4,5
10B	3	1,2,4,5
5PB		1,2,3,4,5
10PB		1,2,3,4,5
10P	4	1,2,3,5
5RP		1,2,3,4,5
10RP	4,5	2,3

[a] From Helson and Lansford, 1970, with the permission of the Optical Society of America.

[b] Key to sources: 1 = 6500 K filtered filament; 2 = 2854 K filament; 3 = 3000 K fluorescent; 4 = 4500 K fluorescent; 5 = 6500 K fluorescent (Macbeth Daylight).

TABLE 7–4

Differential Background Effects on Ratings of Eight Color Families by Men and Women [a]

Color family	Number of backgrounds on which object colors were rated higher by women	Number of backgrounds on which object colors were rated higher by men
10R	23 (92%)	2 (8%)
5YR	25 (100%)	0
10YR	25 (100%)	0
5GY	8 (32%)	17 (68%)
5P	2 (8%)	23 (92%)
10P	4 (16%)	21 (84%)
5RP	3 (12%)	22 (88%)
10RP	8 (32%)	17 (68%)

[a] From Helson and Lansford, 1970, by permission of the Optical Society of America.

results but with some reservations: Closely related *unitary* and almost unitary hues, like 5R and 10R, 5Y and 10Y, 5G and 10G, and 5B and 10B, make equally good or poor combinations with other colors. We venture the guess that the reason for this is that binary hues such as GY, PB, or RP, are subject to double contrast effects with one of the components accentuated at the expense of the other, thus reducing the overall liveliness of the color.

Our study of color preferences demonstrates very clearly that the aesthetic effects of colors depend not only on their specific hue, chroma, and lightness but more importantly upon the backgrounds on which they are viewed, the context of other colors in the field of view, and upon the spectral energy distribution of the source illuminating the entire visual field. Adaptation-level theory provides an economical way of treating the pooled effect of all these factors.

Measurement of Affective Responses

We must finally deal with the problem of measuring affective responses, since the main emphasis in modern scaling has been concerned with measuring fairly neutral sensory processes. Like the classical Weber and Weber–Fechner laws, the power law merely substitutes another monotonic function in place of the older formulations (Stevens, 1957). The psychophysical functions so far proposed do not take into account the bipolarity of affective and motivational behavior nor even the affective aspects of sensory processes. The power law never even hints that a sound 110 dB above threshold is unbearably unpleasant while one 10 dB may be too soft for comfortable hearing, or that a sound of a given intensity may be judged loud in the quiet of night and soft against the noises of a busy street. It is not enough to give the scale values of two stimuli whether on an interval, ratio, or whatever kind of scale, for two stimuli x units apart on one side of AL are quite different from two stimuli x units apart but on different sides of AL. If AL is between two stimuli, their qualitative, often affective, differences are much more important than their mere intensity difference. This is especially important when the stimuli concern affective and emotional reactions for stimuli on one side of AL may be accepted while those on the other side are rejected. The literature on contrast effects in reinforcement (Bower, 1961, 1962) bear this out and its importance for sensory and cognitive processes in animal studies has been shown by Martha Wilson (1972) who found that rhesus monkeys discriminated stimuli on opposite sides of visual ALs for length, orientation, and density better than equally spaced stimuli on the same side of prevailing AL. Scales must therefore provide for the bipolarity of responses in cognitive as well as in affective–emotional types of responses.

Still other problems require consideration within the framework of AL theory. It has often been said that a good theory raises problems as well as solves them. Among problems that have been raised anew as a result of AL considerations is the nature of the intensity–affect function: Is it unimodal or bimodal (cf. Berlyne, 1967) Looft (1971) maintains that unimodal curves are the result of averaging across subjects, that individual curves are always bimodal. This position may be true for affective value of simple, sensory processes where intensities near AL are neutral and affects increase in pleasantness on both sides of AL for a time and then fall to become unpleasant with wider departures from AL as in the so-called butterfly curve of Haber (1958). However, monotonic functions containing provision for neutral, indifferent states and for degrees of pleasantness on one side of AL and unpleasantness on the other side of AL are possible as Woodworth (1938) pointed out when he stated that various kinds of esthetic objects may be arranged from least to most pleasant on a single continuum. Indeed, as already pointed out, order of merit and rank order methods are examples of monotonic orderings of affective stimuli (cf. Guilford, 1954, whose "composite standard," or series as a whole, is essentially similar to the AL concept). A final problem, the existence of multiple ALs simultaneously and more or less independent of one another has been solved in the case of ALs within and across sensory modalities by Bevan and his co-workers (cf. Bevan, 1968; Bevan & Pritchard, 1963; and Helson & T. Kozaki, 1968).

In closing, there is one cardinal principle that summarizes all AL theory and may be stated as follows: There is no change in behavior, at any level, without a change in the internal norm (AL) underlying that behavior. Norms may be changed by varying input (focal or background stimuli) or by varying residuals (prevailing ALs, past experience, and other factors within the organism). With this principle in mind, no further summary of AL theory is necessary.

References

Beebe-Center, J. G. The law of affective equilibrium. *American Journal of Psychology*, 1929, 41, 54–69.

Beebe-Center, J. G. *The psychology of pleasantness and unpleasantness*. Princeton, New Jersey: Van Nostrand-Reinhold, 1932.

Berlyne, D. E. Arousal and reinforcement. In D. Levine (Ed.), *Nebraska Symposium on Motivation, 1967*. Lincoln: Univ. of Nebraska Press, 1967.

Bevan, W. An adaptation-level interpretation of reinforcement. *Perceptual & Motor Skills,* 1966, **23,** 511–531.

Bevan, W. The contextual basis of behavior. *American Psychologist,* 1968, **23,** 701–714.

Bevan, W., & Adamson, R. Reinforcers and reinforcement: Their relation to maze performance. *Journal of Experimental Psychology,* 1960, **59,** 226–232.

Bevan, W., & Adamson, R. Internal referents and the concept of reinforcement. In N. F. Washburne (Ed.), *Decisions, values, and groups,* Vol. 2. Oxford: Pergamon, 1963.

Bevan, W., & Pritchard, Joan F. The anchor effect and the problem of relevance in the judgment of shape. *Journal of General Psychology,* 1963, **69,** 147–161.

Boring, E. G. *A history of psychology.* (2nd ed.), New York: Appleton, 1950.

Bower, G. H. A contrast effect in differential conditioning. *Journal of Experimental Psychology,* 1961, **62,** 196–199.

Bower, G. H. The influence of graded reductions in reward and prior frustrating events upon the magnitude of the frustrating event. *Journal of Comparative and Physiological Psychology,* 1962, **55,** 582–587.

Fehrer, E. V. Shifts in scale values of attitude statements as a function of the composition of the scale. *Journal of Experimental Psychology,* 1952, **44,** 179–188.

Guilford, J. P. The affective value of color as a function of hue, tint, and chroma. *Journal of Experimental Psychology,* 1934, **17,** 342–370.

Guilford, J. P. *Psychometric methods.* (2nd. ed.). New York: McGraw-Hill, 1954.

Haber, R. N. Discrepancy from adaptation level as a source of affect. *Journal of Experimental Psychology,* 1958, **56,** 370–375.

Helson, H. Perception and personality—A critique of recent experimental literature. *United States Air Force School of Aviation Medical Reports,* Project 21-0202-0007, Report 1, 1953.

Helson, H. Adaptation-level theory: *An experimental and systematic approach to behavior.* New York: Harper, 1964.

Helson, H., & Joy, V. Domains of lightness assimilation and contrast effects in vision. *Psychologische Beiträge,* 1962, **6,** 405–415.

Helson, H., & Kozaki, A. Anchor effects using numerical estimates of simple dot patterns. *Perception & Psychophysics,* 1968, **4,** 163–164.

Helson, H., & Kozaki, T. Effects of duration of series and anchor stimuli on judgments of perceived size. *American Journal of Psychology,* 1968, **81,** 291–302.

Helson, H., & Lansford, T. The role of spectral energy of source and background color in the pleasantness of object colors. *Applied Optics,* 1970, **9,** 1513–1562.

Helson, H., & Rohles, F. H., Jr. A quantitative study of reversal of classical lightness-contrast. *American Journal of Psychology,* 1959, **72,** 530–538.

Hinckley, E. D., & Rethlingshafer, D. Value judgments of heights of men by college students. *Journal of Psychology,* 1951, **31,** 257–262.

Hunt, W. A., & Volkmann, J. The anchoring of an affective scale. *American Journal of Psychology,* 1937, **49,** 88–92.

Jones, L. V., Peryam, D. E., & Thurstone, L. L. Development of a scale for measuring soldiers' food preferences. *Food Research,* 1955, **20,** 515–520.

Judd, D. B. Choosing pleasant color combinations. *Lighting Design and Applications,* 1971, **3,** 31–41.

Looft, W. R. The unimodal preference-for-complexity function: Artifact? *Journal of General Psychology,* 1971, **85,** 239–243.

Rethlingshafer, D., & Hinckley, E. D. Influence of characteristics of judges on their psychophysical judgments. *American Psychologist*, 1954, **9**, 454.

Steger, J. A. Visual lightness assimilation and contrast as a function of differential stimulation. *American Journal of Psychology*, 1969, **82**, 56–72.

Stevens, S. S. On the psychophysical law. *Psychological Review*, 1957, **64**, 153–181.

Werner, H., & Wapner, S. Toward a general theory of perception. *Psychological Review*, 1952, **59**, 324–328.

Wilson, Martha. Assimilation and contrast effects in visual discrimination by Rhesus monkeys. *Journal of Experimental Psychology*, 1972, **93**, 279–282.

Woodworth, R. S. *Experimental psychology*. (1st ed.). New York: Holt, 1938.

Additional References Germane to this Discussion

Appley, M. H. (Ed.). *Adaptation-level theory: A symposium*. New York: Academic Press, 1971.

Di Lollo, V., & Beeze, V. Negative contrast effect as a function of magnitude of reward decrement. *Psychonomic Science*, 1966, **5**, 99–100.

Ekman, G. Quantitative approaches to psychological problems. In F. Lindblom (Ed.), *Theory and methods in behavioral sciences*. Stockholm: Norstedt, 1970. Pp. 53–72.

Helson, H. Studies of anomalous contrast and assimilation. *Journal of the Optical Society of America*, 1963, **53**, pp. 179–184.

Helson, H. Some problems in motivation from the point of view of the theory of adaptation level. In D. Levine (Ed.), *Nebraska Symposium on Motivation*, 1966. Lincoln: Univ. of Nebraska Press, 1966. Pp. 137–182.

Helson, H. Adaptation-level theory: 1970 and after. In M. H. Appley (Ed.), *Adaptation-level theory: A symposium*. New York: Academic Press, 1971. Pp. 5–17.

Helson, H., Blake, R. R., & Mouton, Jane S. Petition-signing as adjustment to situational and personal factors. *Journal of Social Psychology*, 1958, **48**, 3–10.

Marimont, R. B. Model for visual response to contrast. *Journal of the Optical Society of America*, 1962, **52**, 800–806.

McClelland, D. C., Atkinson, J. W., Clark, R. A., & Lowell, E. L. *The achievement motive*. New York: Appleton, 1953.

Restle, F. A., & Greeno, J. G. *Introduction to mathematical psychology*. Reading, Massachusetts: Addison-Wesley, 1970.

CHAPTER 8

Acquired Pleasantness and Conditioned Incentives in Verbal Learning [1]

ALBERT SILVERSTEIN

University of Rhode Island

Introduction

Level of performance in the learning of different verbal materials in both academic and professional settings is well known to vary not only with the difficulty of the materials but also with their attractiveness and interestingness; i.e., their incentive value. Speculations about the reasons why materials of differing incentive value produce differences in level of performance must be verified ultimately by attempting to build in such differences experimentally. This raises the question: "What are the necessary and sufficient conditions for neutral verbal stimuli to become incentives for learning?" This chapter will report the results of a number of experiments investigating that question. The fundamental approach used was to attempt to alter the incentive value of neutral nonsense syllables through various manipulations and to delineate the details of the manipulations that do or do not produce alterations in the subsequent speed and style of learning of those syllables.

[1] The research reported here was supported by Grant MH 08974 from the National Institute of Mental Health, U.S. Public Health Service. The author wishes to thank Richard A. Dienstbier, Lionel Blatchley, Alice Marshall, Phillip Marshall and Muriel Kantrowitz for their assistance in the conduct and analysis of these experiments.

189

Much of the difficulty encountered in attempting to deal with the question of how incentives develop stems from the widely held view that this is the same question as that of how a stimulus acquires pleasantness (PL). It is an *empirical* issue however, whether materials which have acquired PL have also, thereby, acquired incentive value. Pleasantness is always defined by a subject's verbal judgments of a generally undefined affective quality, whereas incentive stimuli are specified by the performance of some class of behavior which increases or renews the subject's sensory contact with those stimuli, whether by (a) locomotion toward them, (b) receptor orientation toward them or (c) the performance of acts which the subject has learned will be followed by them. A common and plausible assumption has been that these criteria are highly correlated and are all indices of a generalized approach tendency (Schneirla, 1959), but this assumption has not been firmly proven by the evidence available and it is criterion (c), the selective performance criterion, that will be used in the remainder of this essay. Even this criterion includes such diverse behaviors as consistent turning in a T maze, spending additional hours on the job, purchasing an item or rehearsing certain stimuli more vigorously, but they all indicate that the subject "expects" the incentive to follow his act. Thus, the selective performance criterion, as a whole, is relevant to the level of performance in a learning task and is in keeping with the prevailing definition of the concept of incentive value (cf. Spence, 1956).

The total confusion of the empirically distinct concepts of incentive value and pleasantness is part of the legacy from psychology's introspectionist days, (cf., Beebe-Center, 1932) and even an adroit investigator of human incentives like Thorndike (1931) gratuitously assumed that subjects can reliably judge their own selective approach tendencies toward stimuli, whatever the circumstances of judgment. An early protest against the assumption of identity between affective and incentive stimuli was made by Peters (1935) in formulating his "judgmental theory of feeling," in which he asserted that the relative PL of stimuli refers to no specific conscious content, but only to judgments per se of these alleged affective states. He claimed that such judgments are based upon an assessment of one's *typical* tendency to approach or withdraw from stimuli but are not necessarily coexistent with the occurrence of the emotional stimuli that originally produced such approach or withdrawal. Thus, for example, familiarization with a stimulus may habituate or extinguish the emotional response to it while leaving intact the affective judgment. Berlyne (1971) has provided impressive evidence that judgments of PL often have only moderate degrees of correlation with indices of interest or measures of viewing time, and that the two classes of variable yield different curves in relation to stimulus features like novelty and complexity. Still, the assumption of identity between the two classes of stimuli has been a prevalent feature of the thinking of most investigators of the acquisition of human incentives and has hampered our ability to form clear conclusions about this acquisition process. For these reasons, the experiments to be reported here were also addressed to the question of when increases in the PL of nonsense syllables will and will not be accompanied by increases in their incentive value as indexed by performance in a learning task.

The hypothesis which served as the paradigm for the current studies was the contiguous conditioning hypothesis of secondary reinforcement (Wike, 1966) which is based on the assumption that the contingent presentation of a neutral stimulus with a preexperimental reinforcer will enhance the reinforcing power of the former. Since reinforcement value and incentive value may, but need not, coincide (cf. Berlyne, 1967), this hypothesis was modified in the present case to read that the contingent occurrence of a neutral stimulus with a preexperimental incentive would enhance the incentive value of the former. Prior to the present series of experiments that hypothesis remained virtually untested. However, there is a vast body of relevant experiments demonstrating that contiguous conditioning of neutral to highly pleasant stimuli will enhance the PL of the former, and Staats (1964) has hypothesized that the conditioning of an implicit affective or evaluative response (r_m) to previously neutral stimuli will mediate acquisition of incentive characteristics by the neutral stimuli. Razran (1938a, b, 1940a, b, 1956) found an increase in PL for a variety of different stimuli after subjects ate in their presence, and suggested that this increase was mediated by the concurrent conditioning of the salivary response. His hypothesis received support from Sheridan's (1966) demonstration that degree of shift in evaluation was correlated with amplitude of the conditioned salivary response. On the negative side of affectivity, it was shown that electric shock administered while viewing words can lower their evaluation, and that the degree of this shift is correlated with the amplitude of GSR conditioned to the words (Staats, Staats, & Crawford, 1962). A number of experiments have used emotionally loaded words to alter the evaluation of neutral verbal items with which such words were paired (DiVesta & Stover, 1962; Paivio, 1969; Staats & Staats, 1957; Staats, Statts, & Biggs, 1958; Yavuz, 1963). Since emotionally laden words are assumed to have been conditioned themselves, such experiments demonstrated the occurrence of "higher-order conditioning" (Staats, 1964; 1968). It should be noted that the negative shifts produced by "bad" words were far more impressive than the positive shifts produced by "good" words in these experiments. The degree of shift in the evaluative meaning of the neutral stimuli was shown to vary with the number of pairings with the loaded words (Staats & Staats, 1959b) and to generalize to synonyms (Staats & Staats, 1959a). Shifts in affective judgment have also been obtained by Blandford and Sampson (1964) through the use of the names of famous and infamous people as UCSs, and by Reitz and Jackson (1964) and Silverstein and McCreary (1964) through the use of affectively toned photographs.

The first successful demonstration that contiguous pairing of neutral and incentive (or affective) stimuli is a sufficient condition for the former to become incentives for learning was made by Silverstein and McCreary (1964), who found a selectively higher level of performance in paired-associate (PA) learning for nonsense syllables previously paired with pleasant (P) photographs as compared with syllables paired with indifferent (I) photographs. Subsequently, Lott, Lott, and Walsh (1970) found a greater tendency to respond with syllables previously paired with "liked" persons' names than those paired with "neutral" persons' names. While these studies established contiguous pairing as a sufficient condition for an acquired incentive phenomenon, they did not lay bare the mechanism by which such acquisition took place, and it is the uncovering of this mechanism to which the remainder of the studies here described are addressed.

The strategy used in investigating this issue involved raising the following empirical questions: (1) Are there any nonincentive reasons for the enhanced performance with P-paired syllables that are confounded with the contiguous pairing procedure? (2) Are there any conditions under which pairing syllables with P items does not enhance subsequent performance with them in a learning task? (3) What is the relationship between the acquisition of incentive value by P-paired syllables and their acquisition of increased PL?

Since the remainder of the research to be described here was generated by the Silverstein and McCreary (1964) data, that prototype experiment will be reviewed in some detail. Male subjects learned two successive PA lists conforming to the A–B, C–A paradigm. In List 1, nonsense syllables were the stimuli to which subjects learned to anticipate the appearance of photographs of real scenes by giving short labels for the pictures. The labels were supplied by each subject so that no learning was required to associate them with the pictures. Half of the eight pictures had been judged by an independent group of subjects to be "very pleasant" and half were judged to be "indifferent" on a 9-point rating scale. Highly correlated with the sharp separation in PL ratings of the two subsets of pictures were differences in the amount of time that the subjects spent looking at the P and I pictures and in the percentage of the subjects who selected each as a keepsake of their participation in the rating experiment. This demonstrated a substantial difference in the pre-experimental incentive value of the two subsets, a demonstration that was confirmed by the fact that subjects learned to anticipate the appearance of the P pictures more rapidly than that of the I pictures. In the learning experiment, the specific syllables used were counterbalanced across the subjects with regard to the type of picture they were paired with. List 1 was learned to a criterion of two successive errorless trials. List 2 was composed of the prior syllables as responses to two-digit numbers, and was given to the subject for 12 anticipation trials immediately following the end of List-1 learning. In both lists, the materials were displayed by automatic slide projector, the first slide of each pair showing the stimulus item and the second slide showing the response item for 5 sec each. The percentage of correct responses in List 2 for the P-paired syllables was significantly greater than that for the I-paired syllables (mean superiority was 7.0% and was shown by 18 of the 24 subjects), thereby demonstrating the former's acquired incentive value. An independent group of subjects was given the task of rating the PL of the syllables instead of learning them in a second list, and they gave a significantly higher rating to the P-paired syllables. A replication of this study by Silverstein (1966) with a different set of pictures at a different university yielded essentially the same results, with the mean superiority of the P-paired syllables increasing to 10.5%. In both experiments, the bulk of the difference in performance with the two subsets of syllables was found in the first four or five trials. Most of the remaining experiments to be described used PA learning to assess the syllable's incentive value, because of the analytic power provided by that method.

What Is Being Transferred to P-Paired Syllables?

A primary issue in delineating the precise basis for the effect found in the preceding experiments is that of whether some variable correlated with the pictures' PL was being transferred concurrently to the syllables and played a role in altering their learnability in List 2. The cluster of variables subsumed under the heading of "meaningfulness" (M) was a natural candidate for such a role, both because of its known correlation with PL in words (Johnson, Thomson, & Frinke, 1960; Pollio, 1968;

Silverstein & Dienstbier, 1968a; Zajonc, 1968) and because M has been shown to be such a potent variable in verbal learning (Underwood & Schulz, 1960; Goss & Nodine, 1965). The possibility of confounding by M was rendered more plausible by the discovery that the P pictures used produced less variability in the labels given to them than did the I pictures (Silverstein, 1973). Since measures of associative variability are negatively correlated with M, it appeared likely that the P pictures were also more meaningful than the I pictures. This conclusion was further strengthened by the fact that an independent group of subjects who rated the labels given to each picture for meaningfulness produced a significantly higher mean value for the labels given to the P pictures (Silverstein, 1973).

The next question asked was whether the difference in M of the P and I pictures was transferred to their associated syllables. Word associations were obtained for 12 nonsense syllables paired with P and I pictures (Silverstein, 1973) in a task identical to that used by Silverstein and McCreary (1964). It was found that the P- and I-paired syllables yielded virtually identical mean percentages of response within the allotted 10-sec period and virtually identical distributions of the percentages of those responses that fell in different ranks. While there was a nonsignificant trend for the P-paired syllables to produce a smaller total number of different associations, this trend can be accounted for by a significantly greater number of "picture relevant" associations given to the P-paired syllables (as judged by two independent judges unfamiliar with the purposes of the research). Finally, these syllables' printed frequency (Thorndike & Lorge, 1944) was slightly lower in the P- than in the I-paired case. Thus it seemed that, although the P-paired syllables had acquired a more reliable capacity to evoke images relevant to the pictures with which they had been paired, they had not become more meaningful. To settle the issue, a second study was performed in which the subjects rated the syllables for M, according to a variant of Noble's (1961) procedure, subsequent to their pairing with P and I pictures in the prototype List-1 task (Silverstein, 1973). We first demonstrated that the rating procedure we used was sufficiently sensitive to detect small differences in the M of only eight syllables with a small number of subjects. Despite this sensitivity, the mean values obtained for the P- and I-paired syllables were trivially and insignificantly different.

Perhaps the most conclusive piece of evidence to rule out the possibility that a differential transfer of M was responsible for the superiority of P-paired syllables in PA learning comes from a study by Silverstein and Dienstbier (1968b). The design of that experiment was identical to that of the prototype experiment (Silverstein & McCreary, 1964) except for the use of English nouns instead of pictures as response items for List 1; nouns which differed widely in M. No significant differences were found between the syllables paired with high-M and low-M words in either number of correct responses in List-2 learning or in meaningfulness ratings obtained following the conclusion of List-2 learning. Parker and Noble (1963) had previously shown that pairing syllables with items of differing M did not alter subsequent ratings of meaningfulness of the syllables.[2] On the other hand, Young and Parker (1970) found that serial-learning performance with nonsense syllables could be enhanced by prior pairing with high-M items. As Silverstein (1973) pointed out, however, their data must reflect the operation of a different mechanism than that which produces the acquired incentive effect, since they were obtained under conditions in which no acquired incentive effect is found.

Another variable whose operation required assessment was similarity. The evidence that organizational effects are found even in PA learning (cf. Postman, 1971) raised the question of whether P-paired syllables had become more quickly learned than I-paired syllables because of having acquired a greater degree of similarity or subjective organization among them. It was found that the subjects are able to group syllables according to whether they had previously been paired with P or I pictures beyond a chance level and also that they judge the corporate similarity of the P-paired syllables to be higher than that of the I-paired syllables (Silverstein, 1973). On the other hand, that same study produced several lines of evidence in opposition to the hypothesis that these grouping tendencies play any part in the difference found in PA performance. First, no evidence was found for clustering in free recall of syllables according to the kind of picture they had previously been paired with. The clustering phenomenon is a very sensitive index of the operation of subjective grouping dispositions (Bousefield, 1953; Tulving, 1962). Moreover, there was no correlation found between the amount of clustering shown by individual subjects and the amount of superiority in recall for P-paired syllables. Even more impressive evidence comes from an experiment in which three groups of subjects learned a first list of nonsense syllables as stimuli for nouns of high and low intrasublist similarity. In none of these groups was any significant difference found in the speed

[2] This was not the general conclusion reached by the authors, but it is what their data showed.

of learning the syllables paired with the high- and low-similarity sublists during a subsequent PA task.

Additional evidence against any influence of acquired similarity in the acquired incentive experiments can be found in the fact that the introduction of either task anxiety or a continuous pronunciation task removed the superiority of P-paired syllables in learning, but neither reduced the subjects' abilities to group the syllables according to type of picture with which they were paired (Silverstein, 1972b). Finally, it has been found that the superiority of P-paired syllables in PA learning occurs only when they are response items in the list, (Silverstein, in press) whereas intralist similarity is known to be a far more effective variable in PA learning when manipulated on the stimulus than on the response side (Goss & Nodine, 1965).

A third potential variable for confounding that was carefully assessed was that of subjective confidence in the ease of learning the conditioned syllables. If the subjects felt the P-paired syllables were easier than the I-paired syllables they might have selected them for earlier learning on those grounds and also have been more willing to guess a P-paired syllable when uncertain of the correct response. Evidence against this hypothesis was available from the beginning in the form of the P-paired syllables' superior percentage of correct responses *following the first correct response* (Silverstein, 1966; Silverstein & McCreary, 1964). If P-paired syllables were being guessed sooner but were not truly more available to the subject, they should also have shown more errors following their first correct placement since that placement might have been a lucky guess. More direct evidence against the hypothesis was found in two experiments in which the subjects rated the difficulty of learning the number–syllable pairs (Silverstein, 1972b; Silverstein & Marshall, 1968). In both experiments, the ratings of difficulty dropped steadily across successive trials but were not significantly different for the P- and I-paired syllables either on the first rating trial or for the sum of all trials. Related to the preceding hypothesis is one that claims the greater speed of learning P-paired syllables to be the result of the P pictures in the first list having been learned more rapidly, which gave subjects more time to attend to the stimulus syllables for the P pictures. Evidence against this hypothesis comes from a consistent absence of any correlation between the degree of superiority shown by the subjects for P over I pairs in the two tasks of the experiments in this series. A total of 35 different rank-order correlations have been calculated for the various groups in 14 relevant experiments between the amounts of superiority for P pairs in the two lists and not one of them was significantly different from zero at the .05 level. The values of *rho* ranged from $-.339$ to $+.276$, 18 of them being negative and 17 of them being positive. All in all, it seems quite safe to suppose that only incentive value and PL were being transferred from the pictures to the nonsense syllables in these experiments.

When Are P-Paired Syllables Not Learned Faster?

The data reviewed in the preceding section indicate that nonsense syllables increase their incentive value when they are contiguously paired with P pictures that are already incentives. We also inquired into the sufficient conditions for such conditioning to take place. The hypothesis used to guide this inquiry was that incentive conditioning takes place if a genuine and discriminative positive affect reaction is elicited immediately after a nonsense syllable is presented to the subject, provided that he is making no responses that are incompatible with such a reaction.

TASK ANXIETY

One reaction system which seemed very likely to inhibit any positive affect to P pictures was task anxiety, which Sarason (1960) has shown to involve a heightened disposition to make self-deprecatory and self-critical responses in the face of evaluative or personally threatening situations. For the subjects with high task anxiety, such responses would be very likely to occur following an incorrect response in a rote learning task and be incompatible with the type of response hypothesized to be necessary for incentive conditioning in the type of experiment described here. Attention was first drawn to this possibility in four unpublished experiments using female subjects in which no performance superiority was found either for the P over the I pictures in List 1 or the P- over the I-paired syllables in List 2. The difference between performance with P and I items was not found whether affectively mixed or homogeneous lists were used, whether male or female experimenters were used or whether the pictures used were the same as those used for the men or obtained from independent judgments by female subjects. Nor did the addition of the "potency" and "activity" variables (Osgood, 1952) to PL produce incentive conditioning. In one of those experiments we discovered that female subjects reported substantially higher levels of anxiety about having done well than male subjects typically report (Silverstein, 1972b).

If female subjects failed to show incentive conditioning with the syllables because of the inhibition of positive affect responses by a very high level of task anxiety, then the most direct means of removing such inhibition would be to remove the learning requirement for List 1, along with its attendant possibilities for failure. To test this line of reasoning, female subjects were given the pairs of syllables and pictures in one of two incidental learning tasks: six trials of rating the difficulty of learning to associate the members of each pair, or six trials of judging how well each syllable's meaning matched the scene of its associated picture (Silverstein, 1972b). Following the first task subjects were given 12 trials of intentional PA learning with the syllables as responses to two-digit numbers. Table 8-1 shows the mean percentage correct on all trials and the mean number of trials before a response was first given, correct or not (i.e., the Response-Learning Stage, Underwood & Schulz, 1960), for the P- and I-paired syllables in List 2. The same data are also shown for the previous experiment which used intentional learning as the first list task (Experiment A) and for an experiment to be described subsequently (Experiment II), all of which used the same stimulus materials and a female experimenter. It can readily be seen that subjects in both conditions of Experiment I showed a significantly higher level of performance with the P-paired than with the I-paired syllables. On the other hand, the subjects in Experiment A showed nearly identical performance with the two sublists of syllables and a much higher overall level of performance than the subjects in Experiment I. A postexperimental questionnaire revealed that only 28.1% of the women in Experiment I felt anxious about their performance as compared with 70.2% of the subjects in Experiment A who reported such anxiety.

TABLE 8–1

Experiments on Task Anxiety
List—2 Means

Task 1	Experiment A Learning		Experiment I				Experiment II			
			Matching		Difficulty		Matching		Difficulty	
	P	I	P	I	P	I	P	I	P	I
Percentage correct	65.8	64.0	55.3	50.0	60.5	53.7	57.0	57.4	65.5	61.4
Trials: first response	3.99	3.97	4.33	4.67	4.03	5.05	4.70	4.19	4.03	3.98

A conclusive demonstration that task anxiety was responsible for prior failures to obtain a superiority for P-paired syllables with female subjects required certainty that no other feature of the incidental tasks used in Experiment I was responsible for the P-paired syllables' advantage in that experiment. Accordingly, the conditions of that experiment were replicated with the addition of anxiety-arousing instructions which told the subjects that the skills needed to perform the judgments of difficulty or meaning-fit were "part of a general ability to know one's own capabilities," and were highly correlated with intelligence and professional success, and that following the experiment they would see how well they did as compared with nationwide norms. As Table 8-1 shows, the addition of these anxiety-inducing instructions in Experiment II served both to remove the difference between the P- and I-paired syllables and to bring the overall level of learning approximately up to that of the Intentional subjects in Experiment A.

Since all of the evidence on the role of task anxiety had come from female subjects, it seemed important to see whether the use of anxiety-inducing instructions would remove the typical superiority of P- over I-paired syllables for male subjects in the prototype experimental design. This was accomplished in Experiment III of the preceding study (Silverstein, 1972b). While those subjects who were given the standard instructions (Group S) showed the typical superiority for P pictures in List 1 and for P-paired syllables in List 2, those subjects given the anxiety-inducing instructions (Group A) showed a nonsignificant advantage for the I items in the two lists along with a heightened overall level of performance.

FORWARD CONDITIONING

If the nature of the learning involved in the acquired-incentive phenomenon is Pavlovian conditioning, then one would expect it to be more effective in a procedure in which the syllables preceded the pictures than in a procedure in which the syllables followed the pictures or both were presented simultaneously. In another study (Silverstein, in press), a group of male and a group of female subjects were shown the syllables and pictures simultaneously, side-by-side, for six trials of difficulty ratings. On each trial half the syllables were on the left and half on the right, and each syllable appeared on the left for half the trials. Moreover, the subject was instructed to judge the difficulty of learning the pairs in both directions. The standard 12 trials of anticipation learning of the prototype experiment was used for List 2. The data from the female subjects are directly comparable to those of the women in Experiment I of the preceding study who rated the pairs' difficulty in List 1. While the P-paired syllables still enjoyed a superiority over the I-paired syllables (55.1% versus 50.8%), it was a substantially smaller one than that obtained when the syllables were followed by the pictures and it failed to reach the 10% level of significance with $N = 32$. It is also possible to compare the data from the male subjects with those of male subjects in Experiment III of the preceding study. Since the subjects in Experiment III intentionally learned List 1 to a criterion of two perfect trials (which required an average of 10.1 trials), caution must be used in making the comparison with the present experiment. Nonetheless, the results of that comparison confirm those of the more legitimate comparison of the female subjects in showing a sizable attenuation of the superiority for P-paired syllables by every index used, and none of the differences between P- versus I-paired syllables were significant.

AFFECTIVE CONTRAST

Several theorists of secondary reinforcement have argued that a neutral stimulus will acquire reinforcement value only by a differential conditioning procedure (see Wike's, 1966, review of these); that is, by a procedure in which one CS is paired with primary reinforcement and another CS is not paired with reinforcement. The use of first lists containing both P and I pictures in the experiments previously described, thereby providing the subject with affective contrast, conforms to the differential conditioning paradigm. It is important to discover whether incentive conditioning in verbal learning can be achieved through the use of an absolute conditioning paradigm in which different groups of subjects are give pictures that are all either P or I as responses to the nonsense syllables. A closely related issue is whether the demonstration of incentive conditioning requires contrast of incentives in the second list (Premack, 1969), as has been the case in the preceding experiments, or whether it can also be found when different groups of subjects learn either P- or I-paired syllables as responses to the numbers.

A recent study (Silverstein, 1972a) reported several experiments dealing with these issues, the main results of which are shown in Table 8-2. Let us first take the case in which the second list is composed of all P- or all I-paired syllables, thereby removing incentive contrast. In Experiment I and Experiment II all subjects first learned a PA list with pictures that were either all P or all I and then learned a list in which the prior syllables (all P- or all I-paired) were used as responses. The two experiments differed only in that eight pairs were used in the first and six pairs were used in the second. Both experiments also contained a familiariza-

TABLE 8-2

Experiments on Affective Contrast
List—2 Means According to List—1 Pairing

Experiment	List 1	List 2	Percentage correct				Trials: First response			
			P	Non	I	Non	P	Non	I	Non
I	Homogeneous 8 pairs	Homogeneous 8 pairs	60.8	—	60.0	54.1	4.11	—	4.03	4.19
II	Homogeneous 6 pairs	Homogeneous 6 pairs	74.3	—	70.4	54.1	3.10	—	3.29	3.44
III	Mixed 12 pairs	Homogeneous 6 pairs	70.1	—	63.5	—	3.46	—	3.51	—
IV-A	Homogeneous 6 pairs	Mixed 12 pairs	54.4	48.0	38.6	46.3	4.54	5.20	5.76	5.18
IV-B	Homogeneous 6 pairs	Mixed 12 pairs	46.3	50.5	42.2	52.5	4.64	4.28	5.42	4.67

tion control group that rated the syllables' meaningfulness without seeing any pictures, but in all other details they were identical to the prototype design. The use of six pairs in Experiment II was designed to make it comparable in List 2 to Experiment III, in which affective contrast was introduced in the first list. Clearly, there were no differences in the learning of the P- and I-paired syllables in List 2 of either experiment, although both groups performed at higher levels than did the control group. The absence of differences between the P and the I groups was evident throughout the course of learning. The data from the first list showed tiny, nonsignificant advantages in trials to one perfect recitation for the I groups over the P groups in both experiments.

In Experiment III, affective contrast was introduced in the first list, but the second list was homogeneous with regard to type of syllable used. This was accomplished by first giving the subjects a list of 12 paired associates in which six of the syllables were stimuli for P pictures and six were stimuli for I pictures, and then giving half the subjects the P-paired syllables and half the subjects I-paired syllables in the second list. Table 8-2 shows the percentage of correct responses to be substantially greater for the P group than for the I group, but this difference was only marginally significant ($p. < .10$). The P versus I difference in mean number of trials to a perfect recitation (6.52 versus 8.11) was also significant only at the .10 level. Thus, Experiment III indicated that affective contrast in the first list could produce a superiority for P-paired syllables in a homogeneous test list, but that it is a smaller effect than is typically obtained in a test list that contains both P-paired and I-paired syllables. Moreover, closer analyses of the data revealed that the locus of the P-paired superiority in a homogeneous test list was shifted from being predominantly based upon response learning in the early trials to reliably faster and firmer associative learning later in the task. This shift will be discussed more fully later.

To determine whether or not affective contrast is needed to produce a superiority of P-paired syllables in mixed second list experiments, two concurrent experiments were run (IV–A and IV–B) in which the subjects were given either six P or six I pairs in the first list and then received these "conditioned" syllables mixed with six nonpaired syllables as responses in the second list. In both these experiments the first list was learned for a fixed 8 trials and the second list for 12 trials. The subsets of syllables that were paired with pictures or that were nonpaired were counterbalanced across the subjects. The nonpaired syllables used in the second list of Experiment IV–A were new to the subject, whereas in Experiment IV–B they had been familiarized by four trials of "difficulty" judgment. The reason for the use of the familiarization procedure in Experiment IV–B was a fear that the advantage of the paired syllables in familiarity would obscure any differences in performance that were the result of PL, but Table 8-2 shows how unfounded this fear was. That table also clearly shows a significantly greater superiority for P-paired over nonpaired syllables than for I-paired over nonpaired syllables in Experiment IV–A. There was also a significantly *smaller inferiority* of P-paired to nonpaired than of I-paired to nonpaired syllables in Experiment IV–B. Thus, it is clear that removing affective contrast from the conditioning procedure of a mixed test list experiment does not remove the advantage of P- over I-paired syllables.

The apparent reduction in the amount of superiority for P-paired syllables produced by the removal of affective contrast in Experiments IV–A and IV–B was the result of a general advantage held by the nonpaired over the paired syllables, which interviews indicated was the result of a subjective strategy of selecting for earliest learning those syllables which had not been part of a prior learning task (see Battig, Allen, & Jensen, 1965). This advantage was only partly counteracted by P-pairing and was particularly evident in Experiment IV–B where it was enhanced by familiarization training with the nonpaired syllables.

The safest overall conclusion would seem to be that affective contrast is required in either the first or the second list (i.e., conditioning or test list) for incentive conditioning to occur, but that discriminative conditioning in the first list is not absolutely necessary. Apparently, the more crucial factor for the appearance of incentive conditioning is the opportunity for the subject to select P-paired syllables for earlier learning in List 2. This conclusion is strengthened by the facts that the superiority in learning P pictures over I pictures appears only in mixed lists (Silverstein, 1972a) and that the superiority in learning P words over I words appears only in mixed lists (Silverstein & Dienstbier, 1968b). It is safe to assume that the difference in the conditioning histories of these P and I items are the same regardless of the experimental paradigm used.

Words as Unconditional Stimuli

No incentive conditioning would be expected if the stimuli used to elicit unconditional positive affect are no longer capable of doing so as a result of habituation or extinction. Such stimuli might well continue to produce judgments of "pleasant," however, because of their former ability to produce positive-affect responses (Peters, 1935). This might very well be the case with common words whose pleasant meanings were originally conditioned by potent evironmental stimuli but whose frequent subsequent use for communication in institutionalized linguistic contexts had not been accompanied by these environmental UCSs. Each such communicational occasion would thus constitute an extinction trial for the conditioned emotional responses to these words. While the appearance of a pleasant word like "beautiful" or "delight" in a poetic context might be sufficiently novel to rearouse an authentic affective response to it, it would not be surprising if seeing the word by itself in an experimental list produced no such reaction. Thus, such words would be incapable of conditioning new incentive stimuli. On the other hand, children, who have experienced fewer communicational extinction trials for these words, might still reveal a conditioned incentive value for them. An experiment by Finley and Staats (1967) showed that P words were capable of reinforcing an instrumental act, whereas an attempted replication of their design with college students in our laboratory was unsuccessful. Moreover, words with idiosyncratic pleasant meaning (e.g., your true-love's name) might be expected to escape such extinction of incentive value.

In order to test these expectations, the prototype experimental design was repeated by Silverstein and Dienstbier (1968b) with the substitution of sublists of P and I words (equated for meaningfulness, frequency, and similarity) for the P and I pictures. It was found that, despite a substantial difference in the speed of learning the P and I words in List 1, virtually no differences between the P-paired and I-paired syllables appeared at any point during the 10 trials of the second list for either male or female subjects. In another relevant experiment (as yet unpublished) the most commonly given labels for the pictures were used as List-1 responses. Only a small and nonsignificant difference was found favoring the P-paired syllables in List 2. Thus, the conclusion seems warranted that P words are substantially less potent than P pictures in eliciting positive-affect responses and, hence, less capable of producing incentive conditioning. Subsequent research has shown that the faster learning of the P words than the I words in List 1 is based upon subjects judging them to be easier and selecting them for earlier learning.

Opportunity for Differential Rehearsal

Silverstein and McCreary (1964) had proposed that the mechanism by which the superior incentive value of P-paired over I-paired syllables operated in PA learning depended upon the former being covertly rehearsed more intensely and at a more rapid rate. This hypothesis was supported by the findings previously reported that, without the opportunity afforded each subject by a mixed second list to select P-paired syllables for earlier learning, the superiority of P-paired to I-paired syllables is either removed or markedly restricted. Any condition which eliminates the opportunity for such differences in rehearsal rate should also preclude finding any superiority of P-paired syllables. Two such conditions were investigated: making the P-paired and I-paired syllables stimulus items rather than response items in PA learning and the introduction of a continuous pronouncing task during List-2 learning.

Anisfeld and Lambert (1966) had found faster learning of pleasant than unpleasant words when they were responses in a PA list but no difference when they were stimuli or when serial learning (which confuses stimulus and response functions) was used. A study by Silverstein (in press) attempted to confirm this finding in a comparison of pleasant with indifferent items whose PL was conditioned rather than sampled. It was not possible to make a valid comparison of the effects of response versus stimulus position for the conditioned syllables simply by reversing the positions of the syllables and numbers in List 2, since that would have confounded position with transfer paradigm; i.e., an A–B, C–A versus an A–B, A–C paradigm. To avoid this difficulty, the experiments in the Silverstein (in press) study presented the syllables and photographs as simultaneous pairs during List 1, with spatial position counterbalanced, and gave each subject the task of rating the difficulty of learning such pairs. It must be recalled that this conditioning procedure was found to be less effective than the forward conditioning procedure of showing each syllable before its associated picture.

In Experiment I a group of male subjects and a group of female subjects were each given 12 trials of anticipation learning in List 2 with the syllables in either the stimulus or response position. For the male subjects the P-paired syllables showed a moderate advantage in percentage correct over the I-paired ones when they were in the response position (60.3% versus 53.9%) but virtually no difference when they were in the stimulus position (61.1% versus 59.7%). For the female subjects the P-paired syllables were also somewhat superior when in the response position (55.1% versus 50.8%) but not when in the stimulus position (50.1% versus 53.3%). The interaction between PL and position of syllables was significant for the two groups. In a second experiment of that study, male subjects were given eight trials of judging the difficulty of the syllable-picture pairs, after which the syllables were placed in either stimulus or response positions of a PA task in which four study trials were each followed by either a response-recall (in any order) trial or by an associative-matching test. For both types of test trial, the subjects were given one minute to write their responses and were furnished with no feedback until the following study trial. With both kinds of test the P-paired syllables were significantly superior to the I-paired syllables in the response position, but the scores were nearly identical when the syllables were in the stimulus position.

The effect of introducing a continuous pronunciation task upon P and I items was first investigated in two of the conditions of a Master's Thesis experiment by Alice Marshall (1970). In one of them, she showed the subjects pairs of numbers and words, differing in PL, for three trials with instructions to learn them for future use. In another condition the subjects were instructed to pronounce the pairs continuously in addition to memorizing them. Subsequently, both groups received 10 anticipation trials with the list. Performance was generally hampered by the pronouncing task, particularly for the P words, so that superiority for P over I words occurred only with the nonpronouncing group. A subsequent experiment from our laboratory (Silverstein, 1972b, Experiment III) used a continuous pronouncing task during List-2 learning of the prototype paradigm for conditioning incentive value to nonsense syllables. As compared with a group not encumbered with the pronouncing task, this condition was seriously detrimental to performance with the P-paired syllables, so that it was not significantly different from performance with the I-paired syllables at any stage of learning. Thus, it seems justifiable to conclude that the superiority of P- over I-paired items is based upon differential covert rehearsal of these responses in rote learning.

What Is the Relation of Incentive Value to Pleasantness?

As previously noted, the history of research on the role of incentive value in the learning of verbal materials was clouded by the confusion of that variable with judgments of PL. Though it is obvious that these two variables are often correlated, it is an empirical question whether they actually constitute the same variable measured by two different indices. And the answer to this question will help in formulating a coherent theory about how incentive value is acquired by verbal materials and how it operates. In most of the experiments previously described, ratings were obtained of the syllables' PL following performance with them in the learning task, and in some cases these ratings were also obtained immediately following the pairing of the syllables with P and I stimuli. Thus we can determine whether there are conditions under which a transfer of higher PL values will not be accompanied by increases in their incentive value.

The only experiments in which pairing nonsense syllables with P items failed to enhance their rated PL were those two in which homogeneous lists of P *or* I pictures were first paired with the syllables and then the P- or I-paired syllables were learned in homogeneous second lists. These experiments also produced no learning effect of PL. On the other hand, when mixed lists of P and I pictures were paired with syllables that were subsequently learned in homogeneous lists, the truncation in the learning difference between P- and I-paired syllables was not matched in the PL ratings: A substantial superiority was still found for the P-paired syllables. Judgments of PL have long been known to reflect most of the properties of other psychophysical judgments (Peters, 1935) and one would expect such judgments to require a discrimination by each subject of a P stimulus from other stimuli in the context in which the judgments are made, except for very extreme affective stimuli. Apparently, removing affective contrast from the conditioning of the nonsense syllables to the pictures removed an important condition for the formation of such discriminative judgment. Interestingly enough, even when subjects failed to demonstrate an incentive effect for P-paired syllables in a homogeneous second list, they still showed that some discriminative affective reaction was conditioned to those syllables during List-1 learning by rating them higher in PL.

Discriminatively higher judgments of PL for P-paired over nonpaired syllables were also shown by subjects who received no affective contrast in List 1 when incentive contrast was introduced with a mixed second list (Experiment IV–A, Silverstein, 1972a). Since the above result was not obtained in Experiment IV–B of that study, in which the nonpaired syllables received familiarization training and were learned more rapidly than either P-paired or I-paired syllables, it could be argued that the higher ratings of PL obtained in Experiment IV–A for the P-paired syllables was the result of their having been learned faster. This argument is contradicted by the fact that the subjects in Experiment IV–A rated the P-paired and I-paired syllables in different lists equal in PL, despite a sizable learning superiority for the former. A more likely interpretation is that the subjects' higher PL ratings for the P-paired than the nonpaired syllables reflects some residual contrast between the P pictures and the experimental context and were based upon the recall of the specific pictures the syllables had been paired with. Recall for details of the pictures paired with the syllables was found to be very good in a number of experiments.

The experiments reported which showed that task-anxiety eliminated the incentive value of P-paired syllables (Silverstein, 1972b) also showed the superior PL judgments for P-paired syllables to remain intact. This strongly indicates that, even when no authentic positive-affect response is elicited by the P-pictures to be conditioned to the syllables, the subjects will judge both the pictures and their associated syllables to have such affect. This conclusion is supported by the data of Silverstein and Dienstbier (1968b) which showed that subjects rated the syllables paired with P words higher in PL than the syllables paired with I words, even though the P words were not potent enough elicitors of positive-affect responses to enhance the learnability of their associated syllables. Silverstein and Dienstbier (1968b) hypothesized that the differential PL judgments of the syllables were mediated by specific recall of associated P and I words, and that the higher ratings of the P words failed to index the extinction of their incentive value. Subsequent research has shown that there is a strong correlation between subjects' judgments of word PL and their judgments of how easily a word can be learned, and that the earlier learning of P than I words stems from the latter judgment.

Three other experimental instances were reported in which diminished or no differential incentive value for P-paired and I-paired syllables was accompanied by no decrease in superiority of PL ratings of the former. The first of these involved the two experiments in which the pictures and syllables were simultaneously shown, presumably a less efficient procedure of conditioning than successive presentation. The appearance here of differential PL ratings again reflects the importance of specific recall of associated pictures for subjects who are making a difficult judgment. The other two instances of discrepancy between incentive functioning and PL ratings are experimental arrangements in which the task precluded the operation of incentive value of the items learned: stimulus placement of the conditioned syllables and the introduction of a continuous pronouncing task. In both cases it can be presumed that the P-paired syllables were potentially of higher incentive value than the I-paired syllables, and their higher PL ratings can reflect both this and the recall of their associated pictures.

Finally, it may be asked whether the P-paired and I-paired syllables displayed any other signs of differential incentive value other than the differences shown in rote learning performance. Some scanty evidence is available. At the conclusion of one experiment, each subject was offered a bookmark with one of the syllables printed on it as a souvenir of his participation (Silverstein, 1973). The mean percentage of subjects who selected one of the P-paired syllables was 10.7%, as compared with 5.9% for the I-paired syllables. Of the 12 syllables used in that experiment, 10 were selected significantly more often when paired with a P picture than when paired with an I picture. In another unpublished experiment, subjects spent significantly longer looking at P-paired than I-paired syllables during an unpaced difficulty rating task immediately following List-1 learning. This finding seems to contradict a study by Reitz (1963) involving a stereoscopic rivalry task. He found a small, but persistent, trend for neutrally paired syllables to be perceived more often than pleasantly paired syllables were, and both to be perceived more often than syllables paired with unpleasant pictures. Unfortunately, Reitz used a "backward conditioning" paradigm for his first task, and the stereoscopic rivalry measure should be repeated for syllables that were presented prior to the pictures.

More data on various incentive criteria for neutral verbal stimuli contiguously conditioned to incentives should be accumulated and related to the body of studies showing that neutral stimuli paired with some form of reinforcement can acquire incentive value, as measured by various indices (e.g., the studies of Nunnally and his associates: Duchnowski, Nunnally, & Faw, 1968; Kendall & Nunnally, 1968; Nunnally, Duchnowski, & Knott, 1967; Nunnally, Duchnowski, & Parker, 1965; Nunnally & Faw, 1968; Nunnally, Stevens, & Hall, 1965; also Lott, 1955). The convergence of experiments involving contiguous conditioning of neutral with incentive stimuli with those involving instrumental reinforcement would help to specify the basis for the acquired incentive effects in the latter: contiguous occurrence of the neutral stimuli with reinforcers, contingency of the instrumental response with reinforcement, or discriminating the occasion on which primary reinforcement will occur.

Conclusions: Conditioned Incentive Value as a Performance Effect

The experiments reviewed here produce a consistent picture of the kind of learning involved in the acquisition of incentive value by neutral verbal stimuli. When an incentive stimulus, such as a picture of an appealing scene, is seen by an individual, he will make unconditional approach movements with respect to it; i.e., increase sensory contact with it by looking at it longer and more searchingly, moving closer to it, increasing the illumination, etc.[3] The picture may also elicit anticipatory

---

[3] The use of the term "approach movements" in such a general sense, including all acts that increase the subject's access to an incentive, rather than in the more restricted sense of locomotion toward an object, reflects the assumption of a high degree of learned equivalence between a great variety of actions which can enhance sensory contact with an incentive (Schneirla, 1959). The assumption of such an equivalence is not a logical necessity, but must be verified empirically for each class of incentives and subjects. Some evidence of this assumption in the case of pleasant pictures and P-paired nonsense syllables was presented earlier in this chapter.

responses appropriate to the scene itself which can serve as mediators for instrumental action which, in turn, could lead to the stimuli represented in the picture. Very likely (though this has not been well established experimentally), behavior which leads to the appearance of the picture will be reinforced. If the individual rates the PL of such a picture, he is actually assessing the prepotency of his approach tendency (Peters, 1935). Judgments along the PL dimension are the unique way we have been trained to communicate our tendencies to seek out stimuli, but such judgments are not absolute or fixed. They can be altered by a number of variables relevant to the type of scale employed, its anchor points and the conditions under which the judgments are made. The degree of momentary approach produced by the stimulous will be increased by greater contrast between it and the context. A picture of a frolic at a beach will seem more attractive to a sophomore in the dead of winter than during the summer holidays, and if it is part of a heterogeneous group including some rather dull ones, the individual will be more likely to discriminate it for special approach than if all the pictures are very attractive.

Any neutral stimulus regularly paired with an incentive picture will have some fraction of these generalized approach tendencies conditioned to it. The names of very attractive places and the labels of compellingly alluring events acquire some degree of the incentive value of the scenes they symbolize and have been paired with contiguously. Many of the conditions known to enhance Pavlovian conditioning have been found to enhance such incentive conditioning in the experiments reported here. For example, the most efficient conditioning was found to occur when the forward sequence: name → photograph, was employed with a short delay between the onset of the two stimuli. Again, conditions which prevented the occurrence of approach tendencies to the pictures, such as the introduction of a high level of task anxiety, or of experimental tasks that were void of affective contrast, were found to remove or diminish incentive conditioning. Thus, in general, the stronger the approach tendencies elicited by a picture during conditioning, the greater should be the subsequent elicitation of some fraction of these tendencies by syllables with which they were paired. And these conditioned approach tendencies should both reinforce any behaviors that lead to the occurrence of the syllable and produce a disposition to judge the syllable more "pleasant" (i.e., more approach worthy).

The preceding analysis is based upon Staats's (1964) theory of conditioned reinforcers and word meaning, but adds the specification that the core of the evaluative meaning which he suggests has been conditioned to a positive verbal stimulus (r_m, according to Osgood, 1952) by more primary incentives is a generalized, implicit approach reaction. An obvious way for a subject to produce a nonsense syllable that has become an incentive for learning is to rehearse it, either overtly or covertly. Indeed, such rehearsal is the most obvious form of approach response to any verbal item. It was Peters (1935) who first suggested that judgments of the affective value of stimuli reflected such implicit approach (or withdrawal) reactions, whatever the basis for such reactions. He supported his theory with an ingenious series of experiments (Peters, 1938a, b; 1939a, b) showing that subjects increased their ratings of a Japanese word's PL if they were rewarded for pronouncing it in a discrimination task and lowered these judgments if they were punished for pronouncing it by the sound of a bell. While either unconditional or conditional emotional stimuli produce most of the approach or withdrawal reactions in the natural environment, Peters' studies demonstrated that artificially producing approach or withdrawal could duplicate the resulting affective judgments. Peters also hypothesized that mere contiguity between a neutral stimulus and one judged to be P would not produce significant transfer of PL to the former unless the P stimulus actually evoked an approach response in the presence of the neutral stimulus (Peters, 1939b, p. 123). Our studies have shown that Peters prediction is correct for measures of incentive for learning, but that shifts in PL judgment can occur in the absence of genuine approach responding to nonsense syllables if subjects can recall the P stimuli with which they were paired previously.

The studies reported here also showed that differential rehearsal rate was primarily responsible for the superior level of performance obtained with P-paired syllables. The data on associations to P-paired and I-paired syllables indicated that the representational, stimulus feedback produced by rehearsing a P-paired syllable will serve as an associative cue for some of the imagery from the appropriate picture. This, in turn, would be expected to generate additional approach responding to the conditioned syllable (i.e., further rehearsal), so that the implicit rehearsal of a P-paired syllable will be self-reinforcing and occur with increased vigor. Since it is rare that subjects in verbal learning experiments attempt to distribute their efforts evenly across all the items on a list from the beginning of training, the differences in implicit rehearsal rates produced by P-paired and I-paired syllables amount to a disposition to select the former for earlier learning. Such a selective disposition must be viewed as a performance factor and, like the operation of incentive value in animal learning experiments, is controlled by the activation of stimulus conditions whose influence is totally current rather than by differences in long-term cognitive structures (Tolman, 1932; Logan, 1960). Additional empirical support for this view comes from the experiments showing the superiority of P-paired syllables to operate primarily in mixed lists. As Underwood (1966) has pointed out, a variable that operates only in mixed-list experiments is engaging subjects' momentary selection tendencies, whereas a variable that makes material truly more or less difficult to learn will operate equally well when different values of that variable are placed in separate, homogeneous lists.

It is the response availability of incentive items that is principally, though not exclusively, aided by the selective performance disposition that favors them. This is demonstrated by the facts that the P-paired syllables' superiority was found to take place only when they were responses in the list, not when they were stimuli, and that the bulk of this superiority is found in the early training trials and with measures of response availability (Ekstrand, 1966; Underwood & Schulz, 1960).

The analysis just presented is meant to serve as a model of how verbal stimuli can come to acquire, through their contingent pairing with "pleasant" environmental events, the incentive value by which performance with them in a learning task is enhanced. But it must be remembered that, as an individual becomes a more social communicator, he uses common incentive words and phrases in an increasing number of circumstances without the co-occurrence of the more primary incentives they symbolize. Evidence has been presented that the use of common incentive words in such institutionalized communicational interchanges extinguishes their incentive value and renders them incapable of increasing the incentive value of nonsense syllables through higher order conditioning. Still, an individual can recall, upon appropriate instruction, what such a word stands for; what his history of approach to it had once been and, therefore, continue to judge it as "pleasant." The more rapid learning of P than I words is the result of subjects judging them to be easier to learn, whereas subjects *did not* judge P-paired syllables easier to learn than I-paired syllables. In general, there seem to be a number of situations in which evaluative ratings of stimuli are obsolete, reflecting a prior history of approach or withdrawal tendencies rather than current ones (Berlyne, 1971).

References

Anisfeld, M., & Lambert, W. E. When are pleasant words learned faster than unpleasant words? *Journal of Verbal Learning & Verbal Behavior*, 1966, **5**, 132–141.

Battig, W. F., Allen, M., & Jensen, A. R. Priority of free recall of newly learned items. *Journal of Verbal Learning & Verbal Behavior,* 1965, 4, 175–179.

Beebe-Center, J. G. *The psychology of pleasantness and unpleasantness.* New York: Nostrand, 1932.

Berlyne, D. E. Arousal and reinforcement. In D. Levine (Ed.), *Nebraska Symposium on Motivation.* Lincoln: Univ. of Nebraska Press, 1967.

Berlyne, D. E. *Aesthetics and psychobiology.* New York: Appleton, 1971.

Blandford, D. H., & Sampson, E. E. Induction of prestige suggestion through classical conditioning. *Journal of Abnormal and Social Psychology,* 1964, 69, 332–337.

Bousefield, W. A. The occurrence of clustering in the recall of randomly arranged associates. *Journal of General Psychology,* 1953, 49, 229–240.

DiVesta, F. J., & Stover, D. O. The semantic mediation of evaluative meaning. *Journal of Experimental Psychology,* 1962, 64, 467–475.

Duchnowski, A. J., Nunnally, J. C., & Faw, T. T. Acquired reward value in discrimination learning: Methodological developments and effects on reward magnitude and reward schedules. Privately circulated research report, Vanderbilt University, 1968.

Ekstrand, B. A. note on measuring response learning during paired-associate learning. *Journal of Verbal Learning & Verbal Behavior,* 1966, 5, 344–347.

Finley, J. R., & Staats, A. W. Evaluative meaning words as reinforcing stimuli. *Journal of Verbal Learning & Verbal Behavior,* 1967, 6, 193–197.

Goss, A., & Nodine, C. *Paired Associates Learning.* New York: Academic Press, 1965.

Johnson, R. C., Thomson, C. W. & Frincke, G. Word values, word frequency and visual duration threshold. *Psychological Review,* 1960, 67, 332–342.

Kendall, K. A., & Nunnally, J. C. Effects of reward schedules on the acquisition of conditioned reward value. *Psychonomic Science,* 1968, 12, 239–240.

Logan, F. A. *Incentive.* New Haven, Connecticut: Yale Univ. Press, 1960.

Lott, A. J., Lott, B. E., & Walsh, T. The learning of paired-associates relevant to differentially-liked persons. *Journal of Personality & Social Psychology,* 1970, 16, 274–283.

Lott, B. E. Attitude formation: The development of a color preference response through mediated generalization. *Journal of Abnormal & Social Psychology,* 1955, 50, 321–326.

Marshall, A. The role of instruction to learn, overt rehearsal and word-pleasantness on the acquisition of a paired-associated list. Unpublished Master's thesis, University of Rhode Island, Kingston, R.I., 1970.

Mechanic, A., & Mechanic, J. D. Response activities and the mechanism of selectivity in incidental learning. *Journal of Verbal Learning & Verbal Behavior,* 1967, 6, 389–397.

Noble, C. E. Measurements of association value (a), rated associations (a') and scales meaningfulness (m') for the 2100 CVC combinations of the English alphabet. *Psychological Reports,* 1961, 8, 487–521.

Nunnally, J. C., & Faw, T. T. The acquisition of conditioned reward value in discrimination learning. *Child Development,* 1968, 39, 159–166.

Nunnally, J. C., Duchnowski, A. J., & Knott, P. D. Association of neutral objects with rewards: Effects of massed versus distributed practice, delay of testing, age and sex. *Journal of Experimental Child Psychology,* 1967, 5, 152–163.

Nunnally, J. C., Duchnowski, A. J., & Parker, R. K. Association of neutral objects with rewards: Effects on verbal evaluation, reward expectancy, and selective attention. *Journal of Personality & Social Psychology.* 1965, **1**, 270–274.

Nunnally, J. C., Stevens, D. A., & Hall, G. F. Association of neutral objects with rewards: Effects on verbal evaluation and eye movements. *Journal of Experimental Child Psychology,* 1965, **2**, 44–57.

Osgood, C. E. The nature and measurement of meaning. *Psychological Bulletin,* 1952, **49**, 197–237.

Paivio, A. Mental imagery in associative learning and memory. *Psychological Review,* 1969, **76**, 241–263.

Parker, G. V. C., & Noble, C. E. Experimentally produced meaningfulness (m) in paired-associate learning. *American Journal of Psychology,* 1963, **76**, 579–588.

Peters, H. N. The judgmental theory of pleasantness and unpleasantness. *Psychological Review,* 1935, **42**, 354–386.

Peters, H. N. Experimental studies of the judgmental theory of feeling: I. learning of positive and negative reactions as a determinant of affective judgments. *Journal of Experimental Psychology,* 1938, **23**, 1–25. (a)

Peters, H. N. Experimental studies of the judgmental theory of feeling: II. application of scaling to the measurement of relatively indifferent affective values. *Journal of Experimental Psychology,* 1938, **23**, 258–269. (b)

Peters, H. N. Experimental studies of the judgmental theory of feeling: III. the absolute shift in affective value conditioned by learned reactions. *Journal of Experimental Psychology,* 1939, **24**, 73–85. (a)

Peters, H. N. Experimental studies of the judgmental theory of feeling: IV. retention of the effects of learned reactions on affective judgments. *Journal of Experimental Psychology,* 1939, **24**, 111–134. (b)

Pollio, H. R. Associative structure and verbal behavior. In T. R. Dixon & D. L. Horton (eds.) *Verbal Behavior and General Behavior Theory.* Englewood Cliffs, New Jersey: Prentice-Hall, 1968.

Postman, L. Organization and interference. *Psychological Review,* 1971, **78**, 290–302.

Premack, D. On some boundary conditions of contrast. In Tapp, J. T. (Ed.) *Reinforcement and Behavior.* New York: Academic Press, 1969.

Razran, G. H. S. Music, art, and the conditioned response. *Psychological Bulletin,* 1938, **35**, 532–541. (a)

Razran, G. H. S. Conditioning away social bias by the lunch-room technique. *Psychological Bulletin,* 1938, **35**, 693–699. (b)

Razran, G. H. S. Determinants of the consolidation or *pragnanz* of conditioned preferences. *Psychological Bulletin,* 1940, **37**, 481–492. (a)

Razran, G. H. S. Conditioned response changes in rating and appraising socio-political slogans. *Psychological Bulletin,* 1940, **37**, 564–571. (b)

Razran, G. H. S. The conditioned evocation of attitudes. *Journal of Experimental Psychology,* 1956, **48**, 274–282.

Reitz, W. The role of affect in binocular resolution. Unpublished doctoral dissertation, The Pennsylvania State University, 1963.

Reitz, W., & Jackson, D. N. Affect and stereoscopic resolution. *Journal of Abnormal & Social Psychology,* 1964, **69**, 212–215.

Sarason, I. G. Empirical findings and theoretical problems in the use of anxiety scales. *Psychological Bulletin,* 1960, **57**, 403–415.

Schneirla, T. C. An evolutionary and developmental theory of biphasic processes underlying approach and withdrawal. In M. R. Jones (Ed.), *Nebraska Symposium on Motivation.* Lincoln: Univ. of Nebraska Press, 1959.

Sheridan, T. K. Relationship between conditioned salivary response magnitude and intensity of rated pleasantness. Paper delivered at the meetings of the Eastern Psychological Association, Atlantic City, N. J., 1966.

Silverstein, A. Acquired word value, verbal learning and retention: replication and extension. *Psychological Reports,* 1966, **18**, 357–358.

Silverstein, A. Acquired pleasantness and paired-associate learning in mixed and homogenous lists. *Journal of Experimental Psychology,* 1972, **93**, 111–117. (a)

Silverstein, A. The role of task anxiety in removing the effects of acquired pleasantness in paired-associate learning. *Journal of Experimental Psychology,* 1972, **94**, 173–178. (b)

Silverstein, A. Is the acquired-pleasantness effect in paired-associate learning free from confounding by meaningfulness and similarity? *Journal of Experimental Psychology,* 1973, **97**, 116-118.

Silverstein, A. Acquired pleasantness as a stimulus and a response variable in paired-associate learning. *Journal of Experimental Psychology* (in press).

Silverstein, A., & Dienstbier, R. A. Rated pleasantness and association value of 101 English nouns. *Journal of Verbal Learning & Verbal Behavior,* 1968, **7**, 81–86. (a)

Silverstein, A., & Dienstbier, R. A. Can the superior learn-ability of meaningful and pleasant words be transferred to nonsense syllables? *Journal of Experimental Psychology,* 1968, **78**, 292–298. (b)

Silverstein, A., & Marshall, A. Incidental vs. intentional paired-associate learning. *American Journal of Psychology,* 1968, **81**, 415–424.

Silverstein, A., & McCreary, C. Acquired word value and verbal learning. *Psychological Reports,* 1964, **14**, 499–504.

Spence, K. W. *Behavior Theory and Conditioning.* New Haven, Connecticut: Yale Univ. Press, 1956.

Staats, A. W. Conditioned stimuli, conditioned reinforcers and word meaning. In A. W. Staats (Ed.) *Human Learning,* New York: Holt, 1964.

Staats, A. W. Social behaviorism and human motivation: Principles of the attitude-reinforcer-discriminative system. In A. G. Greenwald, T. C. Brock, T. M. Ostrom (Eds.) *Psychological Foundations of Attitudes.* New York: Academic Press, 1968.

Staats, A. W., & Staats, C. K. Language conditioning using semantic generalization. *Journal of Experimental Psychology,* 1959, **57**, 187–192. (a)

Staats, A. W., & Staats, C. K. Number of trials as a factor in meaning established by classical conditioning. *Journal of General Psychology,* 1959, **61**, 211–223. (b)

Staats, A. W., Staats, C. K., & Biggs, D. A. Meaning of verbal stimuli changed by conditioning. *American Journal of Psychology,* 1958, **71**, 429–431.

Staats, A. W., Staats, C. K., & Crawford, H. L. First-order conditioning of meaning and the parallel conditioning of a GSR. *Journal of General Psychology,* 1962, **67**, 159–167.

Staats, C. K., & Staats, A. W. Meaning established by classical conditioning. *Journal of Experimental Psychology,* 1957, **54**, 74–80.

Thorndike, E. L. *Human Learning*. New York: Century, 1931.

Thorndike, E. L., & Lorge, I. *The Teacher's Word Book of 30,000 words*. New York: Teachers College, 1944.

Tolman, E. C. *Purposive Behavior in Animals and Men*. New York: Appleton, 1932.

Tulving, E. Subjective organization and free recall of "unrelated" words. *Psychological Review*, 1962, **69**, 344–354.

Underwood, B. J. *Experimental Psychology*. Philadelphia, Pennsylvania: Lippincott, 1966.

Underwood, B. J., & Schulz, R. W. *Meaningfulness and verbal learning*. Philadelphia, Pennsylvania: Lippincott, 1960.

Wike, E. L., *Secondary Reinforcement*. New York: Holt, 1966.

Yavuz, H. S. The retention of incidentally learned connotative responses. *Journal of Psychology*, 1963, **55**, 409–418.

Young, R. K., & Parker, G. V. C. Serial learning as a function of experimentally induced meaningfulness. *Journal of Experimental Psychology*, 1970, **84**, 24–26.

CHAPTER 9

Intervening Cognitions in Motivation [1]

HEINZ HECKHAUSEN [2]

Ruhr University, Bochum, Germany

Theory construction in motivation is going more cognitive. Evidence, by now, is so abundant that we should take cognitions more seriously than just placing one or two shadowy intervening variables between stimulus and response terms.

How shall we understand the loose term of "cognition"? I do not use it in order to point to such self-evident facts as that people are conscious beings, that they are cognizant of the situation they are in, that they are aware of their feelings and activities. Instead, I want to invite your attention to the fact that there are, in the course of an action sequence, certain classes of concrete cognitive activities that cannot simply be considered to be epiphenomena because their outcome makes a lot of difference to behavior as we observe it. Here are a few examples of such cognitive activities: weighing the probabilities of possible outcomes of an intended action, appraising the consequences of an action outcome, explaining in advance or in retrospect the result of an action, and comparing the actual outcome with a set standard. These cognitive activities can be partitioned into distinct classes and labeled as perceived success

---

[1] Some of the issues in this paper also are examined by Heckhausen and Weiner (1972) and are reviewed by Weiner (1972) in a forthcoming book.

[2] This paper was written while the author was a fellow of the Netherlands Institute for Advanced Study at Wassenaar.

probabilities, anticipated reward values, causal attribution, and self-evaluation, respectively. For theoretical and explanatory purpose, classes of cognitive activities like these are abstracted into intervening constructs which can be inferred from antecedent and consequent observables. This is the sense in which I shall speak of intervening cognitions.

On a first glance, this approach is not terribly new, but quite traditional. Even in the Hullian system, K, the incentive notion, can be thought of as representing the relevant class of cognitive activities. And still more explicit are, in this respect, the various forms of expectancy $\times$ value theories. What is newer, however, is the profusion of deliberate attempts to get closer to the content of actual cognitive activities within the individual, in order to index the cognitive constructs. In addition, constructs for hitherto neglected classes of intervening cognitions are introduced, although the selection presently used does not pretend to be in any way exhaustive. And last but not least, extensive use is being made of data from individual–difference measures in order to arrive at antecedent observables that permit intervening cognitions to be inferred.

In the first part of this chapter, I will go over various examples of recent research that can hardly be explained by traditional behavioristic theories—or, to say the least, that can only be handled in a very cumbersome manner. They all show that, behavioristically speaking, "lawful" relationships are obviously altered by intervening cognitions. We need to infer meanings as they exist for the individual person rather than to confine ourselves to quasi-objectively defined stimuli, drive states, responses, and consequences. Otherwise, we are left with broken logical relationships between all observable terms in our explanatory equations. In a second part of the chapter, I will sketch a process model of motivation as an attempt to take account of cognitions and to catch, at the same time, more lawful predictability of behavior. In a third part, I will report, by way of illustration, on some new findings on action preferences employing the goal-setting paradigm.

I

Drive theory and, even more so, mediational S–R theories cannot be denied some elegance and efficiency in predicting behavior. It might, however, highlight our problem by way of contrast if I refer briefly to an utterly noncognitive approach, namely the reinforcement theory of functional behaviorism. McGinnies and Ferster (1971) have edited a book on *The Reinforcement of Social Behavior* in which they have selected 73 papers from over 400 studies in order to show that there is no need for the postulation of intervening processes. All that needs to be accounted for, according to these authors, are the manipulable environmental events of which behavior is ultimately a function. Their key explanatory term is reinforcement, i.e., a stimulus—or let me say a consequence—that follows a response. Since, however, an administered consequence does not always alter subsequent behavior, they distinguish this reinforcement as a *procedure* from reinforcement *as a process*. The latter can be inferred when the frequency of a response shows an increase.

Thus, functional behaviorism has to rely heavily on postdiction to determine whether reinforcement as a procedure has or has not induced a reinforcement as a process. I will not quarrel with postdiction. Let me quote Niels Bohr who once said that prediction is extremely difficult, especially if it refers to the future. Nonetheless, I am a little dissatisfied with the functional behaviorist's modesty, or shall I say, defeatism. First, I think we can do a bit more about prediction if we take account of cognitions or "private events"—a neat term revealing the ambivalence about this kind of phenomena. Second, if we exclude cognitions from consideration, we deliberately blind ourselves from the possible discovery of lawful processes within the black box.

I will not use the term "reinforcement," because it is bound up with learning theories. And even in the explanation of learning, reinforcement as a process appears to be a superfluous concept. As Edward Walker (1969) has shown, it is a psychological kind of glue, thought to strengthen the connection between a stimulus and a response. Behavior changes, called learning, can sufficiently be explained as "pull" effects of changing incentives depending on the motivational or "push" conditions within the person.

Instead of going into this further let us stick, for the time being, to the difficult but worthwhile distinction between acquisition and performance—introduced through Tolman's latent-learning experiments and, nowadays, revived by results of observational learning (e.g., Bandura, Ross, & Ross, 1963). Motivation, whatever that means, might not always be involved in the acquisition of new responses. There is, however, less dispute that motivational processes are always involved in performance. At any rate, I will concentrate on performance rather than acquisition problems. I will refer mainly to behavior choice under the pull and the push of situational and person-specific conditions, respectively.

The explanatory burden that is carried by the reinforcement concept in the domain of learning is, in the domain of performance, placed on the concept of reward. This, however, does not imply that reward is just another term for reinforcement as a procedure. It is true that reward signifies the positive (or negative) consequences that are contingent on an action. But, first, a reward might or might not coincide with reinforcement as a physically or intersubjectively defined procedure. Again, like stimulus, drive, or performance outcome, reward, as a physically or intersubjectively defined event, implies private meanings, i.e., subjective reward values varying between individuals and, also, within individuals over time. Second, one consequence of a performance outcome may be self-reward and such a phenomenon is hardly covered by the notion of reinforcement as a procedure. To finish these introductory remarks, let me just add that in motivation theories the salient concept, replacing "reward," is "incentive." More precisely, anticipated reward values of the consequences of one's own action are called incentives. This, at least, is my terminological decision, which I shall follow later.

Let me, then, start with a quick review of some recent findings (see also Heckhausen & Weiner, 1972). They all have in common that one must infer cognitions in order to maintain the existence of lawful relationships between stimulus and response, between drive state and response, between response and consequence, between performance outcome and subsequent response. In order not to complicate matters in presenting my purpose, I shall use a simple sequence scheme of stimulus–response–consequence. The "stimulus" term encompasses antecedent information input of external sources of the environment or internal sources within the organism like drive state. The "response" term encompasses ongoing activity as well as performance outcome. And the "consequences" term encompasses emotions, success and failure experiences, reward values of an object, self-rewards.

Cognitions Intervening between Stimulus and Response

A first example comes from studies by Lazarus (1968) and his colleagues on fear arousal, monitored by autonomic indicators like heart rate while subjects are watching a "threat" film, e.g., a primitive circumcision rite. Subjects are told either prior to or during the film that circumcision is actually not painful—or given other coping devices facilitating denial or intellectualization—show reduced fear responses as compared to a control group. The induced cognitions appear to have reduced the aversive properties of the film stimuli and/or changed the information processing responses. In any case, the same stimuli, intersubjectively speaking, lead to different emotional consequences. Intervening cognitions can alter the tie between S and R as Fig. 9-1 indicates.

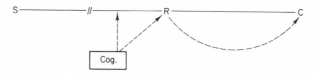

Fig. 9-1. Aversive stimuli of a threat film (Lazarus, 1968). Induced cognitions lead to efficient coping behavior (R) and less fear and discomfort (C).

Research in the area of cognitive dissonance provides ample evidence that other resultant emotions, perceptions of drive state or drive-related bodily sensations are influenced by intervening cognitions. Again, in the following examples, cognitions seem to alter the otherwise "lawful" relations between S and R.

In a carefully executed study by Mansson (1969), thirst was aroused by having subjects eat salty crackers and a specially prepared sauce that created a sensation of a hot and dry mouth. Subjects were offered either low or high justification for committing themselves to go without drinking for a 24-hour period. After that and before the supposed deprivation period started, several response measures were obtained, comprising respondent, consummatory, behavioral, and fantasy indices of third effects. As predicted by dissonance theory, individuals who had committed themselves to endure the deprivation without sufficient justification reacted as if they had almost no thirst. Their attempts at cognitive dissonance reduction led them to report less thirst, to drink less water, to perceive fewer thirst words in a recognition task, to learn thirst-related associates more slowly and to produce fewer need-for-water content in writing a story to a thirst-related TAT picture, compared with subjects with the same high thirst arousal but either in the low dissonance or in a control condition.

The scheme in Fig. 9-2 indicates that dissonance reducing cognitions arise from the imbalance of R and C, i.e., the unjustified commitment to continue with the experiment and the expected unpleasant consequences

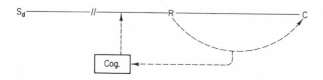

Fig. 9-2. Thirst stimuli (Mansson, 1969). High cognitive dissonance for going without drinking, i.e., commitment for staying in the deprivation experiment (R) compared to insufficient justification (C), leads to reduced thirst perception.

of the deprivation, respectively. These cognitions work on the perception of stimuli arising in the organism, S_D. (drive stimulus). A closer analysis of the data suggests a coping activity denying the burning sensations in the mouth.

Further examples for cognitions intervening in an otherwise simple and lawful S–R relation can be recruited from recent research on emotional behavior instigated by Schachter and Singer's (1962) two-factor theory of emotion. According to this theory, both physiological arousal and a cognitive causal attribution appropriate to the state of arousal are required for the formation, perception, and expression of an emotion.

In a well-known study by Schachter and Singer (1962), subjects received injections under some pretext. Actually, half the subjects were injected with adrenalin, the other half with a placebo. One subgroup in each of both conditions was informed about the true arousing effect of adrenalin, a second subgroup was not informed, and a third was misinformed. Immediately after the subject had been injected, he was placed in a waiting room, where a stooge behaved either in a euphoric or in an angry manner. Individuals not informed or misinformed about the arousal effects of the injection acted more euphorically or more angrily, according to the situation produced by the stooge, as compared with individuals given placebo injections or with individuals given adrenalin injections but informed about their arousing effects. Moreover, the critical subjects also reported the resultant emotions appropriate to the perceived situation. Emotions, therefore, are dependent upon cognitive interpretations concerning the causes of one's internal arousal state.

In a similar vein, Valins (1966) has even shown that the perception of one's arousal state need not be veridical. His subjects overheard their heart-rate feedback while viewing slides of seminude females. To half of the slides a change of the heart beats was faked, and these were the slides that subjects found more attractive and that they would choose as remuneration for participation in the experiment. Obviously, the evaluative response was influenced by a causal attribution to the changed heart-rate like: "That girl has affected my heart beats; she must be very attractive."

Cognitions Intervening between Drive State and Response

Let us now turn to cognitions affecting the otherwise "lawful" relation between drive state and response. By "otherwise lawful" I mean lawful according to the well-known drive theory propositions of Hull and Spence. I have chosen two studies that employ a classical learning paradigm, i.e., pain avoidance in eyelid conditioning and the multiplicative effect of drive and habit in paired-associates learning.

Grinker (1969) put the eye-lid conditioning procedure within frame conditions that created cognitive dissonance in the subjects. After 20 acquisition trials, the experimenter announced an unexpected prolongation of the experiment with increased intensity of unpleasant puffs of air. Subjects were offered a choice between continuing or not continuing the experiment. The committed subjects who remained were given either a high or a low verbal justification for undergoing increased pain. The latter group with high cognitive dissonance (choice and low justification) showed much less elevation of the conditioning level than the low-dissonance group (choice and high justification). Actually, the intensity of the unconditioned stimulus had not been changed. The announcement of the increased threat elevated the conditioning level only in the low-dissonance group. The other group had obviously reduced cognitive dissonance by lowering or blocking the drive state aroused by the experimenter's announcement of increased pain. As a result, they seem to have expected less fear than the low-dissonance group and were therefore less motivated to avoid the air puff.

The second study challenges a well-established explanation of paired-associate learning under different levels of anxiety and of task difficulty. According to drive theory, anxiety is conceptualized as a drive. Therefore, anxiety increases the reaction potential of responses elicited in a given stimulus situation. This will facilitate learning when correct responses are dominant over incorrect responses, as is the case in easy paired associates, i.e., those with minimal intralist competition. Conversely, if incorrect responses are dominant or many diverse responses compete for dominance, as in tasks with high intralist competition, anxiety will impair learning. In line with these propositions, Spence and his colleagues (e.g., Spence, Farber, & McFann, 1956) have demonstrated that anxious subjects are superior in easy tasks whereas nonanxious subjects are superior in difficult tasks.

A certain development in the theory of achievement motivation (see Weiner, 1965) offers an alternative explanation, according to which the interaction between anxiety and task difficulty is mediated by cognitions of success or failure feedback. Easy tasks are learned quickly and provide, relatively speaking, success feedback: The reverse holds for difficult tasks. What would happen, then, if subjects working on an objectively easy task were given continuous failure feedback and, conversely, were given continuous success feedback when working on an objectively difficult task? Under these conditions, achievement motivation theory provides predictions contradictory to drive theory: Anxious subjects should perform better than subjects low in anxiety on difficult paired associates when given success feedback. On the other hand, subjects low in anxiety should perform better than anxious subjects on easy paired associates when given failure feedback.

This is exactly what was found in an experiment by Weiner (1965) and in a replication by Weiner & Schneider (1971). Moreover, similar results were obtained when the individual-difference measure for anxiety, the Test Anxiety Questionnaire, was superseded by a standard TAT procedure for measuring both tendencies of achievement motivation, hope of success and fear of failure, and using the difference score.

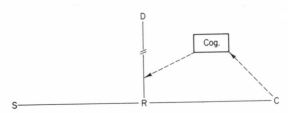

Fig. 9-3. Anxiety as a drive state (Weiner, 1966; Weiner & Schneider, 1971). Rate of paired associates learning is not dependent on interaction between drive level and intralist competition but on interaction between achievement motive type and performance feedback.

In summary, the anxiety-learning relationship is mediated by perceptions of performance outcome. Figure 9-3 indicates the intervention of these feedback cognitions between drive state and response, altering the influence of a drive level that was otherwise believed to have the opposite effects quite regularly on learning under the conditions given. Drive level per se is not what improves or impairs learning in interaction with the degree of response competition. Performance outcome is affected, rather, by the momentary arousal of a motive which, in turn, is mediated by cumulative success or failure perceptions.

Cognitions Intervening between Performance Outcome (or Consequence) and Subsequent Response

The outcome of an activity often invites interpretations concerning what the causes of the outcome might have been. In the case of unexpected outcomes, reinterpretations force themselves upon the actor: causing attributing cognitions influence subsequent responses. Again, cognitions alter a relation from what in some theories is thought to be lawful. I will present examples referring to the frustration–aggression hypothesis and to extinction.

Within the framework of Hullian learning theory, the hypothesis was advanced that frustration creates aggression (Dollard, Miller, Doob, & Mowrer, 1939). It has raised many issues that are still far from having been settled. There are, by now, many studies stressing the role of cognitive determinants in the expression and manifestation of aggression. For instance, Mallick and McCandless (1966) had a stooge frustrate 9-year-old subjects trying to complete block construction tasks, so that the corresponding monetary rewards were lost. In one condition, the experimenter explained the disturbing interference afterward, by pointing out that the frustrator was "sleepy" or "upset." These subjects, as compared with those not given an explanation for the frustration, showed a decline in aggressive feelings and acted less aggressively against the frustrator when given a chance.

Figure 9-4 indicates that the explanatory cognition changes the meaning of the stimulus, the frustrating stooge, and that this, in turn, alters the relation between C and R. The same consequence is now no longer followed by the "lawful" amount of anger and aggression.

Extinction is another field where the influence of intervening cognitions were demonstrated, after it was taken for granted that extinction was strictly dependent on the reward contingency during learning. For instance, if 50% of the correct responses were rewarded, extinction takes longer than with 100% reward conditions. Research stimulated by Rotter's (1954) social learning theory finds this to be true only when subjects believe that the task is governed by chance. If, however, they think the performance outcome to be caused mainly by their skill, extinction takes longer in the 100% than in the 50% reward condition (see Rotter, 1966).

This result, contrasting the animal learning literature, is easily understood when one puts oneself in the shoes of a human being (which is what even a functional behaviorist cannot help doing). Expectation of

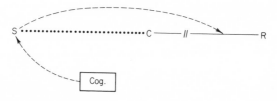

Fig. 9-4. Aggression after frustrating consequences (Mallick & McCandless, 1966). Post hoc explanation of performance-blocking intervention (S) reduces aggressive behavior against the blocking agent (R).

future goal attainment is not only dependent on the numerical rate of goal attainment in a task on past occasions but also on a general belief about the causes of goal attainment in that very task. Rotter (1966) has postulated a general belief dimension ranging from internal to external control of the outcome of one's actions. If a person believes he has internal, i.e., personal, control over a future outcome, as is the case in a skill-related task, it is obvious that a series of failure takes him longer to change his causal inference built up in previous 100% than 50% success series.

In comparison with Rotter's dualistic characterization of the locus of control region, the impact of causal inferences has been much more differentiated in recent causal attribution theory, originally stimulated by Heider (1958). Weiner (in Weiner, Frieze, Kukla, Reed, Rest, & Rosenbaum, 1971) has cross classified the locus-of-control distinction with stable versus variable causal factors, a stability-over-time distinction. Thus, ability and effort are internal factors, ability being a stable factor, and effort a variable factor on the internal side of control. Task difficulty and luck are external factors but task difficulty is a stable factor and luck (or bad luck) a variable factor of the environment (see Table 9-1).

This differentiated causal attribution pattern has proved very powerful in the clarification of individual differences in extinction. In our laboratory at Bochum, Meyer (see Weiner, Heckhausen, Meyer, & Cook, 1972) has shown that, during continual failure, expectancy of further success drops rapidly in those subjects who tend to ascribe their failures to stable causal factors, i.e., to low ability or high task difficulty; whereas, under the same conditions of extinction, subjects who tend to ascribe their failures to variable factors, i.e., to lack of effort or bad luck, have almost no expectancy decrements. It is worth noting that each of the two different

TABLE 9-1

Classification Scheme for the Perceived Causes of Performance Outcome [a]

Stability over time	Locus of control	
	internal	external
stable	Ability	Task difficulty
variable	Effort	Luck

[a] According to Weiner et al., 1971.

causal attribution patterns is preferred by individuals in whom one of the two tendencies of the achievement motive is predominant (Meyer, 1973; see also in Weiner *et al.*, 1971). Hope-of-success individuals tend to explain their failures by the two variable factors and show, consequently, a small expectancy decrement. Fear-of-failure individuals tend to explain their failures by the two stable factors and show, therefore, a marked expectancy decrement. Finally, let me add that decrement of expectancy is accompanied by a decrease in speed of performance.

Still another case in point is goal setting. In a series of trials the setting of the next goal is influenced by the causes to which a person tends to attribute his last action outcome. As with the extinction results, there are two clearcut causal attribution patterns that lead to a raising or lowering of the level of aspiration above or below the attained performance level, respectively (resulting in a positive or negative goal discrepancy score). Those subjects who tend to attribute their unsuccessful trials to lack of effort rather than to an insufficient ability of their own, will prefer high over low risks and will have, in consequence, a positive goal discrepancy score. On the other hand, subjects with the reverse causal attribution bias (i.e., high effort attribution after success and lack-of-ability attribution after failure) prefer low to high risks and have a negative discrepancy score. More generally speaking, a bias—in the case of success—toward stable causal factors (ability and task difficulty) and—in the case of failure—a corresponding bias toward variable causal factors (lack of effort and back luck) is the attribution pattern of offensive risk takers. The reverse bias toward variable factors after success and stable factors after failure is the attribution pattern of defensive risk patterns. These predictions have been confirmed by Meyer (1973).

Cognitions Intervening between Performance Outcome and Consequences

There is still only one relation left in our action scheme; the relation between R and C, between performance output and self-administered consequences. Let me cut the last link within the scheme. In order to do this, I am going to demonstrate that, intersubjectively, the same performance output may lead to differential consequences, dependent on intervening cognitions.

A case for self-administered consequences is self-reward. If we consider the affective consequences of performance outcome, like feelings of success or failure, to be self-rewards (as I am inclined to do), then it is clear that the consequences depend, among other factors, on prior standard setting.[3] Standard setting is often a private cognitive event, as in the case of an intention. The research literature on level of aspiration, e.g., gives ample evidence that the same performance outcome may mean success to one individual and failure to the other, dependent on the individually held performance standard.

We know, however, more about the self-evaluative process, intervening between performance outcome and consequences, than just these generalities. Again, causal attributions enter the scene. Consider a simple case. If a performance outcome is ascribed predominantly to external causes, to very high or very low task difficulty or to sheer luck, no self-rewarding consequences are likely to occur.

As Meyer (1973) has shown, individuals with different motive types possess different causal-attribution patterns for mediating self-reward. He has given ninth-grade students digit-symbol substitution tasks with induced success and failure. After each trial, the subjects assigned the perceived causes of their success and failure to the four factors of ability, task difficulty, effort and luck. Moreover, the subjects rated how intensely they felt pleasure and pride after success or anger and shame after failure, respectively. The results are clearcut. Hope-of-success individuals, for instance, tend to ascribe success to high ability, whereas failure is ascribed to a momentary lack of effort and bad luck. In line with this attribution strategy, they experience pleasurable feelings following success whereas, following failure, they remain pretty indifferent. Compared to this happy pattern, fear-of-failure individuals attribute their success less to ability and more to good luck and their failures more to lack of ability and less to lack of effort and bad luck. Accordingly, they feel moderately happy after success and very unhappy after failure.

These results make one wonder how far one could go in construing the concept of motive as a self-conditioning mechanism. The individual himself seems to condition the contingencies of self-reward to a remarkable degree, mediated by his bias in locating perceived causes of his performance outcome. This has far-reaching consequences. Consider the hope-of-success individuals. Their relatively happy attribution strategy insures them a confident outlook and a high persistence, even in the face of failure.

The reported results have been corroborated in a study by Cook (see

---

[3] Highly relevant for problems of standard norms in motivation is adaptation level theory. See Helson (Chapter 7).

Weiner *et al.*, 1971, 1972). Pupils in the fourth and fifth grades, placed in a free-operant setting, rewarded themselves for performance on a puzzle task, with half the puzzles actually being insoluble. The subjects were instructed to "reward themselves by taking as many chips as they feel they deserve" following each successful trial. Likewise, they were told to "punish themselves" in case of a failure by returning the number of chips which "they feel they should." The results are similar to Meyer's. With increasing resultant approach tendency of the achievement motive, as well as with increasing self-ascription for success and failure, more chips are taken following success and fewer chips are returned following failure; i.e., the net outcome of self-rewarding is more positive.

So far I have dealt heavily on causal attributions. However, no less important for, and constituent of, self-evaluation is the standard, the level of aspiration against which the performance outcome is evaluated. This has cogently been shown in several studies by Locke (1967, 1969; Locke, Cartledge, & Knerr, 1970). Let me just add that the relation of performance outcome to the aspiration standard rather than the relation to expectancy (success probability) is what determines self-rewarding affect. We have to conclude that standard as well as causal ascriptions are the determinants constituting the self-evaluative cognitions that give rise to affective consequences of self-reward. (For the role of performance standard for self-evaluation and self-reward see also Kanfer, 1971.)

In sum, the last relation in our scheme has been severed. The same outcome of a performance leads to different consequences, mediated by intervening self-evaluative cognitions, as Fig. 9-5 indicates.

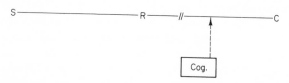

Fig. 9-5. Self-reward for performance outcome (Meyer, 1973; Cook in Weiner *et al.*, 1971, 1972). Amount of self-reward (*C*) dependent on causal self-ascription of performance outcome (*R*).

Motive-Linked Differences in the Reward Value of Money

Since we are concentrating in this volume on reward and preference, it might, perhaps, be worthwhile and illustrative to have a short look at such a highly symbolic reward as money. It is a truism that the same objective amount of money may have quite different weights for different people. But if we control amount by using individuals as their own controls it is remarkable how much the reward value of the same amount of money changes with different uses to which the money is put.

In a recent study in our laboratory, it was predicted that the reward value of various possibilities of using money was closely linked to enduring motive types of individuals (Regelmann, 1972). Subjects had to imagine an unexpected legacy bringing them 1000, 10,000, or 100,000 D-Marks. They could choose among several ways to use the money, but, having once decided, they had to stick to that decision for at least 2 years. The uses ranged across wide areas of consumption, saving and investment; e.g., various consumer goods, a trip, furniture, a normal savings account with a statutory term of notice, life insurance, a private house, bonds, stocks, a property account, a share in a firm, the establishment of an own enterprise. In a multiple paired comparison of all possibilities, ratios of indifference in reward value between all possible uses were determined for each subject.[4] For instance, an individual might prefer to invest the inherited 10,000 D-Marks in a small firm rather than place the same amount of money in a property account. Then, the amount for the property account was raised until the subject was indifferent in his preference for the one or the other possibility so that, finally, the value of 10,000 D-Marks for investing equals the value of, say, 13,000 D-Marks for a property account.

As predicted, the indifference ratios for the reward value of various money uses were closely related to achievement motive differences, as assessed by our standard TAT procedure, which scores hope-of-success and fear-of-failure tendencies separately. Hope-of-success individuals prefer investing to saving, and saving to consuming; i.e., they ask less money for investing than for saving and for consuming. On the other hand, fear-of-failure individuals prefer saving to investing, and investing to consuming, etc. It is obvious that the differential reward values are dependent on how instrumental the various possibilities of money use are with regard to the current concerns in both motives. If we diagnose predominant motives with their current concerns, we can predict differential reward values which, otherwise, look equal to the outside observer.

---

[4] With regard to Berlyne's (Chapter 1) scheme of different research streams this study shows that psychophysical scaling techniques used in the research stream of decision theories, are closely germane to incentive value theories. The separation of both streams in Berlyne's "delta" scheme is bound up more with research traditions than with the problems to which research is addressed.

II

Coming to the second part of this chapter, let me first summarize. We have seen that objectively similar antecedent conditions may lead to quite dissimilar consequent effects. Intervening cognitions appear to be capable of altering each "lawful" link between all adjacent terms in any behavioristic theory construction. This holds for the ties between S and R, D and R, C and R, and R and C. A pivotal role in creating apparently nonlawful relations, obviously, is played by cognitions about S and C, i.e., by the perception of the situation and anticipation of possible consequences of the performance outcome. And, lastly, we are left with, if not plagued by, a lot of free-floating cognitions. What can we do about them? Is there any possibility of sorting out the pieces of this cognition puzzle, let alone assembling them all?

At this point, a short epistemological digression might be in order.[5] It is all packed into Fig. 9-6. The uppermost row shows the S, D, R, C scheme as "physically" defined variables, manipulated and described by the experimenter. The short slanting lines interrupting the connections between the terms indicate nonlawful consequent effects. The box is left empty. Other noncognitive or pseudocognitive theorists put in intervening variables like expectancies or incentives.

I have put the terms in quotation marks because the statement that they are "physically" defined, as is sometimes claimed by behaviorists, is an overstatement if not always a fiction. An injection of .5 mg adrenalin is physically defined, but the subject attaches some meaning to this "stimulus" of an injection unless one ventilates "the experimental room with vaporized adrenalin"—an idea Schachter and Singer (1962, p. 388) toyed with. Stimuli and reactions in an experimental setting always convey meanings with the interaction of an experimenter with his subject. These meanings cannot be defined physically but only publicly, i.e., according to the agreement of outside observers. It is therefore nonsensical to draw a straightforward connection between physically defined events and their meaning as indicated in our figure by the dotted lines leading to the second row. Smedslund (1969) has aptly elaborated on this point. It is crucial for the experimenter—with the functional behaviorist being no exception—to establish some communality with his subjects in the public meaning of stimuli and responses. He tries hard to maximize the overlap in shared public meaning of the experimental procedures with his subjects, by giving explicit instructions and by contriving experimen-

---

[5] See also Madsen (Chapter 11 in this book).

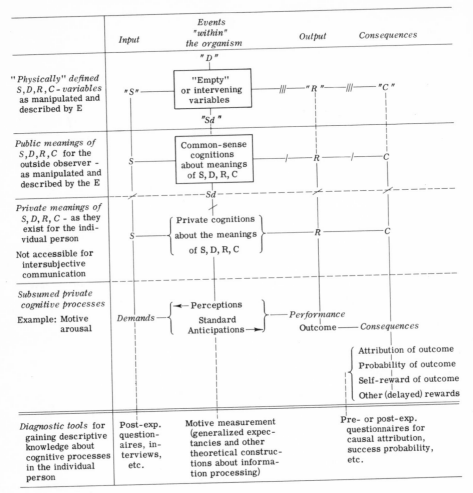

Fig. 9-6. The lawfulness of relationships within the sequence "stimulus–drive–response-consequence" when these terms are defined differently.

tal circumstances. In this sense, we can speak of S, D, R, and C as "objectively" or intersubjectively defined.

In some research areas, e.g., in cognitive–dissonance studies, the experimenter's endeavor to control for meaning has introduced so much artificiality and complication into experimental conditions that subjects become suspicious or confused. As a result, subjects cannot help but search for their own hypotheses concerning what the experiment might all be about. In such a situation, some subjects are eager to conform to what they think the experimenter might be after, whereas others are less inclined to do so. Paradoxically, the experimenter's eagerness to create a maximal overlap of public and private meanings might sometimes create the opposite, i.e., more variance of private meanings among the subjects.

In any case, the public meanings of S, D, R, and C never fully coincide with the private meanings of S, D, R, and C as they exist for individual subjects. Although there are some regularities, there are no universal rules which allow the inference from the public meaning of an experimental condition, as seen by the experimenter, to the private meaning existing for the individual subject. This is precisely why the functional behaviorist has to distinguish between reinforcement as a procedure and as a process. But even if we allow for intervening cognitions and try to manipulate them carefully, as in motivation research, the predicted relationships between S, D, R, and C often turn out to be nonlawful, as shown in the first part of this chapter and as indicated by the interrupted ties in this figure.

This brings us to the next row, to the private meanings of S, D, R, and C, as they exist for the individual person. If we could ascertain them, the necessary conditions for constructing more lawful relationships would be realized. But, we cannot, of course, get hold of private meanings in other persons directly. They are not accessible to intersubjective communication. What, then, could be done to infer the private meaning of all these floating cognitions, e.g., in motive arousal? The next row shows an abbreviated process model of motivation. The S, D, R, and C terms have been translated into cognitive "language": perceived demands of the situation instead of stimulus, anticipated performance and performance outcome instead of response, and anticipated causal attribution of performance outcome, anticipated probability of performance outcome, anticipated self-reward for performance outcome as well as anticipated other and delayed rewards instead of consequence. There has accumulated a substantial body of findings that logical implications exist between these types of cognitions, as we will see later.

But how can we infer the contents of these cognition types in the individual person more closely? We control the public meaning of our experimental variables in the first place. In addition, however, we can gather diagnostic data on the individual's inside world, so to speak. We have to use diagnostic tools for gaining descriptive knowledge about the individual person.[6] The diagnostic tools have to be designed with respect

---

[6] Eysenck (Chapter 6) demonstrates very convincingly the need to take account of individual differences.

to the subsumed private cognitive processes in question, as the bottom row of our figure indicates for the case of motive arousal. For example, the thematic apperceptive procedure for the measurement of motives like achievement, affiliation, or power has proved to be quite useful to gather some descriptive information about a person's generalized expectancies in one motive area. The obtained scores yield something like a frame of reference, within which the person processes incoming information when the situation arouses the respective motive. From the achievement motive scores, for instance, we can to some extent predict the perceived demands of an intersubjectively defined stimulus situations as well as action preferences like risk preference or persistence. We can refine our predictions by obtaining separate diagnostic data about the individual's preferred pattern of causal attribution and the momentarily perceived probabilities of performance outcome, although these special data, assessed by scales, are to some extent correlated with the individual's motive scores.

In sum, diagnostic tools uncover conspicuous portions of individual differences in the private meanings of perceived situations and intended actions within an intersubjectively defined experimental setting. The diagnostic data themselves present, of course, no private meanings. They are intersubjective, as are all data in psychology. Otherwise, they would not be communicable. They enable us to construct more refined models of intervening cognitive processes, whose predictive power can be tested and compared to other models that are less cognitive or noncognitive.

A first step toward pinpointing intervening cognitions for a process model of motivation is to see how they might influence the course of behavior within an action sequence (Heckhausen & Weiner, 1972). Cognitive processes are obviously not distributed evenly over the whole action sequence. There are two stages giving rise to augmented cognitive activity: motive arousal in the preperformance stage and self-evaluation in the postperformance stage. In both stages reward plays a pivotal role. During motive arousal an action preference often is sought which necessitates the weighing of reward values of possible performance outcomes. In the postperformance stage, on the other hand, self-evaluative processes determine self-reward, the immediate consequence of a performance outcome.

I have already pointed out the role of causal attribution in self-reward, citing some findings from Meyer (1973) and Cook (in Weiner *et al.*, 1971, 1972). The present model for self-reward is based on simple logical implications. There is a standard and a performance outcome. The deviation of the performance outcome from the standard determines the self-rewarding consequences, but they are mediated and moderated by attributing causes to the performance outcome. The attribution of causes is partly dependent on the cues of the given situation and partly on the individual attribution pattern linked to the aroused motive. This latter part can be called attribution bias (or attribution "error"). As we have seen, attribution bias makes a great deal of difference and can be conceived as a self-conditioning device stabilizing an individual's motive.

The present model of motive arousal is analogous to the model for self-reward, insofar as the cognitions have the same referents underlying self-reward: performance outcome, deviation from standard, causal attribution, and resulting reward values. But motive arousal cognitions have another grammatical form, so to speak. They refer to what *will* be and *might* be the case under given circumstances. They anticipate future and probable events under the arousing and constraining demands of the present situation.

III

In the last section of this chapter I want to show briefly how the application of combined diagnostic tools sharpens our predictions and yields deeper insight into motivation processes. I choose parts of two recent studies in our laboratory at Bochum. Both studies have explicitly attempted to cover more variance in risk preference, the paradigm in need achievement research most often investigated, than could be covered hitherto. In both studies, individual differences in the subsumed reward values of performance outcomes have been more differentiated by employing additional descriptive knowledge. Besides need achievement, a second motive, need affiliation, was measured in order to predict more precisely the actual risk preference in an experimental situation which is always an interpersonal one.

Let me start off with the well known risk taking model proposed by John Atkinson (1957). As you may remember, only one piece of information about individual differences is needed to have the Atkinson model work: the resultant tendency of the achievement motive. Individuals more highly motivated to achieve success than to avoid failure prefer tasks of intermediate difficulty, whereas individuals in whom the fear of failure tendency is predominant avoid most strongly the intermediate range of task difficulty. According to the model, this differential risk preference is derived from the assumption that, for each task, probability of success and incentive value of success (i.e., the anticipated reward value) form a multiplicative function in which incentive is inversely and linearly related to success probability. This is why the resulting curve of risk preference reaches a maximum for approach motivated subjects when the probability of success is .50. For avoidance motivated subjects the same curve represents risk avoidance. Therefore, no descriptive knowledge is needed about incentive value of success for each individual. It can be derived from experimentally induced probabilities of success.

The logic of the model can best be understood psychologically if we paraphrase it in terms of causal attribution theory. Tasks of intermediate difficulty have a maximal uncertainty with regard to the possibility of success or failure outcome. When performed they will yield the most definite information about one's own ability and expended effort. Information about these internal factors is preferred by a person motivated by hope of success and facing a risk preference situation. On the other hand, success or failure in very difficult or easy tasks depends almost entirely on external factors like task characteristics or luck. And by opting for information about these external factors, a person motivated by fear of failure avoids internal attributions and their self-evaluative consequences.

The Atkinson model has stimulated much research which has, roughly speaking, confirmed the model. However, there have been found repeatedly two main deviations from the model's predictions. Both deviations appear to be caused by the fact that the model construes the role of incentive too simply.

The first deviation refers to the peak of the preference curve (the probability × incentive function). The curve does not reach a maximum at a probability of success of .50 but somewhat lower, between .30 and .40 (Heckhausen, 1967, 1968; Schneider, 1971). This can be understood as a consequence of the asymmetrical self-rewarding strategy of hope-of-success subjects. You will remember that these subjects show an asymmetry in the causal attribution of success and failure. They are much more inclined to ascribe success to their own ability than to ascribe failure to lack of ability. Instead, they tend to ascribe failure to lack of effort or to bad luck. By this happy attribution pattern, the performance outcome on a moderately difficult task promises more self-reward in case of success than in case of failure. When a probability of success of, say, .35 is preferred, it is as though the somewhat lower probability of a positive, as compared to a negative, outcome is compensated, in the long run, by the greater positive reward value of success as compared with the negative reward value of failure.

The second deviation from the model concerns the risk preference curve of fear-of-failure subjects. In almost all studies, the curve does not reach a minimum at intermediate task difficulties, as it should according to the model. Are additional reward values at stake for these subjects? For the researcher this is a typical case where he feels a need to look for more descriptive knowledge in advance, enabling him to formulate more differentiated predictions and uncovering, it is hoped, more lawful relationships than were hitherto established.

A first hint appears in a study by Atkinson and O'Connor (1966). To their surprise, these authors did not find the usual relation between resultant achievement motivation and risk preference. Instead, they did find that high need affiliation, assessed by a TAT measure, produced all the usual effects of need achievement, including preference for tasks of intermediate difficulty. The experiment was conducted by a female experimenter. Subjects were male students and seen individually. Under these circumstances the reward value of social approval might have been the salient incentive arousing need affiliation. Subjects high in this motive might have been very eager to comply with the experimenter's demands. The reward value of social approval is obviously proportionate to the difficulty of a task successfully solved. This post hoc explanation in terms of extrinsic reward values in an achievement situation is supported by the fact that the original hypotheses were confirmed only among subjects weak in need affiliation.

Even in an achievement situation, which is nearly always a social situation, we might have been mistaken in considering need affiliation an "extrinsic" motive which is merely a constant source of "error" in the data. This has been shown, in a recent study at our laboratory. Schneider and Meise (in preparation) obtained TAT measures of both motives, need achievement, and need affiliation. For each motive the approach and the avoidance tendencies were scored separately. With respect to need affiliation, we have developed a coding syst ∴n for hope of affiliation and for fear of rejection. A risk preference experiment was conducted by a male experimenter with male students of eighth and ninth grade as subjects. In one condition, the experimenter was present during the experiment; in another condition he was absent.

It was predicted that, when the experimenter was present, subjects motivated by hope of affiliation would prefer more difficult tasks than subjects motivated by fear of rejection. The results confirm this prediction, especially when hope-of-affiliation subjects are, in addition, moti-. vated by fear of failure. With the experimenter present, these subjects prefer more difficult tasks than when the experimenter is absent or than other fear-of-failure subjects who are motivated by fear of rejection. The results not only explain, to some extent, why the Atkinson model fails to predict risk preference in fear-of-failure subjects more accurately.

They show how necessary it is to take into account multiple reward values, even in a situation strongly directed toward achievement.

In another still uncompleted study by Jopt (in preparation), the interaction of fear of failure with the two tendencies of need affiliation was demonstrated once more. Again, the hope-of-affiliation subjects among the fear-of-failure group preferred more difficult tasks than the fear-of-rejection subjects. In this study measures of risk preference, performance on a digit-symbol substitution task and causal attribution of success and failure were measured in male college students. The same procedure was, however, embedded into two different frame conditions. In one condition, a male experimenter gave an achievement-related instruction but behaved in a neutral manner throughout. In the other condition, a female experimenter behaved in a friendly way and expressed some concern about cooperation in a further and unrelated study on student problems.

The study has been designed in order to disentangle the interactive effects between 2 × 2 motive combinations and two arousal situations involving corresponding incentives. I will only mention some causal attribution results. It is, for instance, a rather important question to what extent attribution bias is more closely linked to the specific motive pattern of a person than to the change in situational demands. Certainly, the results show interactions between the two motives and the two situations. The main effects, however, are, as far as most causal factors are concerned, far more strongly motive bound than situation bound. Let me give just two examples for each case.

First, as you may remember, fear-of-failure subjects tend to ascribe their successes far less to their own ability than hope-of-success subjects do, with all the corresponding self-rewarding consequences. This attitude of minimizing one's own accomplishments characterized most explicitly those fear-of-failure subjects who are motivated by hope of affiliation, with the situation having no effect. What, then, about the other fear-of-failure subgroup motivated by fear of rejection? These subjects should perceive both situations in a double sense threatening, but with different saliency of the one or the other threat, failure or rejection, respectively. Interestingly enough, these subjects have the highest ascriptions of success to ability among all motive subgroups, contrasting most sharply with the other subgroup of fear of failure which is motivated by hope of affiliation. One might speculate why the double bind of a threat of failure *and* of rejection makes these subjects behave like the hope-of-success persons do, even exaggerating the attribution bias of the latter ones; i.e., to identify fully with one's achieved successes. Perhaps, they take resort to what is socially desirable and approved of, but what is, to them, at the same time frightening.

Second, as an example of a situation bound main effect I will mention the attribution of failure to bad luck. This occurs most markedly in the fear-of-failure and hope-of-affiliation group when the situation stresses affiliation but, in contrast, least markedly when the same group works in a situation without explicit affiliation cues. Obviously, in the first situation a need for minimizing self-responsibility for failure is felt more strongly so that expected affiliation rewards shall not be endangered.

I will not go into more detail. I simply want to make clear how descriptive knowledge about persons narrows down the variance in subsumed private meanings as they exist in the perception of a given situation and in the anticipation of reward values. I am quite confident that a cognitive approach to motivation, some beginnings of which I have tried to outline, will provide new and promising glimpses into human behavior, although cognitive theories might soon become so complex that they outrun the power of our present experimental and diagnostic tools.

My last remark is devoted to that term of our three-word volume I have left out deliberately in my paper: to pleasure. Much headway has recently been made in the discovery of underlying brain mechanisms (Olds & Olds, 1965), of antecedents and concomitants like arousal potential and change of arousal level, respectively (Berlyne, 1967). However, I do not see much progress in coming to grips with the psychological nature of pleasure as it is experienced and as it may guide action. Are we not, as psychologists, still stricken with blunt hedonism coming from the time of Aristippus? For instance, when we speak of self-reward in motivation theory we mean something like pleasure. But this something boils down in our theoretical language to a "positive affect" stripped of all constituent cognitive content. Evidently, we need an ultimate something which spurs everybody to action.

However, inner experience at least tells us that this is hardly half the truth. Take achievement goals. Are they always pursued in order to enjoy afterward a positive feeling tone as such? Or do we engage in activities because some future accomplishment will be satisfactory or even pleasurable, for its own sake? In this case it is totally impossible, phenomenologically speaking, to reduce the "reward value" to one self-subsisting affect or hedonic tone, existing by itself. The pleasure feeling rather penetrates the accomplished results of our striving. It cannot be separated from its referent.

The most cogent and incisive analysis I have ever read about pleasure,

its variety and motivational impact, is a posthumous article by Karl
Duncker (1940–1941) "On Pleasure, Emotion and Striving." Let me just
invite you to read the article published over three decades ago in quite
a remote philosophical journal. You might then, perhaps, agree with me
that the old problem of pleasure is still too big a problem for today's
motivation theory.

References

Atkinson, J. W. Motivational determinants of risk-taking behavior. *Psychological Review*, 1957, **64**, 359–372.

Atkinson, J. W. & O'Connor, Patricia. Neglected factors in studies of achievement-oriented performance: Social approval as incentive and performance decrement. In J. W. Atkinson & N. T. Feather (Eds.), *A theory of achievement motivation.* New York: Wiley, 1966. Pp. 299–325.

Bandura, A., Ross, D. & Ross, S. A. A comparative test of the status envy, social power, and secondary reinforcement theories of identification learning. *Journal of Abnormal Psychology*, 1963, **67**, 527–534.

Berlyne, D. E. Arousal and reinforcement. In D. Levine (Ed.), *Nebraska Symposium on Motivation 1967.* Lincoln: Univ. Nebraska Press, 1967. Pp. 1–110.

Dollard, J., Miller, N. E., Doob, L., Mowrer, O. H. & Sears, R. R. *Frustration and Aggression.* New Haven, Connecticut: Yale Univ. Press, 1939.

Duncker, K. On pleasure, emotion, and striving. *Philosophy & Phenomenological Research*, 1940/41, **1**, 391–430.

Grinker, J. Cognitive control of classical eyelid conditioning. In P. G. Zimbardo (Ed.), *The cognitive control of motivation.* Glenview, Illinois: Scott, Foresman, 1969. Pp. 126–135.

Heckhausen, H. *The anatomy of achievement motivation.* New York: Academic Press, 1967.

Heckhausen, H. Achievement motive research: Current problems and some contributions towards a general theory of motivation. In W. J. Arnold (Ed.), *Nebraska Symposium on Motivation 1968.* Lincoln: Univ. Nebraska Press, 1968. Pp. 103–174.

Heckhausen, H. & Weiner, B. The emergence of a cognitive psychology of motivation. In P. C. Dodwell (Ed.), *New horizons in psychology, II.* London: Penguin Books, 1972. Pp. 126–147.

Heider, F. *The psychology of interpersonal relations.* New York: Wiley, 1958.

Jopt, U. Der Einfluss des Anschlussmotivs auf das Leistungsverhalten. Diss. Psychol. Inst. Ruhr-Univ. (In preparation).

Kanfer, F. H. The maintenance of behavior by self-generated stimuli and reinforcement. In A. Jacobs & L. B. Sachs (Eds.), *The psychology of private events.* New York: Academic Press, 1971.

Kelley, H. H. Attribution theory in social psychology. In D. Levine (Ed.), *Nebraska Symposium on Motivation 1967.* Lincoln: Univ. Nebraska Press, 1967. Pp. 192–238.

Lazarus, R. S. Emotions and adaptation: Conceptual and empirical relations. In W. J. Arnold (Ed.), *Nebraska Symposium on Motivation 1968.* Lincoln: Univ. Nebraska Press, 1968. Pp. 175–266.

Locke, E. A. The relationship of success and expectation to affect on goal-seeking tasks. *Journal of Personality & Social Psychology,* 1967, 7, 125–134.

Locke, E. A. What is job satisfaction? *Organizational Behavior and Human Performance,* 1969, 4, 309–336.

Locke, E. A., Cartledge, N., & Knerr, C. S. Studies of the relationship between satisfaction, goal-setting, and performance. *Organizational Behavior and Human Performance,* 1970, 5, 135–158.

McGinnies, E. & Ferster, C. B. (Eds.) *The reinforcement of social behavior.* Boston, Massachusetts: Houghton, 1971.

Mallick, S. K. & McCandless, B. R. A study of catharsis of aggression. *Journal of Personality & Social Psychology,* 1966, 4, 591–596.

Mansson, H. H. The relation of dissonance reduction to cognitive, perceptual, consummatory, and learning measures of thirst. In P. G. Zimbardo (Ed.), *The cognitive control of motivation.* Glenview, Illinois: Scott, Foresman, 1969. Pp. 78–97.

Meyer, W. U. *Leistungsmotiv und Ursachenerklärung von Erfolg und Misserfolg.* Stuttgart: Klett, 1973.

Olds, J. & Olds, M. E. Drives, rewards and the brain. *New Directions in Psychology II.* New York: Holt, 1965.

Regelmann, S. Belohnungsaufschub, Sparmotiv und Leistungsmotivation. Uupubl. Diplomarbeit. Psychol. Inst. Ruhr-Univ. Bochum, 1972.

Rotter, J. B. *Social learning and clinical psychology.* Englewood Cliffs, New Jersey: Prentice-Hall, 1954.

Rotter, J. B. Generalized expectancies for internal versus external control of reinforcement. *Psychological Monographs,* 1966, 30, 1–26.

Schachter, S. & Singer, J. E. Cognitive, social, and physiological determinants of emotional state. *Psychological Review,* 1962, 69, 379–399.

Schneider, K. *Leistungs- und Risikoverhalten in Abhängigkeit von situativen und überdauernden Komponenten der Leistungsmotivation: Kritische Untersuchungen zu einem Verhaltensmodell.* Diss. Monogr., Ruhr-Univ. Bochum, 1971. Also in (K. Schneider, *Motivation unter Erfolgsrisiko.* Göttingen: Hogrefe. In press).

Schneider, K. & Meise, C. Wechselwirkung von Leistungs- und Anschloss motivation auf die Risikowahl. Also in (K. Schneider, *Motivation unter Erfolgsrisiko.* Göttingen: Hogrefe. In press).

Smedslund, J. Meanings, implications, and universals: Towards a psychology of man. *Scandinavian Journal of Psychology,* 1969, 10, 1–15.

Spence, K. W., Farber, I. E., & McFann, H. H. The relation of anxiety (drive) level to performance in competitional and noncompetitional paired-associates learning. *Journal of Experimental Psychology,* 1956, 52, 296–305.

Valins, S. Cognitive effects of false heart-rate feedback. *Journal of Personality & Social Psychology,* 1966, 4, 400–408.

Walker, E. L. Reinforcement—"The one Ring." In J. T. Tapp (Ed.), *Reinforcement and Behavior.* New York: Academic Press, 1969. Pp. 47–62.

Weiner, B. The effects of unsatisfied achievement motivation on persistence and subsequent performance. *Journal of Personality,* 1965, 33, 428–442.

Weiner, B. Role of success and failure in the learning of easy and complex tasks. *Journal of Personality & Social Psychology*, 1966, **3**, 339–344.

Weiner, B. *Theories of motivation: From mechanism to cognition.* Chicago: Markham, 1972.

Weiner, B. & Schneider, K. Drive versus cognitive theory: A reply to Boor and Harmon. *Journal of Personality & Social Psychology*, 1971, **18**, 258–262.

Weiner, B., Frieze, I., Kukla, A., Reed, L., Rest, S., & Rosenbaum, R. M. *Perceiving the causes of success and failure.* New York: General Learning Press, 1971.

Weiner, B., Heckhausen, H., Meyer, W.-U., & Cook, R. E. Causal ascriptions and achievement behavior: A conceptual analysis of effort and reanalysis of locus of control. *Journal of Personality & Social Psychology*, 1972, **21**, 239–248.

CHAPTER 10

Pleasure and Reward in Human Motivation and Learning

JOSEPH R. NUTTIN [1]

University of Leuven/Louvain, Belgium

Pleasure is a goddess with many faces. All living beings adore her and are fascinated by the magic of her name. Her impact on human behavior is subtle and all pervasive. In science, however, her position is uncertain and marginal. In that field, *Reward*, a commoner, is her rival; he lends himself more easily to manipulations. Some would like to limit her reign to the sensory domain, even to food pellets distributed by an automatic dispenser; others extend it to behavior as a whole. This last point of view will be our thesis; but by situating pleasure in its behavioral context it is expected to make it more suitable for scientific treatment.

Pleasure in Its Behavioral Context

First of all, then, an effort will be made in this chapter to situate the concept of pleasure in its full behavioral context. In approaching this problem, one is struck by the fact that in basic research the problem of

[1] The final draft of this chapter was written during the author's stay at the Center for Advanced Study in the Behavioral Sciences, Stanford, California 94305, in the fall of 1972.

pleasurable events and so-called *rewards* has been reduced to its extreme simplicity. In one of his theoretical papers, Neal Miller (1963) says:

> At the simplest level, which is where most of us work most of the time, we use only a few clear-cut rewards, such as giving food to a hungry animal or letting an electrically shocked animal escape. We know very well from experience that these rewards work, at least in the laboratory situations in which we use them, and we give the matter very little further thought [p. 67].[2]

My first suggestion, then, would be that we do give the matter a little further thought indeed (as Miller himself has done). In fact, in recent years a much broader area of complex behavioral patterns beyond "the simplest level" is currently being studied, but the same theoretical models, based on the type of research Miller has in mind, are still prevalent.

THE INFINITE DIVERSITY OF PLEASURE

One of the obvious and, I think, fundamental facts is the overwhelming *diversity* and, also, the *relativity* of human pleasures and rewards as compared with the short catalog of general and stable rewards used "at the simplest level" as just mentioned.

I ask myself what are the psychological processes at the basis of this diversity; can all these types of pleasure and reward be reduced or at least related to one common variable, and, most important, to what extent does this diversity and relativity really matter in behavioral research?

A first source of pleasure is found in the perception of certain stimuli or configurations of stimuli. For many years experimental research has been interested in this field, and current work is trying to find out some basic and common characteristics of the stimuli which are responsible for pleasurable sensations. One thinks in terms of arousal potential, level of stimulation, intensity, etc. [see Berlyne's (Chapter 1), Helson's (Chapter 7), Eysenck's (Chapter 6) contributions in this book]. Moreover, it is well known that the pleasurable effect of some sensory stimuli is considerably increased by their relationship to need reduction (hunger, sex, etc.) or other motivational processes and artistic interpretations. But my point is that besides these sources, man gets more intense pleasure from being behaviorally active in certain ways, from getting some behavioral outcomes, and, also from the fact that other people deal with him according to some patterns of behavioral relationships.

This *behavioral pleasure*, then, is the one I have especially in mind in this chapter. Perceptual and sensory pleasures are not at all excluded by

---

[2] Reprinted from *Nebraska Symposium on motivation, 1963* by Neal Miller by permission of the University of Nebraska Press.

this behavioral point of view, on the contrary; but the emphasis will be on the perceptual *activity* of the behaving subject, rather than on the stimulus characteristics of the perceived object.

One of the behavioral characteristics of human individuals, as compared to other living beings, is the great variety of objects they are interested in and respond to. In an article on Darwin's contribution to psychology, Thorndike (1909) observed: "The demonstrable difference between the year-old baby and the monkey . . . is that the baby responds to more things and in more ways." The objects related to organic needs are only a very small part of the enormous variety of things and events which evoke his interest and his response. It can be said that all behavioral functions are "hungry" for the type of objects suited to their own activity, and that pleasure is gained from this activity.[3] It seems undeniable that people take pleasure in just dealing with objects and events in work and play, and that this pleasure is independent, to a certain extent, of specially pleasurable characteristics of the objects involved. People need objects to be occupied with, problems to solve, information to listen to, other people to perceive in the streets or to meet, etc.

For most of the time in our culture, the flow of information and contact with events is so abundant that satiation is felt. However, in either experimental or natural situations with shortage of objects or events (sensory deprivation in its broadest sense), the need for keeping busy manifests itself, and the pleasure with something happening, or with meeting either new or familiar, nice or odd objects and people is intense and sought for. Moreover, man manifests a great deal of interest and pleasure in experiencing and dealing with life in all its variety and richness: He likes to be involved and participate in all kinds of situations, ways of behaving and living, etc.

It may be possible to formulate this thesis in an even more general way: For the normal or healthy living being, functioning itself, i.e., biological and behavioral interaction with the suitable elements of its world, is basically a source of pleasure. The types of pleasure gained are as varied as the types of activity involved.

STIMULATION PLEASURE AND CAUSALITY PLEASURE

The organism's functioning in interaction with objects and situations can be approached from different angles. It can be looked at as an

---

[3] The type of activity and pleasure meant here is not the *Funktionslust* described by Buehler, but the regular dealing with objects as in ordinary behavior. The *Funktionslust* is just a special and extreme case of the pleasure gained by this normal behavioral activity.

activity of the organism or personality, as was just described; it can be studied also from the point of view of the impinging objects in terms of *stimulation*. In that case one is emphasizing the fact that living beings take pleasure in being stimulated rather than their pleasure in being active. In more technical terms it is often said that stimulation in and by itself (without relationship to the satisfaction of organic needs) re-inforces the response which it follows. (For the problem as a whole, see Berlyne, 1969).

It is not my purpose to underestimate the importance of stimulation as source of pleasure. In fact, I see it as the correlative process corre-sponding to activity in the complex behavioral event which is interaction. But I would like to emphasize the active side of the process as source of pleasure in man. This will be done by showing that man takes special pleasure in the most intense degree of activity which is *being cause of an event*. Let us, therefore, investigate whether man's preference goes either to *being stimulated* by an event or to *being cause of it*. We are at present running in our laboratory an experiment on this problem; a first series of results can be communicated here in a preliminary report.

The theoretical context in which the experiment was planned can be briefly described as follows. Older theories claiming that pleasure is to be identified with absence or a minimum of stimulation have been disproved; current theories hold rather that stimulation as such is reward-ing: A light or sound (without any relationship to organic needs) follow-ing a response reinforces this response (e.g., bar-pressing). Without referring here to the problem of stimulation and reinforcement as a whole, I simply mention one of the first experiments in this field carried out with rats by Kish (1955) and Kish and Antonitis (1956). In this type of experiment, and in the theoretical hypotheses and conclusions related to it, two things are usually considered as equivalent conditions, namely on the one side: "a stimulation *following* the response" and on the other side: "a stimulation *produced by* the response." Even when it is said that the stimulation is a *consequence* of the response, it appears from the context that nothing other than a *temporal sequence* is meant. In fact, Kish's (1955) hypothesis is formulated as follows: "A perceptible environmental change . . . will reinforce any response *that it follows* [p. 261]." More generally, one currently refers to the phenomenon as response-*contingent* light change and light-*contingent* bar pressing (see among others Berlyne, 1969; Russell, 1972).

The purpose of our experiment is to investigate to what extent a light stimulus reinforces the subject's responses in both conditions. In other words: Are these conditions really equivalent, and to what extent do subjects of different ages prefer the situation in which the stimulus (a light following the response) is perceived as *produced* by their own response to the situation in which the stimulus is perceived as happening independently of this response? The experiment was first tried out with children 5 years of age.

EXPERIMENT ON CAUSALITY PLEASURE

After a short period of playing with the experimenter [4] in a separate room, the child is introduced into the experimental room equipped with two identical automats (A and B), each having two colored electrical bulbs and two handles. One handle can be moved in the horizontal direction, the other vertically. The distance between the handles is about 20 cm; the bulbs are about 15 cm above each handle. The two bulbs of *Automat A* are automatically and alternately set on for ¼ second at different intervals of time (see infra the different subconditions). As to *Automat B*, there is no change going on in the bulbs: the lights are either out (condition 1), or on (condition 2), but the machine is constructed in such a way that one of the bulbs goes either on (condition 1), or out (condition 2) for ¼ second when the corresponding handle is moved beyond a certain limit.

The idea underlying the experimental procedure can be formulated as follows: By the very fact of the automatic lighting up of the bulbs in automat A, the manipulation of a handle (response) is actually *followed* by a photic stimulation, but the stimulation is not perceived as *produced* by the subject's response; whereas in automat B the light stimulation following the response is perceived as produced also by that response. The fact that time intervals between manipulation and stimulation should be of the same order of magnitude in both cases was taken care of in three different ways (see the three subconditions 1a, 1b, and 1c).

The child entering the experimental room finds himself in front of automat A (at a distance of about 2 m from the door); 50 cm more to the left stands automat B, a curtain separating the two automats which both are visible from the entrance door. Behind the experimental room is a second room, unseen by the child, with the apparatuses and two observers behind a one way screen. The *subjects* are nine boys of 5 years of age. The child upon entering the experimental room is simply instructed that he is allowed to play here a bit alone with these machines

---

[4] The experiment was run by our collaborator Mrs. Danny Verstraeten and two observers.

(the experimenter points to the handles of the automats), while the experimenter sits down at a small table in the room and does some writing (she also observes the child's behavior and takes note of his motor and verbal reactions).

The following conditions have been tried out in the preliminary phase of the experiment as reported here:

Condition 1a. Each bulb of automat A lights up for .25 sec and goes out for .75 sec. The second bulb of the same automat starts lighting up .25 sec after the first bulb goes out. As to automat B, the bulbs light up only when the corresponding handle is manipulated. This is the same in conditions 1b and 1c.

Condition 1b. The alternations of the automatic lighting up of the bulbs of automat A are slowed down (about once every 4 sec) but from time to time during these intervals the two observers from behind the one way screen push a button commanding the lighting up of one of the two bulbs of the same automat. Especially, when the subject is on the point of stretching his hand to manipulating one of the handles, the observer pushes the corresponding button a series of three or four times at regular and short intervals in such a way that the corresponding bulb lights up one or two times just before the child actually moves the handle beyond the critical point (the same as in automat B), and two or three times immediately after. Thus, the child's manipulation of the handle comes in during one of these series of lightings of the corresponding bulb, which destroys the impression of causation.

Condition 1c. The bulbs of automat A light up in fast alternations. In order to make sure that in this automat a light stimulus follows the subject's response within exactly the same limits of time as in automat B, each of the two bulbs is connected with the opposite handle after the subject is familiarized with the functioning of both automats. These lightings are actually *produced* by the subject's response, but tend not to be perceived as such, although one of the subjects seemed to be puzzled a bit.

Condition 2. Automat A the same as in condition 1a. As to automat B, the two bulbs are on, but the light goes out for .25 sec each time the corresponding handle is moved beyond the critical point.

Each child is free to spend the time he wishes with each automat, and he freely goes from the one to the other. The curtain separating the two automats prevents the child from seeing automat A when he is playing with B, and vice versa. When the child shows signs of satiation and stops playing, the instructor accompanies him to the first room. After playing there for about half an hour in different settings, the child is reintroduced into the experimental room and is allowed to play again. The purpose is to see which automat (A or B) the child spontaneously goes to play with. Afterward, the child is also asked which is the most interesting device to play with, and why.

The following measures and verbal records are registered:

1. The manipulations of the handles (number of times, amplitude, and duration);

2. the total time spent with each of the two automats, which are equally available;

3. the preference shown by each child for going first to either automat A or B at the beginning of the second session;

4. verbal communications of the child, either during or after the session, and observational data of the experimenter and the observers.

RESULTS

The global behavior of each individual child, his absolute number of responses, etc., largely differ, of course, from child to child. However, the comparison to be made here is between the children's handling of automat A and automat B. These results are given in Table 10-1, showing for each condition the average number of responses to automat A as compared to B, the total time spent in A as compared to B, and the preference for A or B as expressed by going to one of these two automats when reintroduced to the room. Six children participated in condition 1, and three in condition 2. Although one could have expected that the children would be more interested by the colorful spectacle of the rapid

TABLE 10-1

The pleasure taken by children in receiving stimulation (automat A) as compared to pro-ducing it (automat B), as measured by average number of responses and time spent with A and B in several experimental conditions. (Conditions 1a, 1b, and 1c have 2 Ss each, condition 2: 3 Ss)

	Responses		Time (in sec)		Preferences
	Automat B	Automat A	Automat B	Automat A	
Condition 1a	86	62	590	195	2 × B
Condition 1b	104	40	454	304	2 × B
Condition 1c	59	33	416	289	2 × B
Condition 2	152	51	583	253	2 × B
					1 × A

lightings in A, it appears from the data that the children are much more
attracted by automat B (causality): The number of responses, as well as
the time spent in B, are constantly and considerably higher than in A.
There is a constant preference also for going back to B in the second
session (except in one case where the child explained that he was most
interested in trying to turn off the lights in A too, as he was able to do
in B).[5]

The general observational data and verbal communication are still
more striking and clear: All the children quite definitely prefer automat
B (causality), and explicitly say so. When it is suggested that A is more
interesting because the lamps are automatically lighting up they object
and say something that means that they prefer to "do" it. When first
introduced into the room the children perceive both automats; spontaneously they go to automat A which is closest to the door; they look at
the alternating lights which obviously interest them, and they try the
handles without any clear effect. After a certain time they approach the
other automat (B) which is identical to A but with its lights out. Here,
then, comes the interesting discovery by the child. From the very moment that he experiences that manipulating a handle lights a lamp, the
whole situation is only looked at from the point of view of *producing
this event*. He will try to do the same in A. This is very striking in condition 2. Here the bulbs of B are continuously lighting and the manipulations of the handles switch off the light. When going back after a while
to automat A with its automatically lighting bulbs, the boy's only interest
in it is visibly to test the possibility of shutting off the lights. The only
boy who first went to automat A when reintroduced in the room (second
session) explicitly says that he would like to try once more to shut off
the lights. One of the boys even became angry with A because it resisted
his efforts; he finally fantasized that the lamps responded to his manipulations and commands, etc. The spontaneous verbal reactions of the chil-

---

[5] If one prefers to formulate the results in terms of *habituation,* it could be said
that the child does not habituate so easily to stimuli which it personally produces,
as to stimuli automatically going on (as to habituation, compare Sokolov, 1960 and
Lettvin *et al.*, 1961). It could be interesting to test the thesis in this last formulation.
Evidence gained from the observation of the child's behavior points to the conclusion that habituation is not the major factor. The expected instrumental character
of the handle in producing the effect is what controls the child's responses. In fact,
the child goes back again and again to automat A to try to influence or change the
automatic event. Stimulation did not act on the child as a reinforcer for responding
as long as the responses were not *perceived* as *instrumental* to the stimulation. The
point is that an instrumental relationship is not to be reduced to a temporal one.

dren give further comments on their obvious interest in being able to produce the effect in automat B and their disappointment in A, overlooking the abundant and colored stimulations received there. Even the fact of producing the *extinction* of the lights (condition 2) gives much more pleasure to the child than being repeatingly *stimulated* by colored lights.

Conclusion

Instead of the current stimulus change explanation of the reinforcement phenomenon studied here, I propose an event *production* explanation. It is admitted that in everyday event perception, temporal sequence tends to be perceived as causal relationship (Michotte, 1963). It is predicted on the basis of the findings reported here, that neither photic stimulation increase and decrease (within certain limits), nor light onset and extinction, will make any important difference, the main factor being that the change is clearly perceived by the subject as *produced* by his response. It would be interesting to carry out comparative studies involving human and animal subjects. I also intend to investigate to what extent the event producing response is better learned than the less productive (active) one. Probably, however, a kind of failure character will be attached to the nonproductive responses when applied to the same subjects.

The fact that *producing* stimulation is preferred to stimulation as such points to the basic behavioral tendency to *produce* events, or to *do* something in the sense of changing something or *making something happen*. This is what could be called *causality pleasure*. The phenomenon fits in with Woodworth's (1958) behavior-primacy theory of motivation as formulated in his *Dynamics of Behavior*. Generally one of the main sources of pleasure in man is *to do things*. Progressively, he will try to produce them according to his plans and projects.[6] It is in this context that the ego-involved pleasure in the successful outcome of an act is to be situated; succeeding in doing, achieving or producing something

---

[6] The first stages of this development (doing things according to plans) in very young children were recently studied by one of our collaborators (Hellings, 1970); see also Bühler and Massarik (1968). As to the pleasure taken in *producing* something, there exists a lot of descriptive literature on the subject, although we do not know about strictly experimental work comparing perception of stimuli with producing them. It was mentioned to us that Groos (1899) used the term "joy of being cause." See also Decharms (1968), and White's (1959) theory of competence and effectance.

(*ego pleasure*). Clinical and abnormal psychology shows that when a man has nothing more "to do" (to produce) in his physical or social environment, no more plans or projects to work at, he is profoundly disturbed and ceases to "respond" to things. His *responding* behavior loses its spring and its rewards by the fact that these responses are no longer "acting-on" processes, but just "going-on" responses.

PLEASURE IN TERMS OF MEANINGFUL RELATIONSHIPS

Besides the sensory stimulation pleasure and the active behavior pleasure culminating in *causality pleasure*, there is a more passive type of pleasure which man gains from being dealt with in certain ways.

What are commonly called affection, esteem, consideration, authoritarian behavior, etc., are, in fact, behavioral patterns of dealing with people. The important fact is that *being dealt with* along some of these lines is pleasant to man; being dealt with in other ways is unpleasant. He tries to avoid being ignored, hated, etc. It can be said that man "needs" to be dealt with in certain ways insofar as these ways of interaction are sought for, or "required" for optimal (or pleasant) functioning of the personality. In fact, being dealt with in some other ways is not only avoided or unpleasant, but may be detrimental to behavioral functions as a whole (cf. data on affective deprivation, and similar phenomena).

An important problem currently investigated with regard to all these sources of pleasure is to find out if some common factor or dimension can be discovered in all of them. It seems rather improbable that the meaningful differences between the pleasing and displeasing behavioral patterns just mentioned could be reduced to stimulus characteristics such as complexity, intensity, etc. In fact, these characteristics can be found in positive and negative patterns. In any case, information about arousal and stimulation level of some behavioral patterns could not replace the information given by the meaningful description of the same patterns. In other words, it is worthwhile to know that it is *producing* something (rather than just *perceiving* changes) that gives pleasure to man; just as it is important to know that it is an authoritarian way of being dealt with which is needed or pleasant in some circumstances, while the opposite way is preferred in other situations and by other people. Information about physical characteristics of the behavioral stimuli involved does not provide us with the same behavioral meaning. Moreover, it seems to me that the common factor eventually underlying all pleasant behavioral patterns should be sought for in *relational* terms, rather than in terms of stimulus characteristics (which are important for stimulation pleasure). In fact, behavior and behavioral pleasure are essentially relational phenomena. I therefore venture to say that pleasurable *events* are those which stimulate or maintain an optimal level of *activity* and *interaction* between the personality (organism) and the outside world in which it exists. This optimal level will oscillate along rhythmic curves (such as circadian periods) and irreversible developments (such as age). The possible value of such general hypotheses lies, of course, only in their suggesting a certain direction of thinking: thinking along lines of stimuli seems less fruitful in this area than research in terms of patterns of meaningful activity and relationships.

MEANS PLEASURE AND END PLEASURE

A great many of the behavioral acts which man performs do not seem to be pleasurable at all. Neutral, and even apparently unpleasant activities, are currently performed without hesitation (see also Walker, Chapter 3). In order to understand this fact, we should carefully investigate the way most human behavior is built up.

When I was invited to contribute to this volume, I was interested in accepting the invitation and I expected a lot of "pleasure" and profit ("utility") from it. After deciding to do so, I constructed (on the representational or cognitive level of dealing with situations) a program, plan or behavioral project via which my motivation to contribute to this volume found a concrete behavioral outlet. Then followed a coordinated and subordinated series of acts, on the "executive" behavioral level, which constituted the preparatory phase of my going to contribute to this volume. This activity went on as long as matching my actual situation with the expected end term did not coincide (compare Miller, Galanter, & Pribram, 1960). Several of the means acts in this coordinated behavioral series were neutral or even tedious to me (getting in touch with travel agencies, with the administration of my university, etc.), others were difficult, sometimes definitely unpleasant (postponing pleasurable activities in order to finish my chapter, doing a lot of unpleasant thinking on pleasure, etc.).

The point I would like to make is that much of our behavior is constructed in the way just described, i.e., as a short or long series of specific acts which can only be fully understood in terms of their role in an overall behavioral task, project or plan. These behavioral "segments" receive their meaning and their motivation from the molar unit in which they are a functional part. They are "pleasurable" to the extent that they bring the subject closer to the end from which some reward value is expected. The parts participate in the pleasure of the project as a whole. It is characteristic for highly developed cognitive behavior that not only events in close temporal contiguity with a rewarding object can be associated this way (secondary reward). Expectations and means–end relationships between acts and events can be *constructed*, bridging long periods of time and without any previous association or confirmation. Hence, this is the importance of the study of time perspective with relation to human motivation.

In this context, i.e., as means or functional parts in a broader behavioral program, practically all events can be endowed with some element of reward value. A student preparing for his exams may really be happy that a friend has said he will not be coming to see him, because it makes staying at home and studying easier for him (*means pleasure*). According to the subject's degree of cognitive inventiveness, all kinds of objects and events can be interpolated as active means in behavioral tasks and plans. Moreover, the plasticity and constructiveness of means–end structures become more evident when specifically human types of behavioral needs are at stake. In fact, the behavioral ways leading to the reduction of basic physiological needs (e.g., hunger) are rather limited,[7] but the means–end structures which a man sets up to achieve something in his life, to make a career or to gain power, consideration, and esteem, etc. are relatively unlimited. Not only are the means more variable, but even the kinds of situations to be reached in order to gain consideration, power, etc. are infinitely more flexible and varied than the rewarding substances to be attained to reduce hunger. A process of goal setting is involved here. It can therefore be said that, in the human context, different types of rewards and pleasures—and probably the most important ones—are created by man himself, and that they can be made out of practically any material, i.e., any object, real or imagined, within his world. Here, the links which have to exist between the so-called primary and secondary rewards are no longer limited by temporal contiguity. Cognitively constructed relatedness and belonging can unite means and ends over years of time and miles of space. Therefore, our world of secondary pleasures and rewards has practically no boundaries, and processes such as affective transfer often make neutral objects and events become really rewarding and pleasurable in themselves.

---

[7] When the whole behavioral process of "earning one's living" is considered, and not just the reduction of the need by eating, it is obvious that the intervening means-end structures are also broadened according to the cultural situation one lives in.

IMAGINATION PLEASURE

There is another characteristic of human behavioral functioning which is responsible for the unlimited number of situations and events which are sources of pleasure and joy (or distress). The very fact that events and their relationships can be "present" to man on the representational level of behavioral dealing with objects is of the utmost importance for all aspects of conduct. In this way, past and future events, as well as situations which possibly never will be met, can arise or stay present in the behavioral situation and produce profound pleasure or displeasure. It is well known that affectively loaded events are precisely those which most often tend to present themselves; they are, as it were, continuously at hand. The catalog of pleasurable objects is, thus, supplemented with events remembered, expected, or even simply imagined. All of these constructs may be endowed with high degrees of behavioral reality; they play an enormous role in actual pleasure and distress, and extend their radius of action beyond boundaries of space and time. Let it be mentioned also that man's shift from looking for pleasure on the level of reality to the level of imagination and memory is an important problem in the study of motivation and behavior as a whole, as well as in mental health.

THE RELATIVITY OF PLEASURE AND REWARD

Correlated with the fact that practically every event can be endowed with reward value or pleasantness is the fact that the same event can be either pleasant or unpleasant according to its behavioral context or circumstances. Just as silence can become an alerting stimulus (Sokolov, 1960), the same thermal, gustatory, and olfactory stimuli can be either pleasant or unpleasant according to the subject's internal state (Cabanac, 1971). As Pribram (1963) puts it: "At any moment in time the central process provides the context in which stimuli arise. Contiguity of stimuli comes to be seen not as some vague 'association' but a process occurring as a context-content relationship [p. 119]."

In the broader behavioral context, it is well known that the personal motivational context as expressed in the level of aspiration, is able to make either a very pleasant success or a most unpleasant failure out of the same objective outcome. As to the social context, what is generally rewarding (for instance, approval or appreciation expressed by a superior) can become punishing for some subjects with special motivations. A teacher in a school for juvenile delinquents told me how marks of approval and appreciation he once expressed for one member of his class was felt by the youngster as the worst discredit in his group. The highest reward in the social context of this group was to dare to do something that was severely disapproved by the authorities or by society in general. Relativity of reward depending on personality orientation and nature of tasks was shown also by Bass (1967).

With regard to the means–end structure of behavior, it is well known that the means can become the goal and vice versa, the goal object can become the means object. In other words, the role of the reinforcing agent and the activity to be reinforced can be reversed. To give an extreme example: Usually people earn money in order to have something to eat, but in some popular games people engage in eating performances to earn money. Thus, the reinforcement relationship is reversible. This type of behavior is analogous to what Premack (1962) proved to exist also in animals: Water ingestion can reinforce running in an activity wheel, and vice versa, according to whether the animal is deprived either of water or of free running activity, or in the case of our human subject, whether he is in need of money or in need of food.

Let us also mention the fact that in many human situations it is not always clear what is rewarding and what is punishing. In most of such cases, one can say rather that the same event is rewarding and punishing at the same time. In fact, events can be looked at from different angles and motivation can proceed along conflicting ways. As an example, take the type of experiments on attitude change in which the social psychologist asks his subjects to deliver a public address in defense of a thesis that is just the opposite of their own conviction. When the subject agrees to deliver such a counterattitudinal speech, and his audience manifests a lot of disapproval and disagreement during his speech, one may ask the question to what extent the disapproval is rewarding to the subject. In fact, the disapproval reaction of the audience manifests agreement with the speaker's basic attitude, while it remains true that an audience's sign of approval with the arguments as developed by the speaker must also mean some reward for him. When it is found (see e.g., Sarbin & Allen, 1964) that negative reactions of the audience "reinforce" the speaker in his inauthentic attitude (i.e., when he changes his previous attitude in that direction), it is not clear whether reward or punishment is responsible; it is also not clear whether the process of reinforcement can be applied to this type of atttitude *change* in a conflict situation.

Another example can be taken from animal psychology where the behavioral meaning of the situation may be less clear. Sevenster (1972) in a recent experiment showed that a specific response in sticklebacks is positively "reinforced" when a rival male appears in its territory. It is not very clear to what extent the appearance of a rival can be considered a positive reinforcer or reward in the usual sense. Should it be considered a reduction of a need, a satisfying state of affairs, or just a state of arousal produced by the appearance of a competitor? In any case its positive or negative rewarding value is not easy to establish.

Finally, I would like to call attention to the fact that in some cases —not all of them abnormal—physical or moral pain can be a source of pleasure. Without going into the details of many minor cases pointing to the rewarding value of pain, I just would like to illustrate the extreme possibilities of human versatility in this respect by reminding you of the conversation between the masochist and the sadist. The masochist humbly begs the sadist: "Please, dear friend, hurt me." The sadist cruelly replies: "No, I refuse to do so."

Summarizing, one can say that it is impossible to detect stable relationships between specific objects or events and their pleasurable or rewarding effect. Instead of trying to make a catalog of "general rewards" (Meehl, 1950) we rather have to ask the question: "What is rewarding to whom in what circumstances?" And in this list everything real and imagined could be mentioned somewhere. Whether an event in a given situation is rewarding or not will depend, to a large extent, on its behavioral or motivational context.

THE SUBJECTIVE NATURE OF PLEASURE AND BEHAVIOR

In dealing with *pleasure* as a scientific concept, it should be made clear how we conceive of its subjective or introspective nature. It has been suggested that it should be replaced by more objective terms such as *reward,* meaning a *rewarding* substance or event, and the term *rewarding* itself being reduced to a way of functioning of the nervous system, as Thorndike already tried to do.

I propose that the so-called "subjective" phenomena expressed by terms such as pleasure, pleasantness, hedonic value, satisfying state of affairs, etc., be maintained in our science as pointing to an intervening variable or construct whose *scientific* meaning is operationally defined in behavioral terms. In fact, pleasure and similar terms referring to personal experience seem to play a functional role in behavior or, at least, to be systematically related to behavioral phenomena. It is this behavioral role we are interested in.

The old problem about the *private* nature of pleasurable experiences, or of whatever other conscious phenomena, should not be revived here. Although the communication of private feelings via descriptive and suggestive symbolic means may be interesting and important in literature and in daily life, psychology as a science has no access to private experience as such. It would even be illusory to suppose that communication of private feelings could be anything more than a translation in a partially unknown language. In any case, in science we have to resign ourselves to the fact that some aspects of reality and some problems cannot be approached by scientific methods. This is the price we have to pay for objective and quantitative rigor. But apart from this, we have access to every psychological phenomenon via the role it possibly plays in conduct in its broadest sense.

First, it should be emphasized that both terms, *pleasure* and *behavior* or *conduct*, are taken in their broadest sense, i.e., they refer not just to one type of pleasure such as sensory pleasure, and one type of behavior, such as motor or overt behavior. In fact, in certain situations, man's behavior (i.e., *what he is doing*) consists, for instance, in just *looking* at a series of events, or trying to solve a problem by *thinking* or *reasoning*. Thus, an experimenter can give a subject the behavioral task of *judging* an object, or of *comparing* two items. The task can be, for instance, to compare the height or the color and its brightness of two objects, or also the pleasant or unpleasant character of that color, etc. In all these types of behavior, we have access to what the subject is doing (judging or thinking) and to the outcome of it, by way of verbal or other communication (for instance, by the subject's marks on a scale).

In all these cases, as well as in overt behavior, it is possible to infer, from either overt or verbal behavior, that a subject experiences in a more or less intense way a "state of affairs" which he "likes" or which he "prefers" to another state of affairs produced by another stimulus, situation, or act (or by the same stimulus in another context). How this state of affairs is exactly perceived in the private experience of the subject himself, can not be communicated in a scientific way, as was already said. But the subject's experience, judgment, or perception can be identified as being either identical or more or less different in such-and-such a way from the perception produced by other stimuli or events. Moreover, the behavioral and motivational meaning of the state of affairs as experienced by the subject can be inferred from his ways of behaving. Even such more complicated states as subjective *conflict, hesitation, inhibition,* etc. can be identified and inferred from their functional role in behavior.

The reliability of verbally communicated experimental data and their actual role in behavior are problems that do not need to be discussed here. It may suffice to have shown that terms such as pleasure and other experiential data have a behavioral meaning, and that behavioral science should not neglect to study them as components of human conduct and as objects of behavioral activities such as judging and comparing.

Reward, Successful Outcome, and Human Learning

Among the many kinds of pleasure a man is able and eager to enjoy we should certainly count the rewarding or successful outcome of a behavioral act. In fact, succeeding in what one is trying to do is a "pleasant" or "rewarding" event; it should be carefully investigated to what extent this successful outcome of an act and its impact on behavior are to be identified with other types of reward as currently used in basic research, especially in animal psychology.

Our problem, then, is to investigate the influence of a successful outcome of a response on the *learning* of this response. The problem is situated in the general context of *reward and learning* as distinguished from *performance*. In fact, at the level of human behavior the repertoire of responses and information available to the subject (i.e., learned) largely exceeds the informational data and responses actually used in a behavioral act. It may be reasonable to admit that the amount of responses learned coincide with the responses actually performed in organisms at the simplest level of cognitive functioning; but in man, the *acquisition* (learning) of informational data and behavioral or verbal skills has developed so autonomously that nobody can reasonably deny the necessity of distinguishing between what man does and what he learns.

Learning, then, is defined here as a process of acquisition by which a more or less enduring change in the organism is produced in such a way that new behavioral responses and informational data can be used (or activated) in behavior when motivation to do so is given.

As to reward, it is defined in terms of the broad area of *positive* behavioral incentive values (cf. supra) and not just as "anything given for something done [Clayton, 1969]." The rewarding event whose influence on learning has been studied in our research program is the successful outcome as just mentioned. It is communicated to the subject by the experimenter in a verbal way by saying *right* or *wrong* at the end of each task. Our first concern, then, is to see to what extent reward and successful outcome have to be distinguished.

Successful Outcome and Reward

We conceive of *reward* as something following an act, and extrinsic to the act itself; the *outcome* on the contrary is part of the behavioral act itself (its end-term). In fact, the successful outcome is nothing other than the successfully performed act itself, i.e., the response insofar as it is successful. For Thorndike's hungry cat in a puzzle box, the reward is said to be the food outside the box. This food reduces the cat's need. The successful outcome as such is the cat's response insofar as it ends in opening the door; but this kind of achievement is usually not taken into account in animal experiments. By the very fact that only organic needs are considered important, it is assumed that succeeding in opening the door is in itself not rewarding for the animal. It is well known that, more recently, things have changed in this respect. For the nonhungry animal presented with a mechanical puzzle, as in Harlow's experiments, the fact of succeeding in opening a door could in itself be considered a rewarding event. In human subjects, the act of solving the problem, i.e., succeeding in a task, seems always to be a pleasure in itself, insofar as the subject is ego-involved in his task and its achievement. An extrinsic reward, such as candy for a child, may be added or not. The candy-type reward can even be given after or "for" failure, as a kind of consolation prize or compensation; it can also simply follow the act without any perceived relationship to it.

A successful outcome has rewarding value in itself insofar as the behaving subject is interested or involved in the act as such, as a kind of achievement or task. In fact, behavior in man is not just a process or a response; it is a personality doing something. A failing act means "I am failing to do what I intended or expected to do." A successful outcome can be more rewarding than the extrinsic reward to which it is instrumental; whereas a man failing, for instance, in his behavioral effort to earn his living and to make a career, can be much more frustrated by the behavioral failure itself than by the very fact of not being able to buy something as a consequence of it.

It must be recognized that in some cases the distinction between the outcome of an act, and the reward obtained via an act, can be rather difficult to make. However, the distinction is to be made and their respective influence on human behavior can be tested experimentally. The core of the differentiation between outcome and reward is to be found in the more ego-involved character of some types of motivation, and in the personalized character (ego-character) of behavior in man. By the very fact of these characteristics of a behavioral act, its outcome or end-term is evaluated as a success or as a failure.[8]

---

[8] In this paper the term *reward* will be used from time to time to indicate the successful outcome in order to make clear that the factor investigated here (positive

The ego-involved type of motivation has mostly been overlooked in the study of *Motivation and Learning*. In fact, the influence of motivation on learning has been studied in such terms as strength of drive, time of deprivation, amount of reward, more or less severe punishment, stress, anxiety, etc. But the more normal motivational state of the human subject working at a task or a project of action has been less systematically investigated as to its role in learning and reinforcement. In this motivational context, however, the outcome of a response and its informational aspect may play an important role in cognitive learning.

COMPLEXITY AND SELECTIVE ALERTNESS VERSUS CONTIGUITY

In answering, now, the question whether a rewarding event following a response is a necessary condition for cognitive learning, I would, in principle, agree with many psychologists (e.g., Estes, 1969) when they say that contiguity may do it without reward, or that reward is certainly neither a sufficient nor a necessary condition. Several series of experiments have proved that rewarded responses are not learned better than punished ones, and that in other conditions even punished responses may be learned better than rewarded ones. (See, for instance, our experiments in the so-called *closed task* condition, Nuttin and Greenwald, 1968). However, my point would be that in order to produce psychological contiguity—i.e., to cause two events (either S and R, or two S, or two R) to be *perceived* as contiguous, which seems to be the minimal requirement for associative learning—something more than pure physical or temporal contiguity is needed.

Let us once more take into account the real behavioral context in which the learning process takes place. Man lives in a field or world in which the number and the complexity of events happening at the same time (psychological present) are enormous. Most of these perceivable events are not even actually perceived: They are not brought to his "attention." In any case, the limited channels at his disposal and the inhibitory mechanisms at work (see, among others, Hernandez-Péon, 1964)

---

or negative outcome) belongs to the broad category of events usually referred to as reward.

On the other hand, it is not to be denied that linguistic differences among languages may account for the fact that the need is felt, or not felt, to use different terms in this respect. For instance, I feel that a certain outcome can be said to be *rewarding*, although I prefer to make a distinction between *reward* and *outcome*. In any case, the difference as explained here is a real behavioral phenomenon, and this is what matters.

prevent man from registering and processing the bulk of informational data available. At the same time, man is confronted with a number of things to do, needs to satisfy, tasks to fulfill, etc. In other words, he is in a motivational state which implies that he is preferentially oriented toward certain types of data or events. The concrete learning and behavior problem is to know how, in this situation, man will gather the information he needs for efficient or adaptive behavior; and how he will deal with this situational and behavioral complexity.

There are many ways to deal with complexity according to the type of complexity at stake. For the type Walker (Chapter 3) is concerned with, *chunking* seems to be the solution. For the type of complexity described here, the *selective* attitude, alertness or attention as spontaneously adopted by the subject in such situations is the only possible strategy. That means that in the behavioral situation we are dealing with, subjects spontaneously have their attention (directed alertness) focused on *screening* and *selecting* the data or events which present themselves. Some signals or characteristics of the events in presence alert the subject's vigilance system and, thus, transform objective stimuli into actually perceived data, i.e., objects or events perceived as being there and *contiguous* with some others.

From the experiment reported on page 247, it appears that special attention is paid spontaneously by human subjects to the fact that one event is *produced* by something done by the subject. This is the old problem of belongingness which seems to be essential in cognitive learning.

Contiguity, therefore, is a condition more complex than it is usually conceived to be. Some directed vigilance or attention, produced by a motivational state, need, task, or interest, or by some structural factor (relief), has to bring out the items perceived as contiguous and having something to do with each other. *What* they have to do with each other may be vague and even unknown, or perceived as a question mark, as a relationship of pure togetherness in time, etc.

As to the motivational factor involved, as just described, it is safe to admit on the basis of various experimental and observational data that in normal situations (without stress and deprivation) the cognitive or observational interest of man is varied and broad, as was shown for instance with regard to the eagerness of the child to respond to innumerable stimuli and to learn from what happens (cf. page 245). Without any *special* task to fulfill or goal to pursue, man is practically always motivated to acquire information along some preferential lines of interests. Incidental learning is to be considered the normal and most important learning process of the adult human being; it also seems to be important in several other species.

The Cognitive Attention Type of Learning

In any case, the concrete way to formulate the cognitive learning problem in the human behavioral context is to put the question as follows: From amid the enormous quantity of potential information with which we are presented, what informational and behavioral data will be actually perceived, acquired, and stored in the organism in such a way that they remain there ready for activation or use in further current behavior?

This, then, is our hypothesis with regard to the role of the successful or rewarding outcome in the cognitive type of learning: First, a successful outcome (e.g., the word *right* as pronounced for each response by the experimenter) has the value and meaning of a *signal* pointing to the useful, i.e., interesting response in the frame of the motivational orientation of the behaving subject. It has no direct learning effect in itself. Second, the signal function or informational aspect of rewarding outcomes *alerts* the subject, thus increasing his level of attention or activity. Third, responses related to an increased activity level tend to be better acquired and preserved. Let us now expand somewhat on these points, referring to experimental data supporting them.

First, it should be noted that according to this hypothesis reward plays an active role in cognitive learning; but a nonreinforcement type of explanation of its function is given. This explanation accounts for the fact that rewarded responses may or may not be learned better, insofar as the role (as signal), usually played by reward (successful outcome), may also be fulfilled by other signals according to certain circumstances.[9] At the same time, the contiguity principle is not denied, but its dependency on other factors (motivational orientation and selective attitude) is emphasized.

---

[9] As to the signal function and information value of reward in general, compare also Muenzinger's (1935) experiments on *emphasis,* and Egger & Miller's (1962, 1963) interesting data on information in secondary reinforcement. With relation to the general theme of this paper it may be interesting to note that pleasure, or the pleasant character of an event, may have a cognitive or informational value as a signal, besides its main emotional aspect. This idea goes back to old biological and philosophical sources (*sensus aestimativus*). However, the reward aspect of the successful outcome is not at all denied here. The successful outcome is rewarding indeed with regard to the past performance, but this rewarding aspect does not play a role in learning itself (except in the second type of learning to be discussed).

Several experimentally tested predictions, deduced from this hypothesis, have been confirmed and will not be described here (see Nuttin & Greenwald, 1968). I mention only one experiment, carried out in our laboratory by G. d'Ydewalle, but not yet published. It is related to the selective alerting function of the successful outcome. The prediction is as follows: When the subject is given the prior opportunity to become familiarized with the complexity of a task, his attitude will become more selective when it is impossible for him to take advantage of all the information contained in both the right and wrong responses given. Thus, for instance, his alertness will be concentrated on the *right* outcomes (providing him with directly useful information) and the wrong responses will be, to a greater extent, neglected. This increased selective attitude toward the "rewarded" responses will result in better learning of these responses as compared to the "punished" ones. On the contrary, subjects who were not given the opportunity to familiarize themselves with the task attend to all informational signals given. This results in a lower learning effect for the rewarded responses than in the previous group of subjects. In other words, the difference between rewarded and punished responses will be greater in the group with familiarization as compared to the group that is unfamiliar with the complexity of the task.

DESCRIPTION OF THE EXPERIMENT ON COMPLEXITY AND REWARD

The verbal material used in the experiment was of the Thorndike type as illustrated in the well-known experiment with the Spanish words. The subjects were 50 freshmen students of the University of Leuven Law School. Half of them (group A) were familiarized with the learning task by being given a preliminary task of the same kind. The others (group B) were not. The main part of the experiment to which both groups were submitted runs as follows. Each subject is instructed individually to learn the translation, in a completely unknown foreign language, of a list of Dutch words which will be successively presented to him. The Dutch word (mother tongue) is the first on each line and is followed by the five foreign words (actually nonsense syllables). The presentation is made by an S/R programmer, and the exposition time for the whole line is 5 sec (light signal). The subject chooses one of the five foreign words; the experimenter says whether the choice is wrong or right. The "right" or "wrong" is pronounced by the experimenter at the very moment that the following line is to appear, in order to prevent the possibility of rehearsal. There are 40 Dutch words. The responses said to be *right* or *wrong* are randomized for each subject. To make conditions realistic, 30 responses are punished and 10 rewarded. This structural isolation (10 rewards against 30 punishments) condition is the same for both groups. The subject is instructed that only one learning trial is given and that, thereafter, a second presentation of the series will follow. The task is to give as many *correct* translations as possible in this second trial.

In fact, the instructions are changed *after the first trial*. At that very moment each subject is instructed to *repeat*, for each line of words presented again, the foreign word which he chose during the first trial for the corresponding Dutch word.

Before starting with this experiment, group A is given a preliminary task which is identical with the experimental learning task, except that the list is short and the words are different (12 Dutch words, each followed by 5 foreign words). Here, the instructions are not changed after the first presentation. Thus, in the second trial the subject gives as many *correct* translations as he can. He is then told that the true experiment will now start, and that a much longer list will have to be learned. It is assumed (and it appears from the reactions of most subjects) that they realize the complexity of the task. In fact, during the second trial, they had to avoid the wrong words chosen during the first trial, and to repeat the right ones. Not all the information received could be used. It was also realized that in this experiment the outcome *wrong* contains less information than *right* (in fact, after each wrong response it is not made clear which of the four other words is the right one). It is assumed that in such a complex situation the subject's attitude will become more selective and will concentrate on the *rewarded* responses as being the most directly useful ones.

RESULTS

Table 10-2 shows that rewarded responses, as predicted, are learned better by subjects of group A (with previous experience of the complex-

TABLE 10-2

Percentage of rewarded and punished responses learned after familiarization and without familiarization of the Ss with the degree of difficulty of the task

Group A (familiarization)		Group B (no familiarization)	
Rewarded	Punished	Rewarded	Punished
54.67	42.58	38.26	41.10
(t = 4.848; p < .005)		(n.s.)	

ity of the task) than in group B. In fact, in group A 54% of the rewarded responses are correctly repeated, against 42% among the punished ones. This difference is highly significant ($t = 4.848$; $p < .005$). As to group B (subjects without familiarization), rewarded responses were not learned better than the punished ones. On the contrary, there is some nonsignificant difference in favor of the responses punished (41% against 38%).

The results of this experiment should be interpreted in the light of many other confirmations of the hypothesis that the rewarded outcome functions as a signal in the framework of a selective attitude. Heightening the level of selectivity (by previous experience) influences the rate in which rewarded responses are favored in comparison with the punished ones.

To conclude on this point, sufficient evidence from different sources is available to assert that a pleasant event, reward, reduction or satisfaction of psychological or organic needs, a successful outcome and the like, are not in and by themselves responsible for learning. The learning process by which new informational data are acquired and more or less consolidated in the organism, can, in our opinion, be conceived of along the following hypothetical lines. Due to a specific task motivation or to general interests, the subject finds himself in a state of either actively directed attention or rather latent vigilance. Some events such as successful outcomes, rewards, or other characteristic changes in the field, function as signals which arouse the subject's attention (see also the *attention learning* mentioned by Olds, Chapter 2, and Trabasso & Bower, 1968). This means that, as a result of the signal, the subject's activity level is increased or aroused, and some specific responses and relationships (pointed to by the signal) are put forward as the objects of this increased activity, attention, or arousal.

The last point of our hypothesis says that responses, objects and events, by the very fact of being related to a higher degree of neuropsychological activity as just described, are better picked up and preserved by the psychophysiological networks of the organism. Some experimental data give support to such an hypothesis. In experiments on discrimination learning in rats by Bloch, Denti, and Schmaltz (1966), Deweer, Hennevin, and Bloch (1968), and Lecomte, Deweer, and Bloch (1969) it was found that stimulation of the reticular system, immediately following the only learning trial, significantly increases learning of the response. Moreover, in memory and verbal learning tasks, several experiments suggest that motivation affects the capacity to retain material in storage (see, among others, Weiner & Walker, 1966). It was also found that associated pairs of items which are part of a still-active motivational system such as a task still to be fulfilled ("open" tasks), a field of interest, etc. are better preserved in the organism. In fact, we found that new translations of words which are part of an active task system remain more available for correct reproduction than those which are part of a completely finished task (Nuttin, 1947, 1968). In general, events and relationships between events which are signaled to the subject as fitting into his field of interest, his task to be fulfilled, or need to be satisfied, were said to become a part of the dynamic means–end system. It was assumed that elements integrated in such a dynamic system are better consolidated. In fact, it seems sound to speculate that by the very fact of being integrated or incorporated in a more or less active motivational system as just mentioned, the behavioral or informational items involved, as well as their neurological correlates, remain in a state of higher activation, even when not used in actual behavior. Thus, the activation hypothesis and our earlier task integration hypothesis seem to be compatible and related to each other. Moreover, there is a large amount of empirical evidence in favor of the relationship between interest, task tension, or dynamic systems at the one side, and retention at the other. Allport's (1946) comparison can be quoted here: "Interest, in this sense, seems to operate almost like a sponge. Anything that has interest-relevance is absorbed—subject, of course, to the limitations of fatigue, intellectual capacity, clear perception and other similar conditions [pp. 180–181]."

The Direct Influence of Reward

The cognitive type of learning just described is not the only way in which man learns: It is the way in which *information* is acquired ("what leads to what," and other information). Important other things to be learned are directly related to the response side of behavior: the acquisition of readily available response patterns such as skills and concrete behavioral forms of wants, desires, or needs. A lot of information and *know how* may go along with the acquisition of these behavioral patterns, but something more than this *know how* is learned and acquired: The behavior pattern itself gets as it were ingrained in the behaving organism; it becomes part of a readily available behavioral repertoire which may function more or less independently of the cognitive data, and even (as in the case of habits and automatisms) with neglect of perceivable (cognitive) elements in the present situation which could have made the response better adapted to it. This shows that in this type of acquisition, learning and performance are more closely interwoven.

The patterns learned are at the same time behavioral readinesses and propensities, especially in situations where the subject's cognitive vigilance and discrimination is functioning at a lower level.

This habit formation type of learning which, no doubt, is predominant in infrahuman beings, and plays an important role in human behavior too, should be conceived, I think, in terms of a more direct and automatic influence of outcome or reward on behavioral responses.

The specific pattern of motor reaction of the tennis player hitting the ball and, more generally, the response leading to the outcome sought for, gives a behavioral outlet to the motivation or dynamic system involved. This process can be conceptualized, as Murphy (1947) and others have done, as a kind of *canalization* process, rather than a connection-strengthening mechanism. The only point I would like to make here is that in this more automatic type of learning too, it is possible to conceive the process in terms of embeddedness of response patterns in more or less enduring and active dynamic systems such as interests, task tensions, needs, etc. Originally, the dynamic system or need is not cast in a behavioral form. The organism does not "know" what to do. The responses giving a behavioral outlet to such dynamic systems, gradually become the behavioral concretization of an originally rather vague need or response tendency. Insofar as certain behavioral responses become integrated in dynamic systems, i.e., when responses become the behavioral channels and outlets of the dynamic systems, they are supposed to remain on a higher level of potential activation and are, therefore, better preserved by the organism, while other responses having no dynamic role are sloughed off. There are, however, two ways in which behavioral responses become incorporated in dynamic systems: either by cognitively functioning signals (signal function of reward), or by the very fact that the dynamic tension system finds a behavioral outlet via the rewarded response (automatic and slower working influence of reward).

It should be emphasized that cognitive or noncognitive learning processes are not to be considered as two separate ways in which man acquires new behavioral forms of dealing with objects. Both processes contribute in variable doses—according to the cognitive development of the living being involved, and his actual state of cognitive alertness or vigilance—to the man's progressive building of his behavioral and cognitive repertoire.

LEARNING AND HUMAN BEHAVIOR

A theory about the role of reward in learning should be supplemented by some insight into the place of learning in human behavior as a whole.

In that respect, it may be wise to go back to the careful observation of man's everyday behavior. In fact, this is the phenomenon eventually to be explained. Two points, then, demand our consideration: (1) What a normal man is really doing or trying to do in his life is not adequately expressed in terms of reinforcement; he certainly does not simply repeat what he successfully performed in the past; (2) as he does whatever he has to do, a great many of man's behavioral response patterns repeat themselves again and again.

Therefore, it seems necessary to distinguish in man's behavior between two components: (1) the behavioral modalities, "techniques," and means he uses (his way of writing or typing when applying to a university; traveling by car, plane, or railroad in going to attend a congress, etc.); and (2) what he really does when typing or writing the characters of his letters, etc. Compare the concept of *actone* in Murray (1938, p. 55).

A striking characteristic in what man really performs is the fact of the ever-changing rewards or goals he is trying to reach. The same writing or typing skills he learned several years ago are activated today in applying for admission to a university, tomorrow for breaking off an engagement, or proposing a research project to his supervisor, etc. Although he is writing in all these cases, he is certainly not repeating the same behavioral act. The fact that man does not just *repeat* successful or rewarded responses is not because he does not look for pleasure (in its broadest behavioral sense), but because the pleasures, rewards, and successes he pursues do not consist for him in always satisfying the same (organic) needs by the same objects. In other words, man's typical pattern of behavior clearly contrasts with the behavior model of the rat in the maze, or the pigeon in front of a food dispenser. What these animals do can be adequately expressed by saying that they repeat with a certain frequency the same rewarded responses leading to identical rewards, satisfying the same automatically and periodically recurring needs. This type of behavioral pattern by which most of the problems and theories in basic research have been moulded, is very alien indeed to what man is really doing when he is working for a degree, planning his vacation, preparing a new research program, making arrangements for building a house, strolling in the park, taking a rest, trying to solve a problem, etc. Although some micromechanisms intervene, of course, in all types of learning and performance (skills, as mentioned earlier), it is very doubtful that the most basic processes involved in man's behavior can be studied in the context of this pattern.

The important process to be added in our theoretical construct of behavior, and whose way of functioning psychologists and psychoneurologists are beginning to concentrate on, can be referred to as programming, planning, making projects, elaborating tasks, goal setting, and the like. In our opinion, this process is to be identified neither with purely cognitive mapping, nor with programming computer operations. It is a complex process in which dynamic and cognitive functions are involved, trying to build up the means–end structures leading to goal-objects beyond limits previously reached (cf. among others such concepts as *plan* and *image* in Miller *et al.*, 1960; *ordination* and *prospection* in Murray, 1959; Nuttin, 1964).

Reinforcement is not able to account for the most characteristic features of man's behavior. As already said, its role as direct "strengthening" of responses by reward (or unconditioned stimulus) is to be confined to a limited, but important area of learning, providing man with some of the essential elements in his behavioral repertoire. It provides *man-the-architect* with the ready-made bricks allowing him to construct an infinite variety of buildings. It is true that on a certain level of behavior (skill learning behavior), man's main activity consists in making bricks; but we are not brickmakers all the time; we are architects too.

The opinion I just expressed is not very different, I think, from Neal Miller's (1963) ironical distinction between "stupid" and "intelligent behavior," when he says that S–R reinforcement theories do well in predicting stupid behavior, but are much less convincing in predicting intelligent behavior; whereas cognitive theories seem to do well in dealing with intelligence, but have trouble in dealing with stupidity. Miller asks the question: "Is there some way to deal adequately with both?" Our position is an attempt to take a step in that direction.

It should finally be noted that reinforcement terminology is currently used so loosely and in so many contexts that it covers a variety of complex processes very different from each other. Two examples may be sufficient to illustrate what is meant here. Social psychologists investigating attitudes seem to like reinforcement terminology. My assumption is that changing one's attitude in a more or less extreme direction in function of a rewarded or punished counterattitudinal speech, is a more complex process than what is traditionally meant by reinforcement (see e.g., Sarbin & Allen, 1964; J. M. Nuttin, Jr. 1974). I would also assume that the process via which the frequency of bar-pressing is increased by receiving food pellets in some temporal sequence is different from the process via which a researcher goes ahead with his research program after successfully solving a first problem (abstraction made of the stimulus aspect of the situations). Bringing together under the same name the wide range of behavioral change processes may mask important differences. Scientific study of these differences is of no less importance than emphasis on their similarities. (Compare also the differences within so-called adaptation processes, especially the so-called active *versus* passive adaptation, Nuttin, 1967).

PERCEPTION OF SUCCESSFUL OUTCOMES

There are other fields of current research with regard to successful outcomes and rewards which I would have liked to report on in this chapter. I will be able to formulate the problems only briefly. In fact, successful outcomes are events which are *perceived* by the behaving subject and by his fellow man. A behavioral unit conceived as a series of subordinated acts (as previously described) will normally end in a series of outcomes, some of which will be more or less successful, others unsuccessful. It is investigated how a sequence of such partial successes and failures (as event–stimuli presented in random order) is perceived in various conditions. In a series of experiments on this topic (see among others D'Amorim & Nuttin, 1972) it was shown how some environmental, social, and personality factors influence outcome perception. The same is to be said about *recall* of outcomes.[10] The main problem is to know to what extent, and in what ways, distortions on the level of perception and recall of rewarding outcomes interfere with the influence of reward on learning and behavior in general. Other aspects of this problem have been discussed elsewhere (Nuttin, 1969; Lietaer, 1966).

CONCLUSION

Talking about pleasure and reward is talking about man's preferential directions toward some types of situations and objects. To a large extent, this problem coincides with motivation. Pleasure, in the language of science, is the construct, or intervening variable, underlying behavioral "likes" and preferences. A living being's capacity for pleasure depends on the variety and intensity of his preferential relationships with objects in its behavioral world.

The role of pleasure and reward in learning is related, in our hypothesis, to their function either as signals (cognitive learning), or as direct behavioral outlets for dynamic systems, and to the organism's activation level implied in both. Moreover, it should not be overlooked that, besides

---

[10] See among others our earlier experiments on the role of recall of outcome in the phenomenon called 'spread of effect' (Nuttin, 1949).

learning, dynamic programming or planning is an important process in human behavior. Man's own pleasure is in planning and realizing objects not yet obtained.

References

Allport, G., Effect: A secondary principle of learning. *Psychological Review,* 1946, Vol. 53, 345–346.

Bass, B. M., Social Behavior and the Orientation Inventory: A Review. *Psychological Bulletin,* 1967, Vol. 68, 260–292.

Berlyne, D. E., The reward-value of indifferent stimulation. In J. T. Tapp (Ed.), *Reinforcement and behavior.* New York and London: Academic Press, 1969, 179–214.

Bloch, V., Denti, A., & Schmaltz, G., Effets de la stimulation réticulaire sur la phase de consolidation de la trace mnésique. *Journal de Physiologie,* 1966, Vol. 58, 469–470.

Bühler, Ch., & Massarik, F. (Eds.), *The course of human life. A study of goals in the human perspective.* New York: Springer, 1968, 422 pp.

Cabanac, M., Physiological role of pleasure. *Science,* 1971, Vol. 173, 1103–1107.

Clayton, Keith N., Reward and reinforcement in selective learning: considerations with respect to a mathematical model of learning. In J. T. Tapp (Ed.), *Reinforcement and behavior.* New York and London: Academic Press, 1969, 96–119.

D'Amorim, M. A., & Nuttin, J. R., La perception des réussites et échecs personnels en fonction des résultats d'un partenaire. Influence de l'intérêt pour la tâche et du niveau d'aspiration chez des sujets masculins et féminins. *Psychologica Belgica,* 1972, Vol. 12–1, 9–31.

Decharms, R., *Personal causation. The internal affective determinants of behavior.* New York and London: Academic Press, 1968.

Deweer, B., Hennevin, E., & Bloch, V., Nouvelles données sur la facilitation réticulaire de la consolidation mnésique. *Journal de Physiologie,* 1968, Vol. 60 (supplément 1-2), 430.

Egger, M. David, & Miller, Neal E., Secondary reinforcement in rats as a function of information value and reliability of the stimulus. *Journal of Experimental Psychology,* 1962, Vol. 64, 97–104.

Egger, M. David, & Miller, Neal E., When is reward reinforcing? An experimental study of the information hypothesis. *Journal of Comparative and Physiological Psychology,* 1963, Vol. 56, 132–137.

Estes, W. K., Reinforcement in human learning. In J. T. Tapp (Ed.), *Reinforcement and behavior.* New York and London: Academic Press, 1969, 63–94.

Groos, K., *Die Spiele der Menschen.* Jena: Fisher, 1899, VIII + 538 pp. In English (translation by E. L. Baldwin), *The play of man.* New York: Appleton, 1901, IX + 412 pp.

Hernandez-Péon, R., Attention, sleep, motivation, and behavior. In R. G. Heath (Ed.), *The role of pleasure in behavior.* New York: Harper, 1964, 195–217.

Kish, G. B., Learning when the onset of illumination is used as a reinforcing stimulus. *Journal of Comparative and Physiological Psychology,* 1955, Vol. 48, 261–264.

Kish, G. B., & Antonitis, J. J., Unconditioned operant behavior in two homozygous strains of mice. *The Journal of Genetic Psychology,* 1956, Vol. 88, 121–129.

Lecomte, P., Deweer, B., & Bloch, V., Consolidation et conservation de la trace mnésique: Effets respectifs de la stimulation réticulaire. *Journal de Physiologie,* 1969, Vol. 61 (supplément 1-2, 334–335).

Lettvin, J. Y., *et al.,* Two remarks on the visual system of the frog. In W. A. Rosenblith (Ed.), *Sensory communication. Contributions to the symposium on principles of sensory communication.* M.I.T., 1959. New York: M.I.T. Press and Wiley, 1961, 757–776.

Lietaer, G., Experimenteel onderzoek naar de invloed van het prestatie-niveau van een socius op de perceptie van eigen slagen en mislukken. *Psychologica Belgica,* 1966, Vol. 6, 86–102.

Meehl, P. E., On the circularity of the law of effect. *Psychological Bulletin,* 1950, Vol. 47, 52–75.

Michotte, A., *The perception of causality.* London: Methuen–Basic Books, 1963.

Miller, G. A., Galanter, E., & Pribram, K. H., *Plans and the structure of behavior.* New York: Holt, 1960, 226 pp.

Miller, Neal E., Some reflections on the law of effect produce a new alternative to drive reduction. In M. R. Jones (Ed.), *Nebraska symposium on motivation, 1963.* Lincoln: Univ. of Nebraska Press, 1963, 65–112.

Muenzinger, K. F., Motivation in Learning, I. Electric shock for correct response in the visual discrimination habit. *Journal of Comparative Psychology,* 1935, Vol. 17, 267–277.

Murphy, G., *Personality. A biosocial approach to origins and structure.* New York: Harper, 1947, 999 pp.

Murray, Henry A., Explorations in personality. London and New York: Oxford Univ. Press, 1938.

Murray, Henry A., Preparations for the scaffold of a comprehensive system. In S. Koch (Ed.), *Psychology: a study of a science.* Study 1. Conceptual and systematic; Vol. 3: Formulations of the person and the social context, 7–54. New York: McGraw-Hill, 1959.

Nuttin, J., Respective effectiveness of success and task-tension in learning. *The British Journal of Psychology* (general section), 1947, Vol. 38 (part 2), 49–55.

Nuttin, J., Spread in recalling failure and success. *Journal of Experimental Psychology,* 1949, Vol. 39, 690–700.

Nuttin, J., The future time perspective in human motivation and learning. *Proceedings of the 17th International Congress of Psychology.* Amsterdam: North Holland Publishing Company, 1964, 60–82; also in *Acta Psychologica,* 1964, Vol. 23, 60–82.

Nuttin, J., Adaptation et motivation humaine. In F. Bresson, J. Nuttin, J. Piaget, *et al., Les processus d'adaptation.* Paris: P.U.F., 1967, 127–137.

Nuttin, J., Elaboration d'une nouvelle approche expérimentale en matière de la perception de la personnalité. Notes sur la formation à la recherche. *Bulletin de Psychologie,* 1969, Vol. 22, 669–675.

Nuttin, J., & Greenwald, A. G., *Reward and punishment in human learning. Elements of a behavior theory.* New York and London: Academic Press, 1968. Pp. 205.

Nuttin, J. M., Jr., *Attitude change after 'rewarded' advocacy: evidence for a non-cognitive dissonance view.* Leuven: Leuven Univ. Press, 1974 (in print).

Premack, D., Reversibility of the reinforcement relation. *Science,* 1962, Vol. 136, 255–257.

Pribram, K. H., Reinforcement revisited: a structural view. In M. R. Jones, (Ed.), *Nebraska symposium on motivation, 1963.* Lincoln: Univ. of Nebraska Press, 1963, 113–159.

Russell, A., The effects of magnitude and duration of change on the light-contingent bar-pressing of hooded rats. *Australian Journal of Psychology,* 1972, Vol. 24, 63–73.

Sarbin, T. R., & Allen, Vernon L., Role enactment, audience feedback, and attitude change. *Sociometry,* 1964, Vol. 27, 183–193.

Sevenster, P., Incompatibility of response and reward. Unpublished paper, Symposium on Learning, Leuven-Louvain, 1972.

Sokolov, E. N. In M. A. Brazier (Ed.), *The central nervous system and behavior, transactions of the third conference.* Josiah Macy, Jr., Foundation, 1960.

Thorndike, E., Darwin's contribution to psychology. *University of California Chronicle,* 1909, Vol. 12, 65–80; In E. Thorndike, *Selected writings from a connectionist's psychology.* New York: Appleton, 1949, 349–363.

Trabasso, T., & Bower, G. H., *Attention in learning.* New York: Wiley, 1968.

Vinckier-Hellings, Hilda, De genese van de processen van doelstelling en project-vorming. *Psychologica Belgica,* 1970, Vol. 10-1, 1–24.

Weiner, B., & Walker, E. L., Motivational factors in short-term retention. *Journal of Experimental Psychology,* 1966, Vol. 71, 190–193.

White, R. W. Motivation reconsidered: The concept of competence. *Psychological Review,* 1959, Vol. 66, 297–333.

Woodworth, R. S., *Dynamics of behavior.* New York: Holt, 1958, 403 pp.

CHAPTER 11

Patterns of Preference and Models of Motivation [1]

K. B. MADSEN

Royal Danish School of Educational Studies, Copenhagen

Introduction

The final contribution to a volume is supposed to provide a summary and attempt to integrate the other contributions.

I should like to summarize and integrate metatheoretically: I shall first present a metascientific frame of reference developed in connection with a comparative study of theories of motivation, which I have worked on during the last two decades. Together with the frame of reference I shall present some results of my comparative study of 42 theories.[2] I shall attempt to place the six main contributions to this volume within this context.

The Frame of Reference

The comparative study of scientific theories—which I call "systematology"—is regarded as a discipline within the broader field of *Metascience*. Systematology is the study of scientific products, i.e., "theories." We use

---

[1] The language of this chapter has been carefully checked by John T. Bruce, M.A.

[2] The results of my comparative metascientific studies are presented in my main books (Madsen, 1959, 1973b). A briefer presentation can be found in my chapter (Madsen, 1973a).

the term "theory" in a very broad sense including all *scientific discourses or texts*. A scientific text may roughly be divided into three parts, levels or strata (cf. Fig. 11-1).

1. *The Descriptive Stratum*—or "Data Level"—is that part of the text which includes concrete descriptions of data from experiments and other kinds of empirical research. The specific concrete descriptions are called

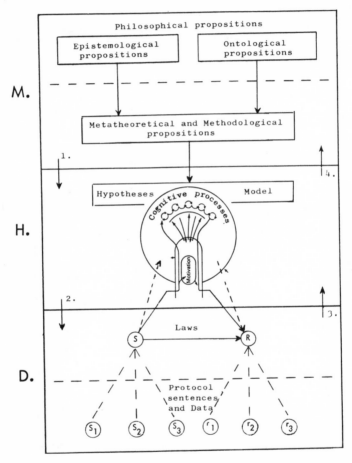

Fig. 11-1. The hierarchical structure of a theory. This diagram illustrates the three strata of a scientific text: "M" = "M-level" or "Meta-stratum"; "H" = "H-level" or "Hypothetical stratum"; "D" = "D-level" or "Descriptive stratum." The four arrows (1, 2, 3, 4) indicate that the top level influences the bottom level. But there is also a "feedback" of influence from the D-level to the H-level and the M-level (otherwise it would not be a scientific theory).

"protocol sentences." In addition, the data level includes the general, abstract descriptions of relationships between data—the so-called "empirical laws."

2. *The Hypothetical Stratum*—or H level—is that part of the text which contains formulations of *hypotheses* and constructions of *models* for explanations and predictions. The H level constitutes the "theory" in the narrow and conventional sense of the term.

3. *The Metastratum*—or M level—is that part of the text which contains the *methodological* principles regarding empirical research methods and the *metatheoretical* principles regarding theory construction. In addition, the M level may also include some *philosophical* presuppositions, such as *epistemological* propositions about knowledge in general and *ontological* propositions about, e.g., the "Mind–Body Problem." These philosophical propositions are usually not explicitly formulated but are found to lie "behind" the principles and hypotheses implicitly.

Although these philosophical presuppositions are frequently implicit, we believe that they are very important as determinants of the whole theory.

In accord with many historians and philosophers of science, we conceive of scientific theories as being determined not only by the *empirical data* obtained from research, but also by the *philosophical presuppositions* which the scientists possess before they start on their research. Furthermore, these philosophical presuppositions influence the whole scientific "strategy": the metatheoretical and methodological positions selected, the kind of hypotheses and models preferred, and the kind of empirical data that are the object of the research.

Patterns of Preferences

From the above exposition, it is clear that the philosophical presuppositions determine *metascientific patterns of preferences.*

We believe that these patterns of preferences are strongly influenced by *the personality of the scientist.* We base this upon the "psycho-epistemological" theory of Joseph Royce. He claims that there are three main theories of knowledge: *empiricism, rationalism,* and *intuitionism* (or "metaphorism" as he also calls it). On the basis of a questionnaire and factor analysis he has found three personality factors. These factors vary in strength from scientist to scientist, and each scientist has his individual "psycho–epistemological profile." This pattern of personality factors determines which main theory of knowledge the scientist adopts.

We think that Royce's psycho–epistemological theory can be expanded into a general metascientific theory: The scientist's personality determines —together with social and historical factors—the metapropositions he prefers, and as a consequence of this what kind of theory he constructs, and what kind of data he collects. We can illustrate this metascientific theory by means of a graphic model (Fig. 11-2).

After this generalization of Royce's theory into a more general metascientific theory, we return to our comparative study of theories in order to present evidence for our metascientific theory. For this purpose we find it convenient to differentiate between two categories of empiristic positions: "radical empiricism" (or "positivism"), and "rational empiricism" (or "logical empiricism").

We can now apply this classification of epistemological positions to the modern and earlier theories of motivation which we have studied. This is presented in the following classification (Table 11-1).

The Mind–Body Problem

The most important ontological problem for psychologists is the psychosomatic or "mind–body" problem. Psychologists are a little more explicit in their theories about this problem than when dealing with the epistemological problem. Of the different theories about the mind–body problem we have only found the following three included in the theories we have studied: *materialism, neutral monism,* and *dualism.* The last one is not formulated so explicitly that we can decide whether it represents parallelism or epiphenomenalism. But we think that the third possible version of dualism, the interactionistic theory, can be excluded, as it is very difficult to defend on the basis of modern scientific knowledge.

We present our classification of the modern and earlier theories of motivation in the following classification scheme (Table 11-2).

The Cognitive Status of Theories

In his well known work about *The Structure of Science,* Ernst Nagel (1961) has a chapter with the same title as we have used for this one. In this chapter he deals with a very important problem, which has also been discussed among theoretical psychologists, namely: What relation do theories have to "reality"? Nagel maintains that there are three different positions, which he describes as the "descriptive," the "realist," and the "instrumental" views of theories.

The descriptive view can be equated with the metatheoretical position which conceives of theories as systems of abstract descriptions of obser-

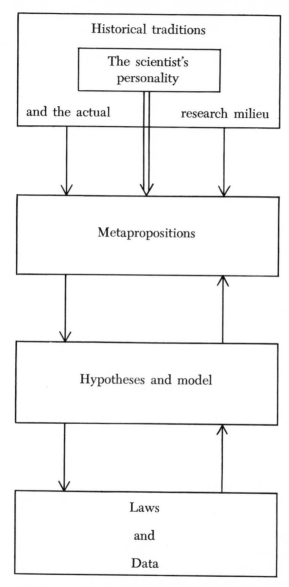

Fig. 11-2. A model of the general metascientific theory: The personal, social, and historical factors determine the M, H, and D levels of the theory. We presuppose critical feedback between the three levels of the theory, but not feedback to the determining factors.

TABLE 11–1

Classification of the modern and earlier theories of motivation according to their presupposed theories of knowledge. Of the earlier theories we have selected 12 of the 20 studied.

Theories of knowledge	Radical empiricism	Rational empiricism	Rational-ism	Meta-phorism
Modern theories	Duffy? Bindra?	Berlyne, Cattell Konorski, Atkinson Pribram Miller Brown Woodworth Festinger		Maslow?
Earlier theories	Skinner Young? McClelland?	McDougall Tolman Lewin Murray Hull Hebb Tinbergen		Allport? Moore

vations. In psychology we find this view among those who—like Skinner —limit the task of science to descriptions of single events or of regular relationships between events ("laws"). This view is also shared by those psychologists who accept intervening variables without any surplus meaning.

The realist view can be equated with the metatheoretical position, which conceives of theories as representing certain unobserved, hypothetical, but "real" entities behind the observed phenomena. In psychology this view is shared by two different groups.

There are those psychologists who have as their final goal the "reduction" of psychology to physiology. If this goal were realized the result would be a physiological, descriptive theory which would belong to the first view. But nobody believes that this goal was reached, and therefore conceive of their theories as hypotheses referring to the neurophysiological structures and processes behind behavior—the "conceptual nervous system" as Skinner ironically called it. This view is shared by those—like Hebb and Konorski—who employ hypothetical terms with physiological surplus meaning (S–O–R theories). Merle B. Turner has produced a very detailed and thorough argumentation for the reductionist view (Turner, 1967).

TABLE 11-2

Classification of the theories according to their presupposed psychosomatic theses. The question mark after some of the names indicates doubt about the classification.

Psychosomatic theories	Materialism	Neutral monism	Dualism
Modern theories	Duffy? Bindra? Kornorski?	Pribram Miller Brown Woodworth Festinger Cattell Atkinson Berlyne	Maslow?
Earlier theories	Hebb Tinbergen Skinner	McDougall Murray Lewin Young Tolman Hull McClelland	Allport Moore

The other group sharing the realist view is composed of psychologists who conceive of theories as referring to the mental structures and processes behind behavior and conscious experiences. This view is held by those who use hypothetical terms with mentalistic surplus meaning (S–M–R theories).

The difference between the two subgroups of psychologists sharing the realist view is to be found in their presupposed theory of the psychosomatic problem. The mentalistic realists have a dualistic theory of the "mind–body" problem, whereas the reductive realists have a materialistic or a neutral monistic theory of this problem.

The instrumentalist view is the metatheoretical position that conceives of theories as "instruments" or "tools" for making explanations and predictions. This view has also been called "conventionalism," which was the name given to it by the famous mathematician and physicist, Henri Poincaré. In psychology the instrumentalist view is represented by well known psychologists such as Freud, Lewin, and Tolman. Tolman made it popular among American psychologists under the label "constructive" (in opposition to "reductive" theories). In the past few years the instrumentalist view has gained many adherents, because mathematical and cybernetic models have demonstrated their utility in psychology. The instrumentalist view is shared by all those psychologists who use hypothetical terms with neutral surplus meaning (S–H$_N$–R theories).

We can summarize this section by making a classification scheme encompassing the modern and earlier theories of motivation which we have studied (Table 11-3).

HYPOTHETICAL TERMS

Practically all psychological theories employ terms referring to unobservable "intervening variables" or "hypothetical constructs." We also refer to these terms as "hypothetical" or "H" terms. They differ from theory to theory according to the kind of surplus meaning they carry with them.

Some psychological theories use explanatory H terms referring to "intervening variables" in the narrow sense. Therefore, these H terms have *no* surplus meaning.

Other theories employ H terms referring to "hypothetical constructs," which are components in a Conceptual Nervous System. These terms do

TABLE 11–3

Classification scheme of modern and earlier theories of motivation according to their view of the metatheoretical status of the theories.

Metatheoretical positions	Descriptive view	Realist view: Reductionism	Realist view: Mentalism	Instrumentalist view
Modern theories	Duffy?	Bindra Konorski Pribram Miller (II)[a]	Maslow	Miller (I)[a] Brown Woodworth Festinger Cattell Atkinson Berlyne
Earlier theories	Skinner	Tinbergen Hebb Young	Allport Moore	McClelland McDougall Murray Hull Lewin Tolman

[a] Miller is presented in two places, because his first theory is instrumentalistic, and his second reductionistic.

not refer to physiological data, but to hypothetical variables which are conceived of as part of a brain model. Therefore, they are called H terms with physiological surplus meaning or "H_0 terms" ("O" referring to the organism).

A third group of theories uses H terms referring to hypothetical constructs, which are components of a mental structure. These terms do not directly refer to phenomenological *data*, but to inferred processes, states, and structures in other peoples "minds," which are akin to the phenomenological data we experience in ourselves. Therefore, these H terms are called H terms with mentalistic surplus meaning or H_M terms

A last group of theories uses H terms referring to hypothetical constructs, which are components of a "neutral" model, which can be borrowed from various fields, e.g., mathematics, cybernetics, and information theory. As these models are "neutral regarding the mind–body problem," we have called them H terms with neutral surplus meaning or H_N terms.

As it is very difficult to draw a sharp line between these H_N terms and those referring to intervening variables and having no surplus meaning, we have—in accordance with Tolman—combined them under the label H_N terms.

Thus it is possible to classify all psychological theories according to the H terms they employ. They can be divided into three main categories:

1. *S–O–R theories* using H_0 terms.
2. *S–M–R theories* using H_M theories.
3. *S–H–R theories* using H_N terms.

In addition to these three main categories there is an additional one, i.e., the S–R theories, which is purely descriptive and do not use any H terms. But as Skinner's theory is the only one we have found belonging to this category, we have included it with the S–O–R theories because we believe that Skinner's theory is actually more similar to this group of theories than to the others. We can now summarize our classification of the earlier and the modern theories of motivation in this classification scheme (Table 11-4).

THE DATA LANGUAGE

There are two main data languages: the behavioral and the phenomenological. Most modern psychologists have used the behavioral data language, but a few have used the phenomenological. Many psychologists have used a mixed data language, but often with the behavioral

TABLE 11-4

Classification of the earlier and modern theories according to their preferred hypothetical terms.

Preferred H terms	H$_O$ terms [a]	H$_N$ terms [b]	H$_M$ terms [c]
Earlier theories	Young Tinbergen Hebb (Skinner)	McDougall Tolman, Lewin Murray, Hull McClelland	Allport Moore
Modern theories	Duffy Bindra Berlyne Konorski	Miller, Woodworth Brown, Festinger Cattell, Atkinson Pribram	Maslow

[a] H$_O$ terms, i.e., H terms with physiological surplus meaning.

[b] H$_N$ terms, i.e., H terms with neutral—or without any—surplus meaning.

[c] H$_M$ terms, i.e., H terms with mentalistic surplus meaning.

as the basic one. There has not, however, been much discussion of the problem in the last decade. Most psychologists seem to have found the behavioral data language to be the most convenient, without committing themselves to a classic behavioristic metatheory and methodology. The reason for this is that the phenomenological data is presupposed to be translatable into the behavioral data language. Even the humanistic psychologists seem to have accepted a behavioral data language, although they criticize the biological philosophy of man as well as the naturalistic philosophy of science, which is a common trait among American psychologists.

The most serious attack upon the dominance of behavioral data language has come from a number of modern philosophers. The *hermenutic* school of metascience has claimed that there is a basic, qualitative difference between behavior and acts. Behavior—even verbal behavior—can be described, explained and predicted in accordance with the naturalistic concept of science. Human acts—to which language belongs—can neither be explained nor predicted, but the intention (or "meaning") of the act and the linguistic message may be interpreted and understood in accordance with the *hermeneutic* conception of science.

This philosophically important distinction between behavior and human acts and language has not only been set forth by the *hermenuetic* philosophers (cf. Radnitzky, 1970), but also by analytic philosophers belonging to the so-called "Oxford school of philosophy." Thus the Danish philosopher, Justus Hartnack, has presented a very thorough analysis of this problem (cf. Hartnack, 1971).

But, unfortunately, these European philosophers' analyses of the problems of behavior and language have not yet come to the attention of any American psychologists. On the other hand most European philosophers seem to be unfamiliar with Tolman's original distinction between molecular behavior and molar behavior acts (cf. Tolman, 1932). This distinction is similar to the philosophers' distinction between behavior and acts (including language). But Tolman thought it was possible to deal with molar behavior acts in the S–R paradigm, if supplemented with the intervening hypothetical variables and thus expanded into an S–H–R paradigm.

We must leave this philosophical discussion and return to our systematological classifications. In our next classification scheme (Table 11-5), we bring the classification of the modern and earlier theories according to their preferred data language.

TABLE 11–5

Classification of the modern and earlier theories according to their preferred data language.

Preferred data language	Behavioral data language	Mixed or combined data language	Phenomenological data language
Modern theories	Duffy Berlyne Bindra Brown	Konorski Pribram Miller Woodworth Festinger Cattell Maslow? [a] Atkinson	Maslow? [a]
Earlier theories	Hebb Tinbergen Hull Skinner	Allport McDougall Murray McClelland Lewin Young Tolman Moore? [a]	Moore? [a]

[a] Two theories—Maslow's and Moore's—were a little difficult to place.

Concluding Remarks

The reader may have noticed that in this chapter we have mentioned the possibility of relationships between the different positions concerning the philosophy of science. These remarks are expressions of our general metascientific hypotheses. If the personality of the scientist determines his preference for some of the major philosophical propositions—such as the epistemological and psychosomatic—then it is logical to assume that these first preferences or choices[3] may well imply some of the later preferences of metapropositions. In turn this should imply some consequences for theory construction and the collection of data. In other words, we expect some relationships between the preferences or some patterns in the metatheoretical positions adopted by a particular psychologist. For example, we expect a radical empiricist to be a materialist rather than a dualist, a descriptivist rather than a realist or instrumentalist, a behaviorist rather than a phenomenalist and so on.

Such a metatheoretical pattern should influence the H level and the D level of the same theory.

We shall illustrate our theory by means of a table (Table 11-6) and later we can see how "correct" the evidence for the theory is in terms of our material.

As can be seen from Table 11-6 we have arranged the different metascientific classifications in such a way that there are three possible patterns of preference or paradigms.

The first paradigm is for convenience called the Empiricist Paradigm. This includes the following pattern of preferences: Radical empiricism + materialism + descriptivism or reductive realism + preference for H_o terms and a behavioral data language.

The second paradigm is called the Rationalist Paradigm. It includes this pattern of preferences Rationalism (pure or empiristic) + neutral monism + instrumentalism + preference for H_N terms and a combined data language.

The third paradigm is called the Intuitionist Paradigm. It includes this pattern of preferences: Metaphorism + dualism + mentalistic realism + preference of H_M terms and phenomenological data language.

These three paradigms are the possible patterns of preferences. We shall now try to ascertain to what degree these paradigms are real pat-

---

[3] We think that the term "preference" is more adequate than the term "choice," because it is rarely a matter of consciously choosing a particular metascientific "strategy" but rather a matter of unconscious personal preferences.

TABLE 11–6

A classification scheme presenting the different metascientific views which psychologists may have on different problems.[a]

	Radical empiricism		Empiristic Rationalism / Pure Rationalism	Metaphorism
Epistemological theories	Radical empiricism		Empiristic Rationalism / Pure Rationalism	Metaphorism
Psychosomatic theories	Materialism		Neutral monism	Dualism
Metatheories	Descriptionism	Reductive realism	Instrumentalism	Mentalistic realism
Preferred H terms	H_O terms		H_N terms	H_M terms
Preferred data languages	Behavioral		Mixed or combined data languages	Phenomenological

[a] The scheme is made so that it is easy to conceive of three metascientific patterns of preference or "paradigms":

(1) The Empiricist paradigm: The empiristic–materialist–descriptionist (or reductionist)–H_O terms—behaviorist pattern.

(2) The Rationalist paradigm: The rationalist–neutral monist–instrumentalist—H_N terms—integrationist pattern.

(3) The Intuitionist paradigm: The metaphorist–dualist–mentalist H_M terms—phenomenologist pattern.

terns of preferences. In other words: How the theories we have studied are distributed over the five classifications. We have placed the earlier and modern theories of motivation in a classification scheme in which the columns indicate the three possible patterns of preferences and the rows indicate the five possible metascientific classifications (see Table 11-7).

If we inspect this classification scheme it can readily be seen that some theories consistently follow a certain pattern of preferences. Thus Duffy, Bindra, and Skinner consistently follow the empiricist paradigm. And it is also easy to see that there are three theories which just as consistently follow the intuitionist paradigm, namely those of Maslow, Moore, and Allport (although Allport is not completely consistent). In the rationalist paradigm we find nine consistent theories, those of Miller, Woodworth, Festinger, Cattell, Atkinson, McDougall, Tolman, Lewin, and Murray.

TABLE 11-7

Classification of 24 theories according to metascientific paradigm.

Metascientific paradigms	Empiricist paradigm	Rationalist paradigm	Intuitionist paradigm
Epistemological theories	Duffy Bindra Skinner McClelland Young	Miller, Woodworth Brown, Festinger Cattell, Atkinson McDougall, Tolman Tinbergen, Lewin Murray, Pribram Hull, Berlyne, Hebb	Maslow Moore Allport
Psychosomatic theories	Duffy, Tinbergen Bindra Skinner Hebb Konorski	Miller, Woodworth Brown, Festinger Cattell, Atkinson McDougall, Tolman Lewin, Murray, Young Hull, McClelland Pribram, Berlyne	Maslow Moore Allport
Metatheories	Duffy, Konorski Bindra, Young Skinner, Tinbergen Hebb Pribram	Miller, Woodworth Brown, Festinger Cattell, Atkinson McDougall, Tolman Lewin, Murray Hull, McClelland Berlyne	Maslow Moore Allport
Preferred H terms	Duffy, Young Bindra, Tinbergen Skinner Berlyne Hebb Konorski	Miller, Woodwroth Brown, Festinger Cattell, Atkinson McDougall, Tolman Lewin, Murray Hull, McClelland Pribram	Maslow Moore Allport
Preferred Data Languages	Duffy, Hebb Bindra, Tinbergen Skinner Brown Hull Berlyne	Miller, Woodworth Allport Festinger, Cattell Atkinson, McDougall Tolman, Lewin, Murray Young, McClelland Pribram, Konorski	Maslow? Moore

These 15 theories are those which most consistently follow one pattern of preferences. And among these Allport was not completely consistent, only in four of the five possible cases. Thus we can call Allport's "80%

consistent." There are some theories beside Allport's which are 80% consistent, namely those of Pribram, Brown, Hull, Hebb, McClelland, and Tinbergen. Together with Allport this makes eight theories which are "80% consistent."

Thus we can conclude that among these 24 theories there are 14—or 58%—which are "100% consistent." And, in addition, there are seven theories which are "80% consistent." We can combine the "100% consistent" theories with the "80% consistent" in one category, the "80–100% consistent theories." This category encompasses 21 of the 24 theories. In other words 88% of the theories are 80–100% consistent. We regard this as fairly good confirmation of our metascientific theory of the patterns of preferences.

Before leaving this topic we shall classify the six main contributors according to their metascientific paradigm. We have placed them in the same classification scheme (see Table 11-8).

SUPPLEMENTARY COMMENTS

The above results about "patterns of preferences" were presented by the author at the symposium. In one of the sessions H. J. Eysenck proposed a very interesting hypothesis: The three paradigms constitute a "dimension" if they are arranged in this way:

Rationalism	Empiricism	Institutionism

And this dimension is according to Eysenck, correlated with the Introversion–Extraversion personality dimension. He has found the same correlation between this personality dimension and the selection of courses, as Royce found between his "psycho-epistemological profile" and the selection of studies. Thus mathematicians and physicists are introverts and rationalists, whereas chemists and biologists are ambiverts and empiricists and humanists and artists are extraverts and intuitionists.

If this hypothesis proposed by Eysenck is confirmed, we have made a step toward the integration of systematology and the psychology of scientists.

Models of Motivation

We have found it convenient to classify the basic hypotheses—axioms or postulates—of motivation into four categories. We call them "models of motivation" because they are often systems of interrelated hypothetical

TABLE 11-8

Classification of the six main speakers according to the metascientific paradigm they prefer.

Metascientific paradigms	Empiricist paradigm	Rationalist paradigm	Intuitionist paradigm
Epistemological theories	Helson Olds	Eysenck Heckhausen Nuttin Walker	
Psychosomatic theories	Helson Olds	Eysenck Heckhausen Nuttin Walker	
Metatheories	Eysenck? [a] Helson Olds	Eysenck? Heckhausen Nuttin Walker	
Preferred H terms	Eysenck? Helson Olds	Eysenck? Heckhausen Nuttin Walker	
Preferred data languages	Helson Olds	Eysenck Heckhausen Nuttin Walker	

[a] The doubt about classification of Eysenck is caused by his important change in metascientific paradigm in his last book. Berlyne is not included in this classification because he already is in the main study.

variables, which can be represented by a "model." These models may be concrete, diagramatic models, but in many cases they are only verbal analogies. In some cases they are mathematical models.

According to the main content of the basic hypotheses in the models, we can classify them into four categories: (1) The "homeostatic" model; (2) the "incentive model; (3) the "cognitive" model, and (4) the "humanistic" model.

1. *The Homeostatic Model.* This is the oldest model in the history of motivational psychology. The concept of "homeostasis" was formulated by the famous American psychologist Walter B. Canon in 1915 (see Canon, 1915). He was inspired by the French physiologist Claude Ber-

nard's conception of the "internal milieu." Besides, a similar conception was formulated by Freud at the same time as Canon (see Freud, 1915).

The special feature of the homeostatic model is that all biological processes—including behavior—are determined by a disturbance of "homeostasis," i.e., the optimal conditions of equilibrium in the organism. And the biological processes—including behavior—go on until homeostasis is restored (or the organism is dead). Formulated in more familiar psychological terms the homeostatic model indicates that: A disturbance of homeostasis constitutes a need which in turn determines a central drive. Together with cognitive processes this drive determines behavior, which reduces—or "satisfies"—the need, and thus reestablishes homeostasis (cf. Fig 11-3).

This homeostatic model is found in such influential theories as those of Freud and Hull. And many other psychologists have adopted this model, because it has several advantages. The most important of these are: (1) it is a simple model, which is always an important quality for scientists and (2) it is a biological model, which was important for psychologists in the post-Darwinian period.

The popularity of the model led psychologists to misuse it and to ignore for a long time facts, which did not fit into the model. Finally, the homeostatic model was so severely criticized that it could not retain its position as the only valid motivational model. Other models were created as alternatives to the homeostatic model.

2. The Incentive Model. The "homeostatic period" lasted from about 1915 (the year of Canon's first formulation) until about 1953 (the year of the first Nebraska symposium on motivation). Thus H. F. Harlow criticized the homeostatic model as being too narrow at the first Nebraska symposium. He pointed out that there were other biological primary motivations besides homeostatic drive. He was especially concerned with the existence of a visual exploratory drive (see Harlow, 1953).

Later it was demonstrated by many experiments that even the so-called "homeostatic drives" (especially hunger, thirst, and sex) cannot be completely explained by the use of a homeostatic model. The earliest and strongest experimentally based attack on the narrow homeostatic model was made by P. T. Young. As early as the beginning of the 1940s he presented experimental evidence regarding food preferences in animals which were not based on homeostasis (see Young, 1941 and 1961; also the chapter about Young in Madsen, 1959, 1968).

The main propositions contained in the incentive model are summarized below.

Certain external stimuli have a *dynamic* effect, i.e., they determine a

state of activation or energy mobilization in the organism. This dynamic
state determines, together with cognitive processes, the behavior of the
organism. This behavior often results in a reduction of the external,

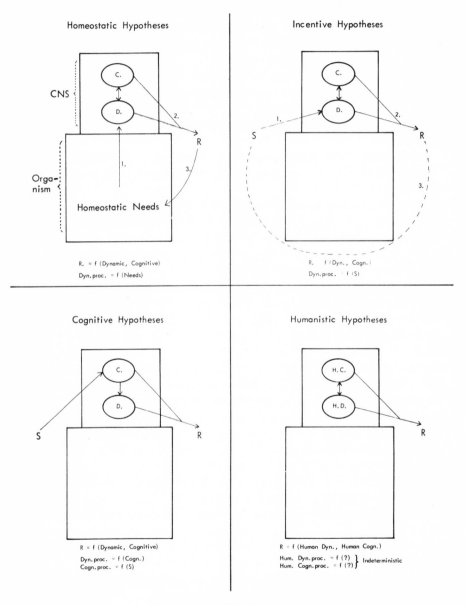

Fig. 11-3. Models of motivation.

dynamic stimuli (cf. Fig. 11-3). These stimuli have their origin in stimulus objects called "incentives," i.e., motivating (dynamic, activating, energy mobilizing) stimulus objects. In some theories incentives include "reinforcers" and "goal objects."

There are two kinds of incentives: primary and secondary. The primary incentives are S variables which have an innate dynamic effect. These primary incentives play an important role in the so-called "hedonistic" theories, among which P. T. Young's is the most elaborate we have studied. He claims that external stimulation has affective as well as sensory consequences, and that the "affective arousal" orients the organism toward or against the stimulus object, and thus influences choice and preference.

Among other well known hedonistic theories we have studied we can mention Hebb's (1949) earliest theory, McClelland's (1953) theory and Tinbergen's (1951) theory.

We should mention that the hedonistic theory is very old, even older than the homeostatic theory. It goes back to the ancient philosophers such as Epicurus and the so-called "Utilitarians" (e.g., J. Bentham) in the 1700s. The hedonic conception is also inherent in Thorndike's "law of effect" and Freud's "pleasure principle."

The secondary incentives are S variables which have an acquired dynamic effect. Therefore such incentives play an important role in modern learning theory. Thanks to K. W. Spence's (1960) incentive motivation was included in Hull's theory (denoted by the symbol "K," in honor of K. W. Spence). This "incentive motivation, K," together with "drive, D" and "habit strength, sHr" determine the "reaction potential, sEr" and the subsequent behavior. K is thus a hypothetical variable which is determined by the S variable: Magnitude and quality of the reward (e.g., food) used in the learning experiments to which the theory refers.

Spence developed the conception of incentive motivation on the basis of Hull's earlier concept of the "$r_g - s_g$ mechanism" or the so-called "fractional antedating goal response." In Hull's theory this "$r_g - s_g$ mechanism" had only a directive effect, but Spence pointed to the possibility that the frustration of R_G—the complete goal response—has an activating effect similar to drive. This activating or dynamic effect of $r_g - s_g$ was separated from the directive effect by the label "K".

In Spence's later version of his own theory (see Spence, 1960), K was more important than D as a determiner of behavior. They were here supposed to interact in an additive way, so that Spence's version of Hull's well-known formula reads:

$$sEr = f\,[sHr \times (D + K)].$$

K is thought to be acquired by reinforcement, defined as drive reduction, while sHr is acquired, according to Spence, by contiguity.

Among the modern theories of motivation we have dealt with we find Atkinson's (1964) to be the most elaborate one based upon an incentive model. Among the earlier theories we should especially like to mention K. Lewin's (1935) because it contained the "valence" concept. Atkinson was strongly influenced by this concept. Freud's concept of "cathexis" is also similar to the modern incentive concept.

After this survey of different incentive theories we now turn to the third model of motivation.

3. *The Cognitive Model.* This model of motivation was implicitly included in many earlier theories of perception and cognitive processes, but without being elaborated as a theory of motivation.

Thus there was—according to Fritz Heider (see Heider, 1960)—a motivational hypothesis contained in the classic Gestalt theory. The "tendency to closure" or "to create the good figure" was treated by the classic Gestalt psychologists as a dynamic variable, a "force." This conception was never elaborated into an explicit motivational hypotheses and the "tendency to closure" was perhaps only intended to explain the motivation of cognitive processes. But the Gestalt psychologists inspired K. Lewin, who elaborated a general theory of motivation and personality, which was, as already mentioned, an incentive rather than a cognitive theory.

The Gestalt psychologists also inspired, via K. Lewin, E. C. Tolman. His original theory (see Tolman, 1932) included both cognitive and motivational variables in order to explain purposive behavior in animals and man. And some of the variables—especially Tolman's "Sign–Gestalt–Readiness—were mixed cognitive motivational variables. Later Tolman (Tolman, 1951) elaborated these mixed variables into his "Belief–Value Matrix," which together with his "New System" and "Behavior Space" determined behavior. He has himself called his theory "A Cognition Motivation Model" (see Tolman, 1952).

Modern theories of motivation contain two slightly different versions of a cognitive model. According to one version cognitive processes determine dynamic processes, and thus cognitive processes have both a directive—and indirectly—a dynamic effect (see Fig. 11-3). As a good example of a clear and consistent theory of this type we can point to Festinger (1957).

Another version of the cognitive model of motivation presupposes that cognitive processes have their own "intrinsic motivation." The best illustration of this we have found is Woodworth's (1958) theory. This theory contains a generalization of the idea of "intrinsic motivation" into a "behavior primacy theory," which claims that the most basic kind of motivation consists of dealing actively with the environment. This theory does not exclude the fact that "extrinsic" motivation—needs and incentives—also may sometimes codetermine behavior. But the main idea is that even without these "extrinsic" sources of motivation the organism would be active.

In a very thorough and thought-provoking paper J. McV. Hunt (see Hunt, 1965) presents a modern "information theory version" of earlier cognitive models of motivation. In the same paper he claims that Jean Piaget's theory contains an implicit hypothesis of intrinsic cognitive motivation. Hunt also claims that Karl H. Pribram's (1971) theory belongs to the same category. The present author believes, however, that the latest version of Pribram's theory, which we have analyzed is a broader and more comprehensive theory, although it comes nearer to the cognitive model than to any of the other models of motivation.

As the more complex cognitive processes are exclusively concerned with human beings, the cognitive model comes nearer to the following model of motivation.

4. *The Humanistic Model*. This model of motivation is not so clearly defined as the three others. But we think that there is a group of motivational theories which have so much in common that they can be differentiated from the other theories and classified together in one class. They have two important features in common: (1) A humanistic conception of psychology; (2) the hypothesis that a special class of human motivation exists. This class of motivation, or human behavior as a whole, is conceived of as being *un*determined (cf. Fig. 11-3).

We have studied two theories which typify the above class. G. W. Allport presented his theory in his well-known book, *Personality* (1937, rev. ed., 1961). In this book he made a distinction between idiographic and nomothetic science, which comes near to the two conceptions of "natural science" and "hermeneutic science." He also introduced the conception of the "functional autonomy" of motivation, which was inspired by an idea presented in Woodworth's (1918) first book. According to this concept there is evidence for a class of motivation in adult, mature, and mentally healthy people which is functionally independent of the basic, primacy motivation found in animals and infants. Allport claims that the motivational theories contained in learning theories are too narrowly based on animal experiments and that the motivation theory contained in psychoanalysis is too narrowly based on studies of neurotic people, who are more infantile in their motivation than healthy mature adults. (See our chapter about Allport's theory in Madsen, 1959, 4th ed., 1968).

Abraham Maslow's theory which we have studied and presented in Chapter 15 of Madsen (1973b), was inspired by Allport as well as others. He was the leader of the "humanistic psychologists" and exposed the necessity of another humanistic conception of science in opposition to the naturalistic, which dominated American psychology until the 1960s. In connection with this he also defended a special humanistic conception of man in opposition to the prevailing biological one. Included in Maslow's conception of man is his hypothesis about a special humanistic adult kind of motivation, the so-called "growth need" or "metamotivation."

A less well-known example of a humanistic theory is that of Thomas V. Moore (see Moore, 1948), which we have studied as one of our earlier theories (see Madsen, 1959). This theory is very much influenced by scholastic, Thomistic philosophy. It presupposes a humanistic conception of science and an indeterministic "free will" theory about human motivation.

We can conclude this section about models of motivation by presenting the results of our study in a classification scheme (Table 11-9). In this scheme we have presented the modern and earlier theories of motivation according to the *dominant* hypothesis of motivation. But the reader must bear in mind that many of the theories studied are so comprehensive that they include two or three kinds of motivation.

A Combined Model

The present author has considered the possibility of making a synthesis of the different models of motivation. We have at the moment integrated the first three models, but have not succeeded in including the last one, the humanistic model.

Our synthesis is based upon a metatheoretical presupposition and a hypothesis. The metaproposition states that all three models are "partly true" as they correspond to different categories of motivation. Or, in other words: the models of motivation are all true, but have limited applicability. Thus each model is supposed to be valid for a special category of motivation.

Our hypothesis states that each category of motivation involves a specific structure in the brain (in addition to the reticular arousal system

TABLE 11-9

Classification of basic motivational hypotheses.

Basic hypotheses	Homeostatic hypotheses	Incentive hypotheses	Cognitive hypotheses	Humanistic hypotheses
Names of psychologists	Pavlov? Freud Hull Murray (1938) Freeman Eysenck?	Lewin Young Tinbergen Helson Hebb Olds Murray (1959) McClelland Atkinson Miller Spence Eysenck? Brown Logan Berlyne Skinner Bindra Bolles	Tolman Woodworth Koch Festinger McV. Hunt White Nuttin Leeper Heckhausen	Allport Maslow Buhler Rogers

which is involved in all kinds of motivation). Thus we have the following categories of motivation:

1. *The Hypothalamic Motives:* [4] This is the category of motivation which is assumed to involve hypothalamic centers as well as the RAS. This is the category of motivation for which the homeostatic model is most valid. But even in this instance we cannot regard the homeostatic model as completely true, as the homeostatic motives include, for example, the sex motive, which is not a completely homeostatic motive. Incentives may also determine this kind of motive as well as other organic motives: hunger, thirst, pain avoidance, cold avoidance, heat avoidance, etc. Thus we could call this category of motivation "organic motives," "homeostatic motives," or "hypothalamic motives."

2. *The Limbic Motives.* This is the category of motivation which is

---

[4] The reader may have noticed that we equate the term "motive" with the longer phrase "category of motivation."

TABLE 11–10

Classification scheme representing our integration of the different models of motivation into one classification of motives according to the brain structures involved.

"*Motive*" or category of motivation	Brain structures involved	Model of motivation applicable	Examples of motives
Hypothalamic ("organic" or "homeostatic") motives.	Hypothalamus and the RAS	Homeostatic model	1. Hunger 2. Thirst 3. Sex motive 4. Maternal motive 5. Excretion motives 6. Sleep motive 7. Breathing motive 8. Acquired "hungers" for tobacco, narcotics, etc.
Limbic ("incentive") motives.	Limbic system and the RAS	Incentive model	Emotional motives: 9. Fear 10. Aggression Social motives: 11. Affiliation motive 12. Achievement motive 13. Power motive
Cortical ("cognitive") motives	Cerebral cortex and the RAS	Cognitive motive (first version)	14. Curiosity 15. Dissonance Reduction
The RAS motives (intrinsic activation motives)	Only the RAS	The intrinsic version of the cognitive model	16. Motives for: Motoric activities Sensoric activities Brain activities Autonomic activities

assumed to involve the *limbic system* as well as the RAS. We have adopted Konorski's (1967) hypotheses that "emotional motives" involve limbic "drive centers" and that "social motives" are conditioned to the emotional motives. We find that the incentive model is especially applicable to these motives. Thus the "emotional" and "social" motives could also be called "limbic" or "incentive."

3. *The Cortical Motives.* The category of motivation which is supposed to involve the cerebral cortex as well as the RAS. These are the motives which function in accordance with the first mentioned version of the cognitive model: Cognitive processes determine their own motivation.

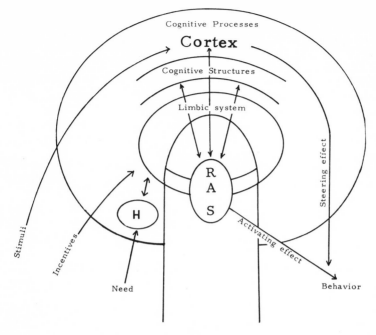

Fig. 11-4.

Consequently the category of motives could be called "cognitive" or "cortical."

4. *The RAS Motives.* This is the category of motivation which is assumed to involve only the reticular arousal system. These motives are those for which the intrinsic model, e.g., Woodworth's behavior primacy theory is supposed to apply here. Therefore, these could be called "intrinsic" or "activation" motives.

We can summarize this combination of the models in the form of a classification scheme (Table 11-10) and a brain model illustrating our integrated model of motivation (Fig. 11-4).

CONCLUSION

It has for many years been a well-known fact that psychology is a science which produces many competing theories. We think that this will continue in the future. Therefore, it is important for psychologists to be able to cope with all these different theories in a rational way. We think that metascientific studies of psychological theories can be of great help to empirical and practical psychologists in their attempt to utilize theories rationally. Therefore, we have tried to develop systematology, the comparative study of theories, into a systematic and exact metascientific discipline. This can be done, among other ways, by the help of computers, which we have utilized in connection with our forthcoming *Modern Theories of Motivation* (1973) to which we can refer the reader who is interested in a more extensive and thorough presentation of systematology than we have been able to give here.

References

Allport, G. W. *Personality: A psychological interpretation.* New York: Holt, 1937.

Atkinson, J. W. *An introduction to motivation.* Princeton, New Jersey: Van Nostrand-Reinhold, 1964.

Atkinson, J. & Birch, D. *Dynamics of behavior.* New York: Wiley, 1970.

Brown, J. S. *The motivation of behavior.* New York: McGraw-Hill, 1961.

Canon, W. B. *Bodily changes in pain, hunger, fear and rage.* New York: Appleton, 1915.

Festinger, L. *A theory of cognitive dissonance.* New York: Harper, 1957.

Freud, S. *Instincts and Their Vicissitudes.* (The Collected Papers of S. Freud. Paperback edition publ. by Collier Books, New York, 1915).

Harlow, H. F. *Motivation as a factor in the acquisition of responses.* In M. R. Jones (Ed.), *Nebraska symposium on motivation.* Lincoln: Univ. of Nebraska Press, 1953.

Hartnack, J. *Mennesket og Sproget.* Copenhagen: Berlingske Forlag, 1971.

Hebb, D. O. *Organisation of behavior.* New York: Wiley, 1949.

Heider, F. The gestalt theory of motivation. In M. R. Jones (Ed.), *Nebraska symposium on motivation.* Lincoln: Univ. of Nebraska Press, 1960.

Hunt, McV. Incentive motivation and its role in psychological development. In David Levine (Ed.), *Nebraska symposium on motivation.* Lincoln: Univ. of Nebraska Press, 1965.

Madsen, K. B. *Theories of motivation.* Copenhagen: Munksgaard, 1st ed. 1959, 4th ed., 1968.

Madsen, K. B. Theories of motivation. In B. Wolman (Ed.), *Handbook of General Psychology.* Englewood Cliffs, New Jersey: Prentice-Hall, 1973(a).

Madsen, K. B. *Modern theories of motivation.* Copenhagen: Munksgaard, 1973(b).

Maslow, A. H. *The psychology of science.* New York: Harper, 1966.

Maslow, A. H. *Motivation and personality* (2nd ed.). New York: Harper, 1970.

McClelland, D. C., Atkinson, J. W., Clark, A., & Lowell, L. *The achievement motive.* New York: Appleton, 1953.

Moore, T. V. *The driving forces of human nature.* New York: Grune & Stratton, 1948.

Murray, H. A. *Explorations in personality.* London and New York: Oxford Univ. Press, 1938.

Nagel, E. *The structure of science.* London: Rutledge & Kegan Paul, 1961.

Pribram, K. H. *The languages of the brain.* Englewood Cliffs, New Jersey: Prentice-Hall, 1971.

Radnidsky, G., *Contemporary Schools of Metascience.* 2nd ed. Copenhagen: Munksgaard, 1970.

Spence, K. W. *Behavior theory and learning.* Englewood Cliffs, New Jersey: Prentice-Hall, 1960.

Tinbergen, N. *The study of instinct.* London and New York: Oxford Univ. Press, 1951.

Tolman, E. C. *Purposive behavior in animals and men.* New York: Appleton, 1932.

Tolman, E. C. A psychological model. In T. Parson and E. A. Shill (Eds.), *Toward a general theory of action.* Cambridge, Massachusetts: Harvard Univ. Press, 1951.

Tolman, E. C. A cognition motivation model. *Psychological Review,* 1952, **59**, pp. 389–400.

Turner, M. B. *Philosophy and the science of behavior.* New York: Appleton, 1967.

Woodworth, R. S. *Dynamic psychology.* New York: Columbia Univ. Press, 1918.

Woodworth, R. S. *Dynamics of Behavior.* New York: Holt, 1958.

Young, P. Th. The experimental analysis of appetite. *Psychological Bulletin,* 1941, **38**, pp. 129–164.

Young, P. Th.: *Motivation and emotion.* New York: Wiley, 1961.

Author Index

Subject Index

Sensitization, 70-71, 76
Sensory processes
  and motivation, 168
Sensory-tonic theory, 168
Series stimuli, 169
Sex differences
  in color preference, 182
Short latency neurons
  function of, 50
Similarity
  and pleasantness effects on learning,
    195-196
Simplicity
  and complexity, 99, 113
Smoking
  and arousal level, 160
  sex differences, 160-162
Social attitude scaling, 9
Standard stimulus, 170
Status of theories
  descriptive view, 278-280
  instrumentalist view, 281-282
    realist view, 280-281
Stimulation pleasure, 245-246
Stimulus characteristics
  and behavioral pleasure, 252-253
Stress
  and personality, 147
Structural information, 101
  amount of, 101-103
  kinds of, 113
  and selective information, 102
"Stupid" behavior, 270
Subjective complexity, 78
  and information, 105

Subjective complexity measures, 100
Systematology, 275

T

Task anxiety, 207
  and incentive formation, 197-199
Task integration hypothesis
  and activation, 267
Tendency to closure, 294
Theories
  cognitive status of, 278-282
Theory, 276
Time series, 42
Time spanning, 143, 144
Transformations, 107
Trophotropic system, 151

U

Uni-dimensional scales, 125
Unity, 111
Unity in diversity, 130
Utility, 9

V

Verbal judgments
  dimensionality of, 127-128
  interactions, 131

W

Word meaning
  and conditioned reinforcers, 210
Words
  and pleasantness role in learning,
    203-204
Wundt curve, 17, 18, 148